FOURTEENTH EDITION

A Student's Guide to History

Jules R. Benjamin

Ithaca College

bedford/st.martin's
Macmillan Learning

Boston • New York

For Bedford/St. Martin's
Vice President, Editorial, Macmillan Learning Humanities: Edwin Hill
Program Director for History: Michael Rosenberg
Senior Program Manager for History: William J. Lombardo
History Marketing Manager: Melissa Rodriguez
Director of Content Development: Jane Knetzger
Developmental Editor: Mary Posman Starowicz
Associate Editor: Melanie McFadyen
Associate Content Project Manager: Matt Glazer
Senior Workflow Project Supervisor: Joe Ford
Production Supervisor: Robin Besofsky
Manager of Publishing Services: Andrea Cava
Project Management: Lumina Datamatics, Inc.
Composition: Lumina Datamatics, Inc.
Senior Photo Editor: Robin C. Fadool
Director of Rights and Permissions: Hilary Newman
Permissions Manager: Kalina Ingham
Director of Design, Content Management: Diana Blume
Cover Design: William Boardman
Cover Image: Historic Map Works LLC and Osher Map Library / Getty Images
Printing and Binding: LSC Communications

Manufactured in the United States of America.

1 2 3 4 5 6   23 22 21 20 19 18

For information, write: Bedford/St. Martin's, 75 Arlington Street, Boston, MA 02116

ISBN 978-1-319-10970-7

Acknowledgments

Art acknowledgments and copyrights appear on the same page as the art selections they cover.

To Elaine, Aaron, Adam, Rose, Vincent, and Solomon

Preface

I love to teach history, and in the classroom I seek to give my students the tools they need to experience the past. The prospect of uncovering truths in history is a long-term goal, but more immediate is the realization that whatever artifact you have—figurine, personal letter, map—can bring you to its time and place. Delving into history is a journey, and I know my students can be fascinated by time travel once they feel confident about their ability to make the trip. I help students chip away at the strangeness that blurs their vision of past places and peoples. I try to make them feel at home in this new world.

In class I used to try to squeeze in as much information as I could, but my students often looked stressed and seemed not to comprehend the material. I eventually discovered, as perhaps you have, that an important reason why my students weren't always able to engage with the material was because I had neglected to lay out for them the skills for mastering (and enjoying) history that we, as historians, acquired long ago. I've realized that these important questions need to be discussed with students first: What kinds of *evidence* do historians work with? How do we *uncover* evidence? How do we figure out what it *means*? And how are we able to *put into words* what we have discovered?

I first wrote *A Student's Guide to History* in response to the barrier I had noticed between my students and the historical material I was teaching. Although this barrier differed somewhat from one student to the next, the core issue was always the need to learn basic study, research, and writing skills. If my students could not take thoughtful and concise notes, tackle common assignments, write clearly, and understand what an exam question required of them, my efforts to explain the meaning of the past would be thwarted by their inability to respond effectively. Since then, new ways of accessing historical evidence have made it possible for students to work with a wide variety of primary sources. To absorb the richness of the new kinds of evidence, students need to master digital searching and visual interpretation, among other skills. This guide complements the basics of study, research, and writing with the skills that students need in today's learning environment.

This book is linear in construction, but its chapters are not tightly bound, and it is designed to be used easily in a wide range of courses and at varying levels. To that end, there are chapters about reading, note taking, and course participation, as well as chapters on what historical evidence looks like, how to find evidence, and how to talk about and write about what such evidence might mean. I hope *A Student's Guide to History* will assist your students in making the most of your course.

New to This Edition

In my ongoing efforts to improve and update *A Student's Guide to History*, I have turned to my own students and to students and instructors across the country, asking what changes they would like to see in future editions. It's my intention that the revisions and additions I have made for the fourteenth edition reflect the needs of today's history students:

- **Updated coverage of contextualization.** A new example in Chapter 1 demonstrates the contextualization of a visual source, highlighting the value of visual sources to historical understanding.
- **New section on "Creating Media Presentations."** Our students have grown up with digital and digitized images of all kinds. Chapter 2 suggests that they learn to use such images to vivify history, not as entertainment but as a provocation to thought. To help foster critical perspectives on media, a new Guidelines box has been added: "Guidelines for Taking Notes on Media Presentations."
- **New section on "Cooperative Learning."** Chapter 2 also includes new coverage on utilizing the internet to find individuals and scholars to aid student research. The new section includes warnings and best practices as students explore intellectual communities outside of the classroom.
- **New section on "What Is a Point of View?"** Chapter 3 includes new coverage on point of view. This discussion brings forward the idea that historians necessarily develop a "perspective" and it is the student's task to understand the author's way of approaching a subject. The terms **perspective** and **point of view** have been added to the Glossary and the definition of **bias** has been revised.
- **New tips on "How to Organize a Short Essay."** This new section in Chapter 5 provides tips and questions designed to target the unique challenges of organizing a short essay. These guidelines are reinforced with an example assignment.
- **New section on "The Problem of Organization."** Chapter 6 takes a wider lens approach to the problem of organization. Students are given three models of organization meant to be used in a more traditional research paper.
- **Updated citation examples.** History students need to know how to cite the materials they use in their papers and projects. Chapter 10 has been updated to include new citation examples that conform to the latest (17th) edition of *The Chicago Manual of Style* formatting.

Organization

Like earlier editions, the fourteenth edition of *A Student's Guide to History* relies on concrete advice, numerous examples, and helpful **Guidelines boxes** to introduce students to the discipline of history and to cover a broad range of skills. It is organized into ten easy-to-reference chapters to emphasize important concepts more clearly. The chapters are paced so that instruction about one skill builds logically upon the next. Students are given practical instruction in research and writing first so they can successfully tackle book reviews and lengthy research papers, where they draw their own conclusions and put forth a persuasive thesis.

Chapter 1 introduces the study of history, the different approaches, and the ways historians think about history. It also explains how history skills can prepare students for a variety of careers.

Chapter 2 covers the basic skills that students need to be successful in a history course: keeping up with reading assignments, taking notes in class, participating in both in-class and online discussions, and giving presentations.

Chapter 3 introduces students to historical evidence (primary and secondary). With more than a dozen examples, students are shown how to read a wide range of sources, including primary texts, scholarly articles, maps, and photographs.

Chapter 4 focuses on how to evaluate historical evidence, with instruction on how to interpret the meaning of a source and then how to summarize and paraphrase what is most important without plagiarizing.

Chapter 5 demonstrates how to respond to different kinds of relatively short writing assignments that students are likely to encounter in a history class: from source analysis to comparative critiques to writing a review of an article or a book. Samples of both effective and ineffective student work are included so students can grasp the different types of assignments more easily.

Chapter 6 unpacks the writing skills that are needed to create an essay that is clear and concise. It goes through the different stages of building an essay: from analyzing the assignment at hand to drafting a thesis statement, to creating a writing outline and a first draft, and to revising and proofing the essay. It breaks down the building blocks of successful writing, including examples of an effective and an ineffective thesis statement as well as examples of clear sentences written in the active voice.

Chapter 7 explains the steps of the research process that are necessary to follow when writing a research paper that requires students to select their own sources and draw their own conclusions. Students are instructed about how to choose a topic, refine it into a researchable project, formulate a research question, and come up with a research strategy. It introduces students to the variety of sources available to them and the most efficient ways of exploring these sources.

Chapter 8 builds on the research skills provided in Chapter 7 and prepares students for what is often the intimidating task of writing a lengthy research paper. It explains how to organize their evidence and how to use this organization to drive their writing toward a central conclusion. The vital role of an effective thesis is reemphasized. It also keeps the student attentive to the mechanics and style of composition that allow the reader to follow the organization of the paper.

Chapter 9 is devoted to providing a full-scale example of a research paper. It demonstrates how one student laid out the results of her research and wrote about them in a way that made a persuasive case for her thesis. The text, illustrations, and notes are annotated so that the student can see how the research paper is structured and how different parts of the paper work together to accomplish the overall goal.

Chapter 10 provides examples of documentation based on the newly updated *Chicago Manual of Style* to answer students' questions about how to provide the reader with source information for a very broad array of resources. A quick reference guide to these documentation models is included at the beginning of Chapter 10 (on p. 188) as well as on the inside back cover.

Appendix A, "Resources for History Research," lists for students hundreds of the best print and electronic history resources, highlighting the most helpful indexes, reference sources, document collections, and periodicals both in print and online.

Appendix B, "Historical Sources in Your Own Backyard," ties popular interest in genealogy to the more broad and complex field of family and local history.

The **Glossary** includes all of the key terms that appear in boldface throughout this book.

Acknowledgments

Every edition has benefited from comments and suggestions made by some of the hundreds of instructors who have assigned *A Student's Guide to History* and by some of the hundreds of thousands of students who have read it over the years. I particularly wish to thank the instructors who reviewed the thirteenth edition in preparation for the revision: Emily Blanck, Rowan University; Michael Clinton, Gwynedd-Mercy College; Cory Davis, Aurora University; Jacqueline deVries, Augsburg College; Brian Leech, Augustana College; Eric Martin, Lewis-Clarke State College; Cristina Mehrtens, UMass Dartmouth; Karen Pastorello, Tompkins Cortland Community College; Carolyn Podruchny, York University, New York; John C. Savagian, Alverno College; Charles Vincent, Southern University.

I want to express my great respect for those at Bedford/St. Martin's who have contributed to this edition of *A Student's Guide to History*: Michael Rosenberg, William J. Lombardo, Mary Posman Starowicz, Melanie McFadyen, and Matt Glazer. This book has been looked after by several generations of Bedford/St. Martin's editors. I doubt that it would have survived so long without them.

Once again, I thank my beloved wife, Elaine, who typed the manuscript of the first edition of this book on an IBM Selectric typewriter over forty years ago — carbon copies and all.

Contents

A Note to Students

I have written this book to introduce you to the world of history that is the heritage of people everywhere. This world is as fascinating as the world of today or as any vision of the future. I hope to convince you that the study of history offers not a journey into a dead past but instead a way to understand and live in the present. You can use the tools of historical research to succeed not only in history courses but in your future career. And you can use them to answer important questions about your own life and your relationship to the rest of the world. This broader purpose is what makes the study of history so valuable.

Jules R. Benjamin
Ithaca College

The Subject of History
and How to Use It

WHAT HISTORY CAN TELL YOU

The Interstate Highway System connects all of the major cities of the United States. The speed limits are high, and local traffic is carried over or under the Interstates. Traveling at 65 miles per hour, you may not realize that these highways have a history—that construction of the Interstate System began in the 1950s and before then such highways didn't exist.

The car that carries you down the Interstate and the music that plays on your car's audio system have a history even older than the highways'. Your car has the same basic components—engine, rubber tires, steering wheel, axles—as the boxy touring cars of the 1920s, whose design was based on the design of horse-drawn carriages. The rock or rap music playing on the audio system is a descendant of country music, folk music, and jazz, with roots extending into the distant past. American folk music traces its roots to the British Isles, from which it was brought to the Appalachian Mountains of the eastern United States in the eighteenth and nineteenth centuries. Jazz traces its roots to the music of enslaved Africans brought to the American South and the Caribbean in the seventeenth and eighteenth centuries.

Looking for the signs of history in the world around us is something like the task of the geologist or archaeologist. However, instead of digging into the earth to uncover the past, the historical researcher digs into the visible, everyday elements of society to find the historical roots from which they sprang. The Interstate Highway System, parts of which are still being built today, is in the uppermost layer of history. If a study of the newest superhighways can take us back sixty years, what about the historical roots of older highways or country roads? How far into the past can we travel on them?

Turn off the eight-lane Interstate, past the huge signs over the multistory motels, and onto U.S. Route 51 or 66—older highways built in the 1940s and 1950s. As you ride along at a slower pace, there are no signs saying "Downtown Freeway 1/2 mile" or "Indiana Turnpike—Exit 26N." Instead, signs say "Lubbock 38 miles" or "Cedar Rapids 14 miles." As you approach Lubbock or Cedar Rapids, you may see small, single-story motels. They may be wooden cottages with fading paint and perhaps a sign that says "Star Motor Court" or "Stark's Tourist Cabins." Instead of fast-food restaurants, you may pass "Betty's Restaurant" or "Little River Diner." The older restaurants, stores, and gas stations that you see provide clues to the history of the road on which you are riding. Places like the Star Motor Court and the Little River Diner probably were built when the road was new. Unless they have been modernized, they are relics of a previous historical period—when Franklin Roosevelt or Harry Truman was president and when cars had rounded hoods, trunks, and fenders. The diner isn't air-conditioned, and the sign over the tourist cabins proudly proclaims that they are "heated." This is the United States of sixty or seventy years ago.

Turn off at State Route 104 where the sign says "Russell Springs 3 miles" or "Hughesville 6 miles." Again the speed limit drops. You are on a road built in the 1920s or earlier (some country roads are a hundred or more years old). Time has claimed many of the buildings that once stood along this road, but a surviving single-pump gas station displays faded advertisements that promote NeHi Orange and Red Man Chewing Tobacco. (Figure 1.1 shows an image from this era.) If you see a restaurant or motel, it may be boarded up because

FIGURE 1.1   Highway Travel in the 1920s
Country stores like this one added gas pumps to serve their new customer—the automobile driver.
Wisconsin Historical Society

the people who used to stop in on their way to Russell Springs or Hughesville now travel on major highways or moved to a nearby city. Many old homes, however, are still standing along Route 104. They were built when only farmland straddled the road, and they may date back to a time when horses pulled traffic past the front door. Relics of early technology such as wringer washing machines and iceboxes may stand on the tilting wooden porches, and a close look behind the tall weeds beside the dirt driveway may reveal the remains of a 1926 Ford. As you stop before one of the old farmhouses, the past is all around you. With a little imagination you can reconstruct what life was like here on the day in 1918 when the Great War in Europe ended.

The line linking past to present never breaks. The farmhouse itself has a history, as do the people who once lived in it. The main bedroom upstairs has a fireplace with the date "1878" carved into the stone. On the table near the bed is the family Bible marked with the year the family came to the United States and the dates in the early nineteenth century when the parents of the immigrants who built the house were born.

The story could extend much further into the past, although the evidence would become slimmer and slimmer. From county records you could find out who owned the land before the house was built, perhaps going back to the time when the people who lived on the land were Native Americans. Evidence of Native Americans could be found not only in written records but in **artifacts**[1] (physical objects) such as arrowheads lying under the foundation of the house. In distance, you may have traveled only ten or twenty miles from the Interstate Highway, and the trip may have taken less than an hour. But while looking in the present for signs of the past, you traveled more than a hundred years into history.

If you think about and study the passage of time between the building of the old farmhouse on the country road and construction of the luxury motel by the Interstate, you may come to understand some of the social, political, and economic forces that moved events away from the old wooden porch and sent them speeding down the superhighway. The more you know about this process, the more you will learn about the time when the farmhouse was new and the more you will understand why the Interstate Highway came into being, what you are doing riding on one, and into what kind of future you may be heading.

HOW HISTORIANS WORK

The past is a fascinating place. Almost everyone feels this. We are easily drawn into films, novels, and histories that bring us vivid images from an unknown time and place. Historians in particular wonder about the past and are motivated to "travel" back into it.

---

[1] Terms in **boldface** are defined in the "Glossary" at the back of the book.

Some historians record their journey of research into the past in order to convey, as best they can, something of the experience of living in a very different world—for example, the life of a Russian serf in the eighteenth century or the building of Great Zimbabwe in southern Africa. Other historians hope to find a storehouse of useful knowledge, even wisdom. They feel that if we can understand the ways of life of past generations, we will better understand our own lives, perhaps because accounts of earlier accomplishments and failures will provide yardsticks by which we can measure the quality of our lives and the success of our social arrangements. Historians are trained to study the past systematically and to use the knowledge they gain to help explain human nature and the roots of contemporary affairs. Many are moved by the possibility that their study of the past will help them understand the problems of the present.

What kinds of answers can history give? What are the ways in which the historian can dig into the complex world of the past? Historians begin their work by asking questions to which they hope historical research can provide answers: What was the effect of the replacement of kerosene lanterns and, later, gas lamps by electric lightbulbs? What **evidence** is there that some of the native peoples of South America may have originally come from islands in the Pacific Ocean?

Special skills are needed to understand the past. Historians must compose important (but not unanswerable) questions. They need to know what kinds of evidence exist, how to examine that evidence, and how to determine what about the past it might explain. When examining a piece of evidence, a historian tries to understand what it means. For example, when analyzing a written document, a historian asks whether it is evidence of something that actually happened (a statement of fact) or whether it reveals instead what the author *believed* happened or wanted a reader to think had happened. As historians, if we learn something about the author of the document and about the world that's described, we may be able to raise questions about the reliability of the evidence. If we read critically, that is, if we ask ourselves what might lie behind the statement, we may learn more about the evidence than if we simply accept it on its face value. When we come across other evidence on the same subject, we need to know how to set it alongside the original evidence in a way that helps explain it. A historian needs to know how to organize the evidence so that the explanation is clear. Finally, historians need to describe the evidence and the conclusions they draw from it; they need to know how to write these results clearly. (For details on how to research a history topic, see Chapter 7.)

HOW HISTORIANS THINK ABOUT HISTORY

A Student's Guide to History focuses on the specific skills you need to master the kinds of assignments you will receive from your instructor. Underlying these practical skills are the ways historians *think* about history. Here is an overview of some of these ways of thinking.

Causation

Historical facts do not explain themselves. They need to be placed in proper relation to one another so that a pattern can emerge. The chronological order of events needs to be established. For example, the automobile was invented in the late nineteenth century. The Interstate Highway System was built beginning in the 1950s. Without knowing the order of these two developments, we would not be able to explain the building of all those highways. Even with a proper chronology, however, explaining one event as being caused by an earlier one can be problematic. The building of the Interstate Highway System was the result of many earlier developments, some of them not as obvious as the invention of the automobile. For example, many Americans were eager to take advantage of the mobility made possible by automobiles.

You should keep in mind that **causation** does not bind events together so tightly that one development *must* lead to the other. Had the automobile industry remained small, or if Americans had preferred to travel by train, perhaps the Interstate System would not have been built. Accurate chronology is merely the first step in the effort to understand patterns in history.

Continuity and Change

In their search for patterns, historians often compare two time periods in the history of their topic. For example, the long skirts worn by women in 1900 became much shorter by 1950. How and why did this happen? To answer this question, historians take a careful look at clothing styles in the period between these two dates. They look not only for differences but also for similarities: those aspects of style that did *not* change. That is, they look for continuity as well as change. After all, despite the significant shortening of skirt lengths by 1950, most women still wore skirts. That had not changed. If a historian were to expand this study to the year 2000, the most important pattern that emerged might be a very different one. By that year, it was more common for women to wear pants than skirts. Looking back from 2000, the rising hemlines of 1900 to 1950 seem to represent continuity as well as change. Historians must keep in mind the idea that patterns of history usually demonstrate some degree of both change and continuity.

Comparison

Comparing a topic across two different points in time is only one of the ways that historians look for patterns. A historian could compare styles in women's clothing in different time periods, but he or she could also compare what clothing styles women wore in different cultures. In 1900 women in Africa dressed very differently from women in Europe. This kind of comparison makes clear that clothing is not simply a matter of style but of ways of life. As a result, the historian's thinking might now focus on African cultural history. Setting one piece of history alongside another deepens the understanding of each. These kinds of connections may bring out some of the broader patterns of history.

Contextualization

The search for patterns in history requires more than looking for similarities or differences. A fuller understanding of each piece of the puzzle of history involves the attempt to discover the ways that each piece connects to those around it. Adjoining pieces may fit into one another at many points. The **historical context** of each piece must be examined in order to have a proper understanding of it. For example, Figure 1.2 is an illustration called "The Mower." It depicts a man swinging a long, sharp-bladed tool known as a scythe. He seems an ordinary farmer working alone in his field. But the artist places this northern farmer in the midst of the American Civil War. The farmer's blade is cutting apart a snake hiding in the grass. The farmer is destroying a "Copperhead," the name given to people in the North who opposed the war against the seceded slave states of the South. Without this context, the emotional power and the historical significance of the simple drawing is lost.

Examining Historical Evidence

Comparison and contextualization are ways of understanding patterns in history. Those patterns are woven from strands of historical evidence. The

FIGURE 1.2   The Mower
Without context, this illustration loses the political and emotional impact that its creator intended.
Fabronius, Dominique C./Library of Congress, Prints & Photographs Division, Reproduction number LC-DIG-pga-10538 (digital file from original print) LC-USZ62-55538 (b&w film copy neg).

historian works to assemble historical evidence to increase our understanding of important events or processes. The history of jazz music, for instance, has patterns, and by using music as historical evidence, historians can find and track those patterns. One pattern might be the rising popularity of this kind of music with larger and more diverse audiences. Another might be the movement of creative centers of jazz music from New Orleans to St. Louis and then to New York City in the early twentieth century. Historians may also discover evidence in melodies and harmonies in the music of Africa, the Caribbean, and the Mississippi Delta. A song sung in the sugarcane fields of Cuba in 1820 or on a cotton plantation in Louisiana in 1850 might be evidence of an important pattern. A historian would examine this music closely to see if and how it fits into the longer view of jazz history drawn from much later evidence in the jazz music styles of New York City. New evidence may reinforce a pattern already seen, or it may raise questions about existing patterns. A historian who has carefully gathered a body of musical evidence might claim that it forms the basis for a very different pattern. Evidence that seems to point in new directions must be examined very carefully. Indeed, historians always ask not simply what evidence says, but also what it means.

Historical Interpretation

History does not have one, unchanging, meaning. That is why historians examine history from many perspectives and why their conclusions are not expected to provide a fully correct answer to a historical question. The past cannot be rerun like a scientific experiment meant to verify or challenge a scientific theory. The facts of history, the meaning of those facts, and the patterns that arise when facts are gathered together are never quite as clear or solid as historians would wish them to be. As a result, historians must be open to new evidence and new interpretations. Historians realize that current understandings of history will be revised or even fundamentally changed by new evidence, new interpretations, and new patterns. The power of the study of history is not in the certainty of its findings, but in the importance of its subject. We cannot know who we are if we have no idea of where we came from. Historians help put us in touch with the ideas and lives of people that we might not know of in any other way.

APPROACHES TO HISTORY

Historians begin their explanation of the past by asking important questions about their subject. A historian's choices among important questions are determined by personal values and experience, by academic training, by the nature of the time in which the historian lives, or by some combination of all of these. The ways in which these influences operate are complex, and historians themselves are not always aware of them.

After the historian chooses a subject, many questions arise. For example, does historical evidence dealing with the subject exist? If it does, where can it be found? If someone wanted to study Gypsy music from medieval Europe, and that music was never written down or mentioned in historical accounts of the Middle Ages, then historical research would uncover little or nothing about this subject. Even when records exist on a particular subject, the historian may be unaware of them or may be unable to locate them. Why? The records may be in a language unfamiliar to the historian, or they may be in the possession of individuals or governments that deny access to them.

If records do exist and they are accessible, the historian still faces a series of formidable questions: How complete is the evidence? Are there significant gaps in it? How credible or reliable is the evidence? Is it genuine? How accurate are the records, and what **biases** were held by the people who created them? If sources of information are in conflict, which source is correct? Or is it possible that most of the sources are in error? Because of these difficulties, historians must carefully examine and interpret the sources they uncover. This may not always be easy to do. The historian's own biases may cloud the picture, making impartial judgment extremely difficult.

Philosophies of History

The historical record is immense. As they explore this world, historians are guided by their understanding of how history works—that is, by their "philosophy" of history. A philosophy of history offers an explanation of the most important causes of specific events and of the broadest developments in human affairs. It explains the *forces* of history, what moves them, and in what direction they are headed. At any particular time, the *dominant* philosophy of history is the one that most closely reflects the beliefs and values of that time, and most of the historians writing at that time write from the perspective of that philosophy.

There are several philosophies of history. Perhaps the most ancient idea is that history runs in cycles (also known as the **cyclical view**). According to this view, events recur periodically—history repeats itself. The essential forces of nature and of human nature are changeless, and patterns of events repeat themselves endlessly. As the saying goes, "There is nothing new under the sun." The Aztecs conceived of history this way, as did the ancient Chinese. This view of history was dominant from ancient times until the rise of monotheistic religions.

For example, the view of history contained in the Old Testament is very different from the cyclical view. Old Testament history is an advancing narrative—the story of the relationship between God and the Jewish people. Societies influenced by Judeo-Christian civilization understood history to be the result of divine intervention. This idea undermined the cyclical view of history. This new philosophy of history, which prevailed in Christian and Muslim states, the **providential view**, held that the course of history is determined by God. Thus, the ebb and flow of historical events represents protracted struggles between forces of good and evil, but the eventual victory of good is inevitable.

The view that history is characterized not by ceaseless repetition but by direction and purpose became an element in the thinking of the more secular age in Europe beginning with the eighteenth century. In this new age of scientific inquiry and material advancement, there arose the **progressive view**, whose central idea was that human history illustrates neither endless cycles nor divine intervention but continual progress. According to this interpretation, the situation of humanity is constantly improving, and this improvement results from the efforts of human beings themselves. The power of human reason directs this process. Each generation builds on the learning and improvements of prior generations and, in doing so, reaches a higher stage of civilization. The idea of history as continual progress remains powerful today. Currently, many variations of the progressive philosophy share the field of historical investigation.

In the eighteenth and nineteenth centuries, political rule shifted from monarchs to parliaments (legislative bodies similar to the U.S. Congress). Progressive historians interpreted the development of democratic institutions as an important sign of progress. The rise of popular government in Europe, however, was accompanied by social problems such as rapid urban growth, exhausting forms of industrial labor, and the growth of poverty.

As a result of the problems of industrialization, progressive historians closely examined the history of "progress" for clues to their solution. The further development of democratic societies in the twentieth century (despite the parallel rise of fascism, communism, and economic depression) gave rise to a variety of progressive perspectives. A very significant new perspective was the study of history "from the bottom up." In this view, the expansion of popular government was not inevitable but was the result of efforts by subordinate groups in society. For example, many historians of the United States began to examine evidence of the roles played by Native Americans, African Americans, Hispanic Americans, European immigrants, and women.

One of the newest philosophies of history is **postmodernism**. This view has not replaced the progressive view but has raised questions about the inherent nature of human progress. Postmodernism has influenced many academic disciplines. In history, it raises the fascinating question of whether the past can truly be understood from the perspective of the present. Evidence from the past, say the postmodernists, takes on new meanings because the present is so different from the past that past and present cannot directly communicate with one another. According to postmodernists, when historians search the records of the past, the understanding of the past that they bring back is heavily influenced by the methods they use or the questions they ask. They do not "find" history or discover how things really were; rather, they "create" history in the process of looking for it.

Few progressive historians wholly subscribe to the postmodernist view, but it has challenged the idea of historical objectivity—the idea that, with time and effort, the historian can avoid bias and uncover the "truth" about history.

Most historians consider themselves capable of discovering and understanding the past. But they are no longer as confident that true objectivity is possible. They believe that some degree of bias always influences historical research, that the facts of history require interpretation, and that historians who undertake this interpretation employ not only reason but intuition as well. Unfortunately, a scientific experiment cannot be conducted on the facts of history to prove the correctness of a particular interpretation.

Historiography

A different approach to the study of history examines evidence taken from earlier writings by historians themselves. This area of study, known as **historiography**, examines changes in the methods, interpretations, and conclusions of earlier generations of historians. Often, earlier studies of historical topics reached conclusions that historians today find surprising. For example, between 1920 and 1939, most of the major histories of World War I placed principal blame for the war on Germany. The prevailing view was that Germany's aggression against its neighbors caused the war. At the end of the war, the Treaty of Versailles required Germany to disarm, to accept blame, and to pay reparations to the countries it fought against for the great damage the war had caused, even though Germany too had suffered greatly. Despite this general agreement on the cause of World War I, the experience of World War II, lasting from 1939 to 1945, led many scholars to rethink the origins of World War I. Historians began to ask how the Nazi movement in Germany, which directed unprecedented brutality against civilians both before and during World War II, had been able to rise to power through elections. Why were so many Germans willing to follow Hitler?

Before coming to power, the Nazi Party repeatedly charged that Germany had to avenge itself for the war guilt placed on the German nation by the Treaty of Versailles. Slowly, historians of World War I realized that the idea that Germany alone was responsible for that conflict had helped the Nazi Party to exploit the patriotism of the German people. Historians looked more closely at the world of 1914 and concluded that there were *many* reasons for the erupting of World War I. Germany was no longer considered to be the sole culprit. Economic and strategic competition among the major powers (Germany, England, France, Russia, and the United States) was seen as an important factor. Intensified nationalism in all these nations—not just in Germany—had increased tensions. Also, it was realized that a series of interlocking alliances among the great powers—which turned a minor conflict in the Balkans into an all-European war—was another source of the explosion. The simplistic verdict of German guilt gave way to a complex explanation of the aims and security concerns of many nations. In this case, an attempt to understand Germany's role in World War II led to a new understanding of the German role in World War I. This kind of reinterpretation is not uncommon in history.

Historians' views of Reconstruction, the period in U.S. history after the Civil War when the defeated South was under the military and political control of the victorious North, also changed. During Reconstruction, for the first time in U.S. history, black people, many of them former slaves, were allowed to be elected to and hold political office. Prior to the 1930s, almost all the books written on Reconstruction (whether by northern or southern historians) concluded that southern politics was corrupted and made ineffective during the Reconstruction period by selfish northerners and ignorant black southerners. Since the 1950s, however, scholars have reached very different conclusions. Most now believe that southern blacks' participation in state and local government was a healthy development and that the standard of politics in the South was generally equal to that of other regions of the nation at that time.

One reason for this new interpretation was the later historians' more effective use of basic sources describing the work of the Reconstruction governments of the southern states. Also, historians compared southern Reconstruction politics with politics in northern and western states of the period (an example of comparative history). And after looking back over the older literature and placing it in the **historical context** of race relations existing at that particular time, most scholars now conclude that an understanding of racist attitudes toward African Americans does much to explain the negative conclusions of earlier historians. Historiography lets historians use the tools of historical research to study themselves and, in the process, come to new conclusions about old questions. This process ensures that the judgments of historians do not fossilize. The reexamination or reinterpretation of earlier research, often called **revisionism**, is constantly evolving and may result from a variety of factors. In some cases, younger scholars examining new topics, or older scholars using new perspectives, may provide new ways of understanding past events. These reinterpretations can be seen in the previous examples: the changing views of Reconstruction and the new perspectives regarding Germany's role in World War I.

Another source for revisionists is the discovery of new evidence. For centuries, there was little hard evidence to support the claim that Thomas Jefferson had several children by one of his slaves. Current DNA testing makes it possible to support this claim, and historical studies of Jefferson now reflect this new evidence.

Fields of Historical Research

When historians investigate the questions that interest them most, they are influenced in their approach by their own values and experiences, their academic training, and their beliefs about which aspects of human nature, human institutions, and the human environment are most important in understanding those questions. As a result, historians might examine their chosen topic from a wide range of perspectives. These differing perspectives or views can be grouped into dozens of major fields (and even more subfields), each of which has a particular focus or concern. For example, when examining the decline of the Ottoman Empire in the late nineteenth century, one historian might choose to focus primarily on political matters, and another might pay more attention to economics. Although the fields of historical study are numerous and varied, they have all evolved over time, nearly all of them influence others, and many of them overlap.

Some fields are more traditional than others. Political approaches to historical questions have been employed by historians for many years. They have studied political parties and elections and have given rise to such fields as military history, diplomatic history, and the history of empire. Political historians are generally concerned with questions of power: who held it, how it was organized and employed, and how it was lost. To answer a question regarding the Ottoman Empire's decline, a political historian might look at the new groups that arose to challenge the power of the sultan (the highest political authority in the empire), whereas a military historian might look at the growing superiority in weapons and training of British, French, and German troops compared to those in the army of the sultan. A historian of empire might compare the ailing system of taxation under the last of the sultans to the more successful systems of the early Ottoman rulers. A diplomatic historian might examine the Ottoman Empire's changing relationship with neighboring powers to explain its demise.

Other long-established approaches to historical questions include views that focus on religious, intellectual, and economic matters. To continue the example of the decline of the Ottoman Empire, a religious historian might compare the roles of Islam and Christianity in the process, whereas an intellectual historian might examine the work of important Muslim scholars (ulama) in the decades leading up to the empire's demise. By contrast, a historian specially trained in the field of economic history might focus on the great increase of indebtedness of the empire to European investors and banks and how this situation arose.

Some economic historians have taken up the field of quantitative history. They use as their primary sources numerical data—election returns, price levels, population figures, and others—that they trace over time. Quantitative data are uniform, allowing study of amounts and rates of change. Different kinds of change can be compared—such as political party affiliation with price levels—in an attempt to describe the conditions under which certain changes occur.

Over time, relatively new historical fields have arisen to probe neglected areas of study such as social and cultural issues. Social historians often focus their research on the development of human communities and their interaction with the larger society, incorporating two of the most rapidly expanding areas in recent decades: women's history and gender studies. Because women have been mostly absent from traditional history texts until recent decades, women's history scholars attempt to fill in the gaps, showing the impact that women have had on all aspects of history. If we return to the example of the decline of the Ottoman Empire, a researcher of women's history might explore the growing use of transparent veils by women in late nineteenth-century Istanbul. Historians of gender study look at the ways in which ideas of masculinity and femininity have influenced history; they might compare the coffee house (male) and the bath house (female) as places of gendered socialization.

In addition, historians of the family and private life have taken up the examination of the structural and emotional development of small, intimate groups and the interaction of these groups with powerful social forces such as wars, depressions, class and ethnic conflict, and technological change. A historian in this field might examine the reasons for the segregation of space by gender in the homes of the wealthy: the drawing room, the sewing room, the study, and the smoking room.

Another fairly recent area of historical study is cultural history—a field in which historians focus on group attitudes and behaviors and how these change over time. If we look again at the Ottoman Empire example, a cultural historian might want to know the significance of the loosening of the clothing laws at the middle of the nineteenth century or of the new forms of public leisure activity, especially among the growing middle class. Numerous subsets of cultural history include the history of entertainment, of sport, and of fashion. A growing field of cultural study is the history of media: newspapers, radio, television, and currently the social media on the internet.

History can be applied to a host of other academic disciplines, resulting in very specific genres. A historian of science, for example, might seek to understand why Islamic medicine, so advanced in earlier centuries, was outpaced by European advances in the nineteenth century. An ethnic historian might study the many non-Islamic peoples of the Ottoman Empire and the status they held in Islamic society.

As fields of historical study slowly but constantly emerge and evolve, they are influenced by many external factors, including current events. For example, just as pollution and climate change have emerged as important issues in our current world, environmental historians have begun to examine the interaction between previous human communities and their habitat. Globalization has influenced the growth of "world" history, which, among other topics, studies large-scale migrations of peoples and the mutual impact arising from the contact of civilizations.

In addition, changes in one historical field, or the emergence of a new field, can influence another. For example, as social history has become more influential, it has led other historians to incorporate a social aspect to their studies. A military historian might expand his or her research of weapons and tactics of the sultan's army to include an examination of the groups in society from which soldiers were recruited.

Historians also welcome ideas and methods of analyzing evidence that arise from disciplines other than history. Some examples include the influence of psychology on family history, the influence of sociology on demography, and the influence of anthropology on ethnohistory. For example, theology might influence a historian of religion to examine the arguments for a return to Islamic law (shari'a) despite the rising secularization of the late Ottoman Empire.

HOW YOU CAN USE YOUR HISTORY SKILLS

The knowledge and skills you acquire in history courses will prepare you for a wide variety of careers. Among these skills are the ability to place evidence in context, to formulate research questions and strategies, and to effectively present evidence in a well-supported and clearly written **argument**. These skills support you in any career you may choose to follow, and they will enrich your life.

There are any number of careers in which the tools of the historian can be directly employed. You could teach history at the secondary or college level. You might acquire an advanced degree in a field such as library science, law, or journalism. You might work in the international arena as part of a nongovernmental organization or in a staff position at the United Nations. Opportunities for work in "public" history are extensive and quite varied. The following section describes only a portion of the options open to you. (See Figure 1.3.)

Public History

The field of public history is a very large one, and many work opportunities for students of history are to be found in public and nonprofit institutions such as libraries, archives, museums, foundations, think tanks, and many more possibilities. Historians work in local, county, and state historical societies and archives. The executive and legislative branches of state governments have staff positions for persons with research skills. The federal government also hires people with training in these skills to staff its vast national and regional archives. Many branches of the government have their own libraries, research staffs, and publishing arms. For example, members of the U.S. Congress have research staff, as do congressional committees. The numerous departments, bureaus, and regulatory bodies of the executive branch all have staffs of researchers. These include positions for historians who work for the various branches of the military, for security agencies, for the State Department, and other Cabinet-level departments. Such well-known government institutions as the Library of Congress, the

Public Sector

American Association for State and Local History   **aaslh.org/jobsonline.htm**

American Alliance of Museums   **aam-us.org/aviso**

American Cultural Resources Association   **acra-crm.org**

Association of College and Research Libraries (ACRL)   **ala.org/acrl**

Association for Documentary Editing   **documentaryediting.org**

American Historical Association: Careers for Students of History
   historians.org/pubs/careers/index.htm

American Institute for Conservation of Historic and Artistic
   Works   **conservation-us.org**

American Library Association   **ala.org**

Association for Preservation Technology International (APT)   **apti.org**

Council of State Archivists   **statearchivists.org**

Institute of Certified Records Managers   **icrm.org**

Library of Congress   **loc.gov**

National Council on Public History: Careers & Training
   ncph.org/cms/careers-training

National Center for Preservation Technology and Training   **ncptt.nps.gov**

National Council for Preservation Education   **ncpe.us**

National Preservation Institute   **npi.org**

National Park Service   **nps.gov/personnel**

National Trust for Historic Preservation   **preservationnation.org**

Society of American Archivists   **archivists.org**

Society for History in the Federal Government   **shfg.org**

Smithsonian Institution   **si.edu**

U.S. National Archives and Records Administration   **archives.gov/**

U.S. National Committee of the International Council on Monuments and Sites
   (ICOMOS)   **usicomos.org**

Private Sector

History Associates Inc.   **historyassociates.com/home**

History Consultants   **historyconsultants.net**

Historical Research Associates, Inc.   **hrassoc.com**

National Council on Public History (consultants)   **ncph.org/cms/consultants**

Milestones Historical Consultants   **milestonespast.com**

Second Story   **secondstory.com**

The History Factory   **historyfactory.com**

The Winthrop Group   **winthropgroup.com**

FIGURE 1.3   Career Opportunities: Public and Private Sector Organizations

Smithsonian Institution, the Museum of American History, and the National Portrait Gallery serve the public through the work of highly trained professionals, including many historians.

There are also professional opportunities in the fields of historic preservation and conservation. For example, the U.S. government maintains hundreds of historic sites, including historically significant parks, communities, buildings, and battlefields, among others. In countless places across the nation, visitors tour preserved or reconstructed sites such as farms, pioneer communities, estates, forts, and gardens where guides known as "docents" explain the lives of the people who once lived in them. These sites must be accurately reconstructed from historical records and developed with the goal of maintaining their integrity and educating the public about them. This work is accomplished by historians, archaeologists, architects, artists, and others. Restoring an ancient Indian community or a Civil War battlefield, for example, requires staff with an understanding of the original look and feel of such a place.

The creation of documentary media employing vintage film footage, sound recordings, artwork, or other historic artifacts requires people with research skills to uncover and interpret source materials. People with these skills analyze these sources, then produce and present them in ways that are historically accurate and that also make them come alive for audiences. Sources need to be documented and interpreted, scripts need to be edited, and museum exhibits need to be displayed in an evocative manner.

The Private Sector

Students often employ the research and writing skills acquired in their study and interpretation of history when they work toward advanced degrees and then practice in the fields of law, journalism, medicine, and many areas of business. There are also opportunities in the private sector for people who possess a historian's skills of writing and research. In some instances, historians will join people with related skills to form a professional group. The group might contract with a corporation, foundation, governmental body, or nonprofit organization to carry out a wide variety of historically oriented projects. Members of such a group might restructure a large but poorly organized company archive. Perhaps a corporation might need to know more of its own history to better formulate its mission, advertise itself to clients, or defend itself from lawsuits. A law firm may need someone to interpret old land records, contracts, or wills so that it can advise its clients on the legal standing of such documents. Genealogical organizations might hire researchers to organize and digitize an immense body of data for their archives. Historical records take many forms and are of uncountable proportions. Media production companies need professionals who can create historically accurate and impactful presentations. Every step back in time creates a need for the talents of someone who can chart this enormous world and reveal it in the present day.

CHAPTER
2

Succeeding in Your History Class

KEEPING UP WITH
READING ASSIGNMENTS

The most common assignment in a history class is reading: many courses have one or more required textbooks, which are often supplemented by **primary sources** and **secondary sources**. (For details on reading primary and secondary sources, see Chapter 3.) Your course syllabus will clearly list the due dates of readings for the entire semester. Don't put off your reading until right before an exam. Keeping up with reading assignments will give you the background knowledge you need to understand the lectures and class presentations. Since many instructors make classroom discussion a significant portion of the grade, it is especially important that you keep current with the assigned readings.

A common mistake students make is to skip required readings altogether, assuming that the instructor's lectures will provide all the necessary information. But in most courses, the lectures are designed to embellish the background material provided in the readings, and instructors assume that students have completed assigned readings in preparation for class. A lecture on the economic aspects of the American Revolution may be confusing if you have not read the textbook discussion of the mercantilist theories behind many of the colonists' grievances.

Navigating a Textbook

A textbook may seem complicated or overwhelming at first, but its sole purpose is to help you understand the course content in the most efficient way.

Before you start reading the first assigned chapter, take a close look at your book. In some textbooks you will find an introduction for students. Its purpose is to familiarize you with the organization of and various features within the book. Read this introduction at the beginning of the semester in order to lay the groundwork for the reading assignments ahead.

Most textbooks have a "brief" table of contents, which lists only chapter titles, as well as a complete table of contents, which includes subheadings and additional features such as chapter summaries, review questions, lists of terms, sources for research, and other aids. The index, of course, provides even more detail than the table of contents does, and you should use it when you are searching for a very specific term or topic. In addition to the tables of contents and index, at the beginning or end of a textbook you are likely to find components such as timelines, lists of maps, appendixes of historical documents, and glossaries, all of which can be useful study and reference guides.

Because textbook chapters typically contain an abundance of information, they usually are designed to help students absorb the content most effectively. For example, most textbook chapters open with an introduction or preview and an image that represents the time period being covered. Within each chapter, headings identify the major topics, and visuals with captions illustrate important concepts. In addition, chapters usually contain tables, timelines, and maps to help contextualize the material being presented. Important terms are usually defined on the spot or in a glossary at the back of the book. Some chapters have sidebars presenting detailed information on particular sources of interest, such as political decrees or historical figures. Textbook chapters typically end with a summary or review, a list of study questions, and a bibliography for further reading.

As you read through each chapter, pay attention to all these features and use them to your advantage. Although they may not be explicitly mentioned in your reading assignment, these features are meant to enhance the main text of the chapter and are therefore worth your time and attention. Many textbooks have companion websites for students that offer further opportunities for exploration and review of the course material via self-assessment quizzes and activities, study aids, and research and writing help.

Reading a Textbook

Before you begin to read, preview the assigned chapter or section to get a sense of its organization. Read any introductory material and scan the headings throughout the chapter. Browse the visuals and their captions to take note of some of the more important aspects of the material contained in the chapter. (Because space is limited, textbook authors typically include visuals only for the concepts that they feel are most important.) Also look at the chapter summary to get a general idea of the territory you will be traveling through.

After previewing the chapter, read through it thoughtfully and actively. (See Figure 2.1 for an example of an annotated textbook page.)

in the formation of the modern global system after 1500. These new crops and the development of the intensified agricultural techniques that often accompanied them contributed to increased food production, population growth, urbanization, and industrial development characteristic of the Muslim Middle East in early Abbasid times.

Technology too diffused widely within the Islamic world. Ancient Persian techniques for obtaining water by drilling into the sides of hills now spread across North Africa as far west as Morocco. Muslim technicians made improvements on rockets, first developed in China, by developing one that carried a small warhead and another used to attack ships.[30] Papermaking techniques entered the Abbasid Empire from China in the eighth century, with paper mills soon operating in Persia, Iraq, and Egypt. This revolutionary technology, which everywhere served to strengthen bureaucratic governments, spread from the Middle East into India and Europe over the following centuries.

Ideas likewise circulated across the Islamic world. The religion itself drew heavily and quite openly on Jewish and Christian precedents. Persia also contributed much in the way of bureaucratic practice, court ritual, and poetry, with Persian becoming the primary literary language of elite circles. Scientific, medical, and philosophical texts, especially from ancient Greece, the Hellenistic world, and India, were systematically translated into Arabic, for several centuries providing an enormous boost to Islamic scholarship and science. In 830, the Abbasid caliph al-Mamun, himself a poet and scholar with a passion for foreign learning, established the House of Wisdom in Baghdad as an academic center for this research and translation. Stimulated by Greek texts, a school of Islamic thinkers, known as Mutazalites ("those who stand apart"), argued that reason, rather than revelation, was the "surest way to truth."[31] In the long run, however, the philosophers' emphasis on logic, rationality, and the laws of nature was subject to increasing criticism by those who held that only the Quran, the sayings of the Prophet, or mystical experience represented a genuine path to God.

But the realm of Islam was much more than a museum of ancient achievements from the civilizations that it encompassed. Those traditions mixed and blended to generate a distinctive Islamic civilization with many new contributions to the world of learning.[32] (See the Snapshot.) Using Indian numerical notation, for example, Arab scholars developed algebra as a novel mathematical discipline. They also undertook much original work in astronomy and optics. They built upon earlier Greek and Indian practice to create a remarkable tradition in medicine and pharmacology. Arab physicians

A Muslim Astronomical Observatory
Drawing initially on Greek, Indian, and Persian astronomy, the Islamic world after 1000 developed its own distinctive tradition of astronomical observation and prediction, reflected in this Turkish observatory constructed in 1557. Muslim astronomy subsequently exercised considerable influence in both China and Europe. (University Library, Istanbul, Turkey/The Bridgeman Art Library)

Margin annotations:

Islamic world disseminated:

1. Technology
– drilling for water
– rockets
– papermaking

2. Ideas
– religion
– politics
– science
– literature

Why did this happen?

Islamic world's contributions:
– algebra
– astronomy and optics
– medicine and pharmacology

FIGURE 2.1   Textbook Page with Student Annotations

This sample page shows how a student might actively read a textbook. Keywords, phrases, and sentences are underlined and circled to highlight the textbook author's interpretations and conclusions. In addition, the student writes notes in the margin, summarizing main points and raising questions to be pursued later.

Underline or highlight the most prominent factual information. Also underline important generalizations, interpretations, and conclusions. Make marginal notes wherever you wish to remind yourself of something important or to raise a question that you might bring up in class. In addition, look for passages that surprise you or with which you disagree, and write your reaction or summary of these passages in the margin. If you are reading an e-book, you can take advantage of note taking, highlighting, search, and other online features. (For more advice on reading, see pp. 45–51.)

If you read your textbook carefully and actively throughout the semester, you will have ready-made study materials when it comes time to prepare for a test: you will be able to reread the underlined material and your comments and obtain a quick review of a chapter's content. Before the exam, however, you may want to reread the textbook itself.

NOTE: Instructors may supplement textbook readings with material of their own. They may hand these out or place them on the class website. Be sure to read and take notes on this material.

TAKING NOTES IN CLASS

The time you spend in class is vital to your learning. True, you can learn on your own outside of class, but the interaction with your instructor and other students is most intense during class time. Learning to record that interaction in your notes is an important skill.

Guidelines for Taking Lecture Notes

- Prepare for a lecture by reading all related course materials ahead of time.
- Write the course information, lecture subject, and date at the top of each page of notes. On a computer, create a new file for each lecture and a name with this same information.
- Be selective. Summarize. Don't try to write down everything a lecturer says or presents visually.
- On the other hand, record more completely anything that the instructor (a) puts on the board; (b) says is important; or (c) emphasizes as he or she speaks.
- Leave room in your notes or files to add material later if necessary.
- Reread your notes or files later in the day on which they were written.
- Underline especially important points.
- Look up the meaning of any unfamiliar words.
- Rewrite any parts of your notes that are poorly organized.
- If something important in your notes is unclear to you, ask your instructor about it.

From Class Lectures and Presentations

The first rule of note taking is simple: pay attention. Learn to concentrate on what is being said. Read assigned texts before going to class so you won't end up taking notes on the material in the book. If everything the instructor says is new to you, you will spend so much time writing that you may not be able to grasp the subject of the lecture. If you have obtained some basic information from outside readings, however, you will be able to concentrate on noting points in the lecture and presentation that are new or different.

An instructor is most likely to prepare exam questions from the material that he or she considers most important. It is therefore essential in preparing notes to determine which points in the lecture and presentations are given most prominent attention. Never fail to note something that the instructor indicates is important. Also note interpretations and generalizations that seem to be stressed, especially when they differ from the approach in the textbook. You should not feel obliged to parrot your instructor's interpretations in an exam, but ignorance of them could work against you.

Write your notes legibly, and begin with the date and subject of the lecture. The notes should reflect a general outline of the material covered, with emphasis on major interpretations and important facts not covered in the textbook. It is often best to write on every other line or to leave a large margin on at least one side of the page. This will allow you to add material later and to underline your notes and write additional comments without cluttering the page. Don't worry about taking down every word; instead, try to summarize major points and put detailed information such as dates, statistics, and particular names into your outline format. If you simply have a list of facts without any organization, the notes will not make sense to you when you review them for an exam.

If possible, reread your notes later in the day on which they were written. If your handwriting is poor or your notes are disorganized, it is best to rewrite them. Check the spelling and definitions of any unfamiliar words, and be sure that your notes are coherent. Remember, your notes are an important source of information in your studies.

To illustrate some of the essentials of good note taking, compare Figures 2.2 and 2.3, which show portions of two sets of class notes taken from the same lecture. Figure 2.2 (p. 22) illustrates many of the common errors of note takers; Figure 2.3 (p. 23) is a well-written set of notes. A third example, Figure 2.4 (p. 24), shows a rewriting of the good notes. The subject of the lecture was early European contact with Africa.

What is it about the poor notes (Figure 2.2) that makes them inferior? First, they are not well organized. They do not even record the title of the lecture, the course number, or the date—omissions that could be problematic if the notes get out of order. They are little more than a series of sentences about gold, trade, spices, Portugal, and slaves. The sentences are not in any particular order and do not say much of anything important.

Even the factual information does not cover the major points of the lecture. By paying too much attention to trivial points about sea monsters, China, Jerusalem, Bartolomeu Dias, and Columbus, the note taker missed or did not have time to record the principal subject of the lecture: the relationship between European-Asian trade and the religious struggle between Islam and Christianity. The note taker also missed another major point: the connection between the enslavement of Africans and the need for plantation labor in the New World. Without those two points, this student cannot write a good exam essay on this subject.

The good notes (Figure 2.3), in contrast, follow the organization of the lecture and touch on the major points made in class. The notes make sense and can serve as the basis for reviewing the content of the lecture when the note taker studies for exams. These notes have a wide margin for extra comments and the marking of important passages. Notice the sections marked "important." The instructor emphasized these points in class, and by specifically identifying them, the student will be sure to master them.

The rewritten version (Figure 2.4), which eliminates unimportant or repetitious phrases and smooths the language into connected sentences, is even better as a study guide. Taking notes during a lecture is difficult, and even a good set of notes can be greatly improved by being rewritten, so these notes were rewritten within a day of the lecture, while the material was still fresh in the student's mind. Notice how much clearer everything becomes.

Colonization of Africa — People were afraid to sail out. Afraid of sea monsters. But they liked the stories about gold in Africa. The Portuguese King Henry sailed south to find the gold mines and built a fort at Elmina.

England and France want to trade with Africa. They begin trading. Competing with Portugal. These countries got into wars. They wanted to control Africa.

China had spices. They traded with Cairo and Venice. The Asians wanted gold, but the Islams stopped all trade. They fought wars about religion for hundreds of years. Fought over Jerusalem. The Pope called for a crusade. This was in the Middle Ages.

Spices came from Asia. In Europe they were valuable because the kings used them to become rich. They also ate them. The Portuguese wanted to explore Africa and make a way to India. Their boats couldn't get around until Bartolomeu Dias discovered the Cape of Good Hope in 1487.

Most of all, the Portuguese wanted slaves. They shipped them back from Africa. Columbus took them after he discovered America (1492). The Pope made a line in the Atlantic Ocean so the Catholics wouldn't fight. The colonies needed slaves. They sent 15 million from 1502 to the 19th century. Slaves did the hard work. They got free later after the Civil War.

FIGURE 2.2   Example of Poor Note Taking

Early European Contact with Africa   *History 200*
Why Did Europeans Come to Africa?   *10/23/18*

1. *Desire for gold*
   - *Medieval legends about gold in Africa.*
   - *Prince Henry (Portuguese nobleman) sent men down coast of Africa to find source of gold. (Also to gain direct access to gold trade controlled by Muslims.)*
   - *Portuguese built forts along the coast. Their ships carried gold and ivory back to Portugal (16th century).*
   - *Then the other European states came (England, Holland, France, Spain) to set up their own trading posts.*
   - *Competed with each other for African trade. (Will talk about rivalry next week.)*

2. *Wanted to trade with Asia and weaken the Muslims (The Muslims had created a large empire based on the religion of Islam.)*
   - *Religious conflict between Christianity and Islam. Fought a religious war in the 11th–12th centuries — the Crusades.*
   - *The Muslims had expanded their empire when Europe was weak. In 15th century they controlled North Africa and they dominated trade in the Mediterranean. They controlled the spices coming from Asia, which were in great demand in Europe. In Europe they were used to preserve meat. So valuable, sometimes used as money.*
   - *Portugal and Spain were ruled by Catholic monarchs. Very religious. The Catholic monarchs wanted to force the Muslims out of Europe. (They still held part of Spain.) Wanted to convert them to Christianity.*

   Important   - *The Muslims controlled North Africa and Mediterranean trade. If the Portuguese and Spanish could sail to the Indian Ocean directly, they could get goods from China and the Muslims couldn't stop them. The way to Asia was the sea route around Africa.*

3. *The Europeans wanted slaves*
   - *When the Portuguese explored West Africa (15th century), they sent back the first slaves (around 1440).*
   - *The Spanish conquered the New World (Mexico, Peru, etc.). (Columbus had made several trips for Queen Isabella I of Spain.)*
   - *In America (the name for the New World), they needed slaves. Most slaves were sent to America.*
   - *Native Americans died from diseases of white men. They were also killed in the wars. There was nobody to work the mines (gold and silver).*

   Important   - *Sugar plantations of the Caribbean (and Brazil) needed labor. Cotton and rice plantations in the south of U.S. also. It was hard work and nobody wanted to do it.*
   - *15 million slaves were brought to work the plantations starting in 1502 until mid-19th century.*

FIGURE 2.3   Example of Good Note Taking

Early European Contact with Africa   *History 200*
What Drew Europeans to Africa?   *10/23/18*

1. GOLD

There were medieval legends that there was a lot of gold in West Africa. Access to the gold was controlled by non-Christian powers (Muslims — believers in Islamic religion). Tales of gold lured the Portuguese (led by Prince Henry) to explore the coast of West Africa in the late 15th century. By the 16th century, the Portuguese had built several trading posts and forts along the West African coast and were bringing back gold, ivory, and pepper.

By the 17th century, English, Dutch, French, and Spanish ships challenged the Portuguese trading monopoly and set up their own trading posts. This was the start of European rivalry over Africa's wealth.

2. DESIRE TO WEAKEN THE POWER OF THE ISLAMIC EMPIRE (MUSLIMS) AND EXPAND TRADE WITH ASIA

Conflict between Christianity and Islam was an old religious conflict (the Crusades as an example in 11th and 12th centuries). The Muslims controlled North Africa and the Mediterranean. They also controlled the spice trade from Asia. Spices were important in Europe because they were the only known way to preserve meat.

The Catholic states of Portugal and Spain wanted to fight with the Muslims. They wanted to drive them out of Spain and challenge the large Muslim empire in Africa, the Middle East, and Asia. They hoped to convert them to Christianity. <u>The Muslims were strong in North Africa, but if European powers could discover a way around Africa into the Indian Ocean, they could outflank the Muslims and obtain direct access to the trade with India and Asia</u>.

3. SLAVES

Portuguese trading posts in Africa had sent a small number of slaves to Europe starting in the late 15th century. With the discovery and conquest of America at the turn of the 16th century, a new and larger slave trade began to European colonies in the New World (America).

The Native Americans died (they were killed in war and by European diseases in great numbers). There was a shortage of labor. In the 17th and 18th centuries, large sugar plantations were set up in the Caribbean and Brazil and rice and cotton plantations in the southern United States. <u>The need for laborers to do the hard agricultural work led to the importing of millions of slaves from Africa</u>. Approximately 15 million Africans were sent to America as slaves between 1502 and the mid-19th century. This slave trade made Africa valuable to the European powers.

FIGURE 2.4   **Example of Rewritten Good Notes**

The greatest value of rewriting notes, however, is that re-creating the lecture material in essay form helps it to become part of the note taker's own thinking. The mental effort that goes into revising lecture notes serves to impress the material and its meaning upon the mind. This makes it much easier to review the material at exam time.

From Multimedia Presentations

Many instructors amplify what they say in class by the use of illustrations, photographs, audio, and videos. To take notes on a multimedia presentation, you need to understand how the different media are being used to support the lecture. Why is your instructor including them; what is there about the specific media employed that gives you a different angle of vision on the lecture topic? Your notes on these kinds of presentations should record not only the basic sounds or sights but also the special quality of the media to remind you of the "nonverbal" nature of their contribution to the lecture topic. For example: you should not simply note that you were shown a satellite photo of the vast Nile River delta but indicate how it was used to deepen your understanding of a lecture on agriculture in Egypt.

A class may include a documentary or commercial movie. Notes that you take about a video should be selective. You cannot possibly describe in words all that you see on screen. Again, understand how your instructor is using the presentation to deepen your understanding of the topic. Use your notes to remind yourself of the overall impression of the video and what it added to your knowledge. Don't fill your notes with long descriptions of images or sounds. Instead, focus on the aspects of the topic that the new media bring to life. Be sure to avoid the temptation to simply "enjoy" the presentation. Some videos may be powerful and beautiful, but use your critical-viewing skills just as you use your critical-reading skills.

If a film is essentially factual (*Walled Cities of the Middle Ages*), note the major facts and interpretations as you would when reading a secondary source or listening to a lecture. If a film is dramatic rather than documentary (*Hotel Rwanda, Citizen Kane*, or *Schindler's List*), examine the emotional message and artistic content as well as any historical facts it describes (or claims to describe). Ask yourself, What is the movie director trying to say, and what dramatic and technical devices does he or she use to say it? Your notes should record important narration and dialogue that illustrate the theme of the film. Finally, you will need to take note of cinematic elements (camera angles, sets, lighting, gestures and movements, facial expressions) because the impact of a dramatic film is essentially visual. Finally, if you have remote or library access to recordings, videos, or photographs used in class, use this access to prepare yourself for exams or discussions. (For more on working with multimedia materials, see pp. 52–66.)

The purpose of incorporating new media is to present you with a richer and more dramatic exposure to a wide variety of historical sources. This

---

Guidelines for Taking Notes on Media Presentations

- Be sure to identify each component of a media presentation. If you do not have this information, ask your instructor where you can find it.
- Include the ways in which the media enhanced or extended the class presentation.
- Describe the information provided by each media component.
- Describe the "emotional" content provided by each media component.
- If the media is available on the class website or elsewhere, view and/ or listen to it again.
- If something in the content of a particular media component is not clear to you, even after viewing and/or listening to it again, ask your instructor about it.

---

material helps to get across the main points that the instructor is covering. Ask yourself, How do the photographs, or timelines, or audio recordings complement the subject of the lecture? Be sure to take notes not only on the media themselves but also on their relation to the subject under discussion. Perhaps your instructor will use media to reinforce a fact—how something looked or sounded. Most likely he or she will also explain the "meaning" of an image or recording: the way it represents nineteenth-century European Romanticism, or the popular culture of a large city in the twentieth century, or the system of dikes in rice paddies next to villages in ancient China.

TAKING EXAMS

When a test is announced, find out what kind of exam it will be: essay, short answer, multiple choice, or a combination of those formats. Determine what topics will be covered and what portions of the reading material and lectures deal with those topics. If you have not done all of the necessary reading, do so immediately and record the important facts and interpretations as indicated in "Keeping Up with Reading Assignments" earlier in this chapter (p. 17). If you missed any lectures, try to obtain lecture notes from someone who knows the rules of good note taking. Then gather together all the materials to be covered in the exam. Reread the parts of the texts that you underlined (or otherwise marked) as being important. Reread all of the relevant lecture notes, paying special attention to any points emphasized by the instructor. Sometimes it helps to do your rereading aloud. If an exam will cover visual materials—slides, videos, maps—be sure to go over this information, even if you have to watch a video a second time.

Guidelines for Writing In-Class Essay Exams

- When you are given the exam, don't panic. Read the entire exam slowly, including all of the instructions. Gauge the amount of time you will need to answer each question. Then choose the question you know most about to answer first.
- Don't write the first thing that comes to mind. Read the question slowly, and be sure you understand it.
- Determine how you will answer the question and the central points you wish to make.
- Write these central points, or even a full outline, in the margin of the exam booklet. As you compose each sentence of your answer, make sure that it relates to one of these points.
- Model your answer on the question. Be as specific or general, as concrete or reflective, as the question suggests. Never allow your answer to wander away from the focus of the question. If the question asks you to "describe" or "trace" or "compare" or "explain," be sure that this is what you do.
- Don't repeat yourself. Each sentence should add new material or advance a line of argument.
- Where necessary, mention the facts that support the points you are making. But the mere relation of a series of facts is not enough. You also must give evidence that you have thought about the question in broad terms.
- Toward the end of an answer, you may wish to include your own opinion. Doing so is fine, even desirable, but be sure that your answer as a whole supports your opinion.
- If there is time, reread and fine-tune your answers. The pressure of an exam may cause you to write sentences that are not clear.

If the test is to be an essay exam, compose sample questions based on the important topics in the readings and lectures. Many textbooks contain sample exam questions or topics for discussion at the end of each chapter. If you do not know how to answer any portion of a sample question, go over your study materials again and look for the information needed. If you are preparing for an objective exam—that is, one requiring short factual answers—pay special attention to the important facts (persons, places, events, changes) and key terms in your study materials. You must be precise in order to get credit for your answer. Make a list of outstanding people, events, and historical developments, and be sure that you can adequately identify them and explain their importance. Again, your textbook may help you by providing sample short-answer questions. Take the time you need to prepare adequately. If tests make you nervous, keep on studying until you master your sample questions and until the material to be covered makes sense to you.

Objective and Short-Answer Exams

Objective exams call for short, factual answers. The three most common objective exam questions are (1) short answer, (2) identification, and (3) multiple choice. Read each question carefully, and don't jump to conclusions. Answer short-answer and identification questions briefly and directly (there is usually a time and space limit). Don't put anything in your answer that wastes space or time. If you are asked to identify John F. Kennedy, don't mention how he was killed (unless that is part of the question); instead talk about some aspect of his presidency that was stressed in class or in course readings. When you have so little room to show what you know, answers that stray from the core of the subject are as bad as wrong answers.

Example of a Short-Answer Question

QUESTION

Describe one of the motives that caused the European powers to explore Africa beginning in the late fifteenth century.

INCORRECT ANSWER

They wanted to dominate Africa and get all the gold for themselves. Columbus wanted to take slaves from Africa, but the Pope said it would start a war. But the war didn't start and the Europeans dominated Africa anyway because they were stronger.

CORRECT ANSWER

The wars between Christianity and Islam were an important factor. The Christian states wanted to weaken the hold of the Muslim religion on Africa and to convert the natives. They also hoped to break Muslim control of trade with Asia by finding a sea route around Africa.

(Check these two answers against the example of good note taking in Figure 2.3 [p. 23]. The notes presented there make clear why the second answer is satisfactory and the first one is not.)

Example of an Identification Question

QUESTION

Identify the "progressive" philosophy of historical interpretation.

INCORRECT ANSWER

Historians who believed that our country was always making progress because Americans were very hardworking people.

CORRECT ANSWER

The interpretation of history that holds that human beings and their condition are continually improving as each generation builds on the foundation laid by previous generations.

(See the "Philosophies of History" section on pp. 8–10 to find the basis for the correct answer.)

Example of a Multiple-Choice Question

The British monarch at the time of the American Revolution was:

a. George II   d. George III
b. Charles I   e. Henry I
c. James II

If you look up the reign dates of those five monarchs, you will discover that George III (who was king from 1760 to 1820) was the ruler of England at the time of the American Revolution.

In-Class Essay Exams

Of course, the best preparation for an essay exam is to be given the question in advance. Some instructors do this (usually in the form of a take-home test), but many give in-class essay exams and hand out in advance a number of possible topics or questions from which they will choose when making up the exam. (For more on take-home essay exams, see pp. 30–34.) If you face an in-class essay exam without *any* questions presented in advance, the key to successful preparation is to come up with potential questions on your own.

Composing Sample Questions

As your instructor probably will tell you, the essay questions will deal with one or more of the major topics covered in the course so far. Using your textbooks, lecture notes, and other course materials, determine what these topics are. Then compose your own questions.

For example, you are told that the exam will cover the decline of the Roman Empire. Many of the factors in the decline have been examined in the readings and lectures so far. Go over this material and try to isolate these factors. Your review uncovers several of them: the cost of defending distant frontiers, declining agricultural output, "barbarian" invasion, the decline of the Roman senate, the cult of the Roman emperor, and the rise of Christianity. The exam is likely to focus on one or more of these factors. Prepare yourself to answer a question about one or more of them. Moreover, become familiar enough with *each* of these factors so that you can comment on how they relate to one another.

Don't prepare for an essay exam by composing questions that are too broad. If the class spent three weeks examining the Cuban Revolution of

1959, don't expect a broad question such as "Discuss the Cuban Revolution." Don't prepare questions that are too narrow either. For example, "Who was Fidel Castro?" is a question for a short-answer or an identification exam.

Here is another example of how to figure out the kind of exam question you might confront. Let's say your class has finished a unit of the syllabus called "Social Hierarchy in Ancient Civilizations." Your textbook presented the material according to geographical region, with separate chapters on China, India, and Greece. In addition to the textbook chapters, you were asked to read primary sources on class, on gender, and on slavery in ancient civilizations. Finally, your instructor's lectures emphasized comparisons between social hierarchies and changes in those hierarchies over time. In this case, you should prepare to answer questions about the important elements in social hierarchy in China, India, and Greece. You should also expect a question that asks you to compare hierarchy in these three civilizations and to describe changes in the hierarchies over time.

Taking the Test

Even if you have prepared properly for an essay exam, you must stay calm enough to remember what you studied, you must understand the questions, you must answer them directly and fully, and you must not run out of time. None of this is easy, but here are a few pointers to follow until you gain the experience to overcome these problems.

Read over the exam slowly. Given the length and complexity of the questions asked, allot the proper amount of time to answer each question. Think about the central points you wish to make, and create a brief outline of these points in the margin of the exam booklet. Directly address the questions asked. If the questions are very specific, respond to them with the amount of detail required. Support the points you make with facts, but avoid composing an answer that is merely a series of facts. Think about the questions asked in broad terms, and pursue your central points. As you write, refer back to your outline and be careful not to repeat yourself. Each sentence should add new material to your answer or advance its line of argument. Finally, try to allow a few minutes to proofread your answers.

Take-Home Essay Exams

A take-home essay exam question requires you to write an original essay of usually two to five pages. Of course, if your instructor asks for a specific length, topic, approach, or format, you need to follow those requirements even when they differ from the information provided here. When you are writing take-home essay exam answers, the tips in Chapter 6 about how to write clearly apply. (See Chapter 6, pp. 110–15, for coverage of how to draft an essay.)

First, note the length requirements of the exam and the due date. Obviously, you will need more time to prepare a six-page essay answer than a three-page one. If your instructor allows you access to sources (which is common), you will need to review all course material that relates to the exam question. If you have not yet outlined or taken notes on this material, do so now. Focusing on the portion of the course material that relates to the question, make a list of the most important points. Try to find from two to six main points for each question, depending on the length of the essay. Compose your answer by introducing and then supporting these points in logical order. Like all essays, your answer should have a clear, central thesis. In this case, your thesis is determined by — and should directly address — the exam question. (See the section on writing in-class essay exams on pp. 29–30.)

Your goal when taking any essay exam is to demonstrate (1) adequate knowledge of the subject, (2) proper organization of points covered, (3) clear and connected writing, and (4) a good understanding of the question. Read the following two answers to an exam question on Chinese history. Do they meet those four requirements?

QUESTION

Explain the origins of the Chinese civil war of 1945–1949. How did the differing political programs of the two contenders affect the outcome of that conflict?

POOR ANSWER

The Guo Mindang (Kuomintang) had a stronger army than the Communists, but the Communists won the civil war and took over the country. Their political program, communism, was liked by the peasants because they didn't own any land and paid high taxes.

China was based on the Confucian system, which was very rigid and led to the Manchu dynasty being overthrown. The Chinese didn't like being dominated by foreigners, and Sun Zhongshan (Sun Yat-sen) founded the Guo Mindang to unite China. He believed in the Three People's Principles. At first he cooperated with the Chinese Communists, but later Jiang Jieshi (Chiang Kai-shek) tried to destroy communism because he was against it. Communism was not in favor of the wealthy people.

The Communists wanted a revolution of the peasants and gave them land. They also killed the landlords. Jiang Jieshi worried more about the Communists than about the Japanese invasion. The Japanese looked to conquer China and make it a part of their empire. Jiang Jieshi wanted to fight the Communists first.

After World War II the Chinese Communists attacked Manchuria and took over a lot of weapons. They fought the Guo Mindang army. The Guo Mindang army lost the battles, and Jiang Jieshi was chased to Taiwan, where he made a new government. The Communists set up their own country, and their capital was Beijing (Peking). That way the Communists won the Chinese civil war.

GOOD ANSWER

The origins of the 1945–1949 civil war can be traced back to the rise of Chinese nationalism in the late nineteenth century. Out of the confusion of the Warlord period that followed the overthrow of the Manchu dynasty in 1911, two powerful nationalist movements arose — one reformist and the other revolutionary. The reformist movement was the Guo Mindang (Kuomintang), founded by Sun Zhongshan (Sun Yat-sen). It was based on a mixture of republican, Christian, and moderate socialist ideals and inspired by opposition to foreign domination. The revolutionary movement was that of the Chinese Communist Party (CCP), founded in 1921, whose goal was a communist society but whose immediate program was to organize the working class to protect its interests and to work for the removal of foreign "imperialist" control.

Although these two movements shared certain immediate goals (suppression of the warlords and resistance to foreign influence), they eventually fell out over such questions as land reform, relations with the Soviet Union, the role of the working class, and the internal structure of the Guo Mindang. (The CCP operated within the framework of the more powerful Guo Mindang during the 1920s.)

By the 1930s, when Jiang Jieshi (Chiang Kai-shek) succeeded Sun, the CCP was forced out of the Guo Mindang. By that time the CCP had turned to a program of peasant revolution inspired by Mao Zedong (Mao Tse-tung). A four-year military struggle (1930–1934) between the two movements for control of the peasantry of Jiangxi (Kiangsi) Province ended in the defeat but not destruction of the CCP.

The Japanese invasion of Manchuria (1931) and central China (1936–1938) helped salvage the fortunes of the CCP. By carrying out an active guerrilla resistance against the Japanese, in contrast to the more passive role of the Guo Mindang, which was saving its army for a future battle with the Communists, the CCP gained the leading position in the nationalist cause.

In the post–World War II period, the CCP's land reform program won strong peasant support, whereas the landlord-backed Guo Mindang was faced with runaway corruption and inflation, which eroded its middle-class following. The military struggle between 1945 and 1949 led to the defeat of the demoralized Guo Mindang army and the coming to power of the CCP.

Let's compare how well the two essays meet the requirements for a well-written answer.

1. *Adequate knowledge of the subject.* The writer of the poor answer omits many important facts, uses vague terms to describe the political programs of the two contending parties, and lists events out of chronological order. The well-written answer illustrates good knowledge of the subject matter. The origins, philosophies, leaders, and relationship of the two contending parties are clearly described, and the writer includes related issues such as nationalism, warlords, guerrilla warfare against Japan, corruption, and inflation, thus indicating knowledge of the historical context in which the Chinese civil war developed. The chronology is clear: events are mentioned in proper time sequence, and the dates of all major events are given.

2. *Proper organization of points covered.* The poor answer is not well organized. The paragraphs do not make separate points, and each succeeding paragraph does not further develop the thesis of the essay. By contrast, the well-written answer uses each paragraph to make a separate important point, and each succeeding paragraph further develops the essay's thesis. The first paragraph sets out the political programs of the two groups and the historical context in which the movements originated. The second paragraph explains the beginning of the conflict in the 1920s. The third paragraph discusses that conflict in relation to the Chinese peasantry during the early 1930s. The fourth paragraph relates the development of the conflict to the Japanese invasion of the late 1930s. The final paragraph summarizes the effects of the conflicts and of postwar developments on the outcome of the civil war.

3. *Clear and connected writing.* Many sentences in the poor answer are badly constructed. Awkward and passive phrases, such as "communism was *liked by* the peasants," lead to unclear sentences that keep the student from getting his or her point across. In addition, repetitious and irrelevant sentences and phrases, such as "Jiang Jieshi (Chiang Kai-shek) tried to destroy communism *because he was against it*," add nothing to the answer. The sentences of the well-written answer are clear, and each adds new material to the essay.

4. *Good understanding of the question.* The poor answer does not deal with the central issue of the question — the political programs of the Guo Mindang and the CCP. It notes that the Guo Mindang was founded on the Three People's Principles, but it does not explain what these were. Of the CCP, it says that there was a belief in communism (which is obvious) and in peasant revolution (which is vague). These are the only references to political programs in the entire answer! It is obvious that the writer of this answer failed to understand that the central focus of the question was on political philosophy. In contrast, the well-written answer is directed to the central issue of political programs and begins on that very point. The remainder of that answer makes clear the relationship of political programs to the origins and course of the Chinese civil war, as called for in the first sentence of the question.

The Dangers of Plagiarism

A problem that sometimes arises with take-home exams is **plagiarism**. Your instructor may allow you to **paraphrase** the sources you use in preparing your essay. Be sure, however, that you write these paraphrases totally in your own words. If you use sentences or even phrases from another source, you are plagiarizing whether you realize it or not. Most schools require instructors to penalize students severely for plagiarizing, which is a very serious matter. If you have questions, turn to "Summarizing and Paraphrasing without Plagiarizing" in Chapter 4 (pp. 76–78).

CLASSROOM PARTICIPATION

In most history classes, you will be expected to actively participate in your own learning. This section discusses some ways of doing so.

Classroom Discussions

Many instructors encourage classroom participation. Some base a portion of the final grade on it. Come to class prepared to answer (and to ask) questions. Follow the discussion as it develops. Don't push yourself into saying something you haven't really thought about simply to join the discussion. When you speak in class, contribute what you know or think. Sometimes the instructor is asking for your informed opinion, and in such a case you won't be judged on whether your comment is "correct" or not. It's important to follow classroom etiquette. If you disagree with the comments of a classmate, speak up respectfully and constructively. If some part of an instructor's presentation or a classmate's comments is unclear to you, don't hesitate to ask a question. If class ends and something remains unclear, raise your question with your instructor after class or during your instructor's office hours.

Oral Presentations

Some instructors require students to give oral presentations in class. Eloquence and effectiveness in public speaking cannot be mastered in a week or two, but you can make a start by taking such an assignment seriously and adequately preparing yourself for it. If you are allowed the option, reading from a prepared text is often the safest procedure. However, this type of delivery can lead to a dull presentation. It is usually better to speak from notes: your presentation will be livelier and more enjoyable for the class. To do a good job, you need to be fully familiar with your subject and pay close attention to getting your points across. Prepare your presentation outline as you would the outline for a short paper. (See "Creating a Writing Outline" in Chapter 6, p. 109). Be sure to cover all the important points and to present them in a logical manner.

Guidelines for Speaking in Class

- Be familiar with the subject under discussion.
- If you are unclear about something the instructor or another student has said, compose and ask your question.
- If you are contributing an opinion, be sure that it is an informed one.
- If you disagree with something said, make your point clearly and constructively.
- Be respectful of others; always treat your classmates as you would expect to be treated.
- If you don't have a chance to raise a question in class, ask your instructor after class.

Guidelines for Giving an Oral Presentation

- If you work from 3-by-5 note cards, put only one or two headings on each card.
- Write neatly and use phrases, not whole sentences. Note any breaks needed for visual material.
- Put a number in the corner of each note card so that the cards will not get out of order. If working from a laptop, be sure that your screens are in the proper order.
- If you have a time limit, rehearse your talk beforehand so that you won't need to rush. Pare down your notes to fit the time needed to present the material clearly.
- Art, audio, or video can make your presentation much more interesting. (See also the next section, on presentation tools.) Make sure, however, that you have the resources you need beforehand and that you know how to integrate them easily and smoothly into your verbal remarks. Remember, visuals may add to the length of your presentation.
- Relax! Speak slowly and clearly, and make eye contact with your audience every few sentences.

Use short phrases rather than sentences in your presentation notes. Suppose you intend to tell the class the following: "Before 1848, most of the large landowners in California were Mexicans. In the decades after the United States annexed California, these Californios, as they were called, lost most of their lands to migrants from the eastern states." Your notes need only say:

(a) Until 1848 big landowners Californios.

(b) Cal. annexed in 1848.

(c) Lost land to easterners.

Once you are fully prepared, practice your presentation before a relative, friend, or roommate (or even in front of a mirror). Be sure that you exhibit knowledge of your subject because this is most likely to determine your grade. Effective public speaking is one of the most important tools for success in many fields of work, and giving a talk in class is a good opportunity to develop your skills in this area.

Creating Media Presentations

Most people know how to put together a slideshow using PowerPoint or similar programs. Slides with text that lists the points you wish to make might be helpful. However, if what you say is more or less the same as what the slides say, your audience will likely read the slides and become disengaged. Instead, use your presentation as an opportunity to create slides that deepen what you are saying, illustrate points you are making, or open the way for a new idea you present. It takes times to create slides that contain more than words or pictures. Combining text, visual, and audio material greatly enhances your presentation. A wealth of documentary pictures, photographs, maps, and so on, are downloadable from the web. Being able to integrate these elements into verbal presentations is becoming a highly valued skill. You could take advantage of your assignment to become more familiar with programs that enable you to layer one kind of media over or under another. Still, your creation should not be so attractive that it pushes the history analysis into the background.

A multimedia presentation takes time to prepare. Go through it at least once to be sure that the sound/video/photograph/art/text combination you create will be clear and comprehensible. Preview the screens for both content and sequence. Take some time to rehearse the presentation to make sure it fits into the time allotted, and that your words can be heard over any audio you have included. Lastly, be sure the technology you need for your presentation is available in your classroom.

Group Work

Your instructor may ask you to be part of a small group and carry out an assignment working with members of that group. Conducting research and preparing a group paper or presentation can be tricky but also rewarding. The key to success is to clarify who in the group is to do what part of the assignment. It's a good idea to choose one person who will check to be sure that each member is prepared when the time comes. Group communications on- or off-line should be more than chats. Group projects are built on serious discussions. It may be helpful to keep a record of these exchanges. This kind of collaboration is even more important if the instructor assigns a group grade, rather than individual grades for the project.

Another kind of group work takes place outside the classroom. Known as **peer reviewing** or **peer editing**, this type of work requires you to evaluate the work of a classmate. For example, you may be asked to read and comment

---

Guidelines for Peer Reviewing

- Don't be overly critical. Your goal is to assist your classmate in seeing the strengths and weaknesses in his or her draft. Your ability to do this comes from your outsider status: you have not been submerged in the research and are able to take a fresh look at the essay.
- Pay special attention to the thesis of the essay. Is it stated in clear terms?
- Does the body of the paper provide important evidence to support the thesis?
- Are the points made in support of the thesis well organized, and are they clear to you as a reader?
- Are the paper's conclusions justified by its arguments and documentation?
- Whether your comments to your classmate are written or oral, be supportive. Give the writer the kind of help you hope to get from your own peer reviewer.

---

on a student's rough draft of an assignment. Your peer review may take the form of an informal one-on-one review in which you go through the paper with the author point by point. Some instructors may ask you to write your evaluation or mark up a draft with comments; others may want your review in the form of a class presentation. No matter what the format is, remember to provide *constructive* criticism that will help your classmates develop their papers. Be sure to point out a paper's strengths in addition to any weaknesses.

If you are asked to peer-edit the work of a classmate, remember also to pay particular attention to the **thesis** of the paper. Ask yourself whether the thesis is stated clearly and whether there is sufficient **evidence** to support it. In addition, you should consider whether the information has been presented in an organized manner, such that your classmate's conclusions are justified. Unless specifically told to do so, don't focus on minor issues, such as misspellings and other typos, especially when reviewing a **rough draft**.

Learning to work collaboratively will be of use when you leave school and enter a working environment in which these kinds of personal and digital interactions are common. Moreover, the ability to accept constructive criticism and use it to improve a piece of work is a skill that will help you no matter what career you choose after your history course. The sooner you get used to sharing drafts via email or posting your comments on a peer project online, the more comfortable you'll feel receiving this kind of feedback. In the end, this give-and-take is an important building block for critical thinking, good writing habits, and a host of other skills necessary for graduate and professional work.

INTERACTIVE COURSE CONTENT

If any aspect of a course is placed online, be sure you know what it consists of and what is expected of you. Your instructor may utilize this element of course work minimally or extensively. Take the time to understand any online aspects of the course. Be sure that you are aware of assignments or exercises that need to be done online. You'll also want to take note of any related material, either embedded in the online syllabus or in any links that take you to digitally stored materials or to websites. Make note of how you will need to respond to online requirements or contribute to interactive aspects of a course. Be sure that your role in any interaction is a serious one. Whether sitting in a traditional or virtual classroom, the same degree of responsibility will be expected of you.

Some professors and students use online resources to enhance or expand their academic experience, or sometimes they may take the course entirely online. Many instructors post the course syllabus and assignments online, perhaps in a secure environment such as Blackboard, Canvas, or Moodle. They may, for example, incorporate links to valuable websites that have primary sources or images as a part of an assignment or as background information. Be sure you are clear about your responsibilities for these elements of the course.

Online discussion may be a formal part of your course work. Again, make sure you know what is expected of you. Learn the ground rules for these discussions: the topic you will need to address, the form of your remarks, and how to treat the people you are talking to. You may be asked to post a more formal comment or write a blog. This may require careful preparation, especially if your comments are part of a thread and will be archived.

Some professors set up interactive environments of a less formal nature to give you the opportunity to raise issues, pose questions, or join in an open discussion. Again, learn the ground rules and then use these opportunities to enrich your learning experience.

Cooperative Learning

Online communication enables you to get in touch with people who may have ideas and experience valuable to your historical research. Such people might become part of your research, especially if your course includes assignments in the world outside your classroom. Your instructor most likely will set out guidelines for such an assignment. The information here is not a substitute for those instructions.

You may know of people with academic training related to your research. You will need to explain yourself and your research to them and be clear about what you are asking for. If they cannot help you, they might let you know of another person who can. Don't expect busy people to assist you, however; they may have other priorities. If you receive a positive response, let your instructor know; there may be dos and don'ts you should be aware of.

Cooperative learning with people outside of academia may provide you with important information as well. Their work or their life history may offer you a new perspective on your research. Also, your own life might be of interest to them. Make your motives clear to these people and treat them with respect. If people offer personal information, be certain you have their permission to include it in your research. (If you offer information about yourself, a similar caution should be exercised.) A legal issue may be involved. Check with your instructor before you enter the world of someone else's privacy. Be sure your instructor is aware of your contacts.

Knowledge of history in books, articles, courses, and documents can make you aware of a world that you can no longer enter but that can enter your mind and be as real as any experience. Being in touch with people whose past and current thinking is new to you offers another kind of connection to the past. This kind of experience may help you understand why the focus of humanistic disciplines is people, whenever they may have lived.

CHAPTER

3

Working with Different Types of Historical Evidence

As we will discuss in Chapter 7, historians usually begin the research process with a pointed question that provides a focus for their study. A historian might ask, for example, "Why did China deemphasize naval exploration and trade by the Middle Ages?" or "What led the Populist Party in the United States to fuse with the Democratic Party in 1896?" Once a historian has settled on a **research question**, he or she will begin looking for **evidence** that can lead to an answer. The evidence available to historians falls into two general categories: primary sources of evidence and secondary sources of evidence.

PRIMARY SOURCES

The raw materials that historians use as they reconstruct the past are known as **primary sources**. These are the firsthand records of an event that come directly from the participants. Witnesses may record what they saw or heard. People caught up in an event may describe what they thought and felt at that time. A drawing of an animal, scratched on a cave wall thousands of years ago, is primary evidence of what that person saw. (It may also be evidence of how that person thought about the animal.) A map of the world drawn in the sixteenth century as well as a later copy of the map (as long as the copy is identical) is another example of primary evidence.

Written primary sources include personal documents, such as letters and diaries, and published works, such as memoirs and newspaper articles. Official statements such as royal decrees, church edicts, advertisements, and political party platforms are considered primary sources, as are official records and vital statistics such as marriage, birth, and death statistics; census

$ _____ **KNOW ALL MEN BY THESE PRESENTS**, That we are held and
firmly bound unto *Colin Clarke* _____
in the just and full sum of *Twelve Dollars of fifty cents ($12.50)*
to be paid to the said *Colin Clarke, his agents* _____ executors,
administrators, or assigns, on or before the *first day of April next* A. D. 1848.
*In the like sum to be paid on the first of July 1848. In
the like sum to be paid on the first of October 1848, and
in the like sum to be paid on, or before the first day
of January in the year Eighteen hundred and forty
nine (1849)* _____
being for the hire of *a negro man slave named, Anthony, to be
employed as a farm hand, or gardner, for the year Eighteen
hundred of forty eight (1848)* _____
Said negro — to be furnished with the customary summer clothing, and to be returned to the said
Colin Clarke _____ or to *his* agent s
in Richmond, on the *twenty fifth* day of *December next*, with
a good winter suit, *a hat and a blanket* _____

For the true and faithful performance of which we do hereby bind ourselves, our heirs, executors and administrators, jointly and severally, firmly by these presents,

As witness our hands and seals this *6th* day of *January*
A. D. one thousand, eighteen hundred and *Forty Eight (1848)*

Robt Baird ⬛ SEAL. ⬛

P W Harwood ⬛ SEAL. ⬛

⬛ SEAL. ⬛

N. B.—Should the above named negro require medical aid in the course of the year, notice must be given to the
said *Colin Clarke* _____ or to *his* agent s in Richmond,
if practicable, if not, Doctor s *R. of R. Cabell* _____ and no other Physician must be employed.

FIGURE 3.1 Example of Primary Evidence (1848)

If you were pursuing the research question "How common was the practice of hiring out slaves in antebellum Virginia?" you might find this 1848 contract to be an informative primary source. Consider the blend of printed and handwritten text on this page. What does the preprinted nature of the form tell us about the practice of slave hiring? What is implied by the schedule of payments and the other conditions of the transaction? Can we learn anything about the "negro man slave named Anthony" from this document?

Robert Baird Papers, David M. Rubenstein Rare Book & Manuscript Library, Duke University

FIGURE 3.2   Example of Primary Evidence (1918)

This World War I–era poster depicts a Red Cross nurse holding a wounded U.S. soldier on a stretcher. What message do you think the artist is trying to promote here? What audience do you think the poster is aimed at? Do you think a similar image would be effective in the United States today?

Library of Congress Prints and Photographs Division, Reproduction number LC-DIG-anrc-08195 (digital file from original) data; property deeds; contracts; and transcripts of legal proceedings. Primary sources can range from a business letter (or an email) to a poem. And a reprinted (or digitized) copy of a primary source is still a primary source.

Eyewitnesses and artists have left us with *nonwritten* primary sources such as maps, illustrations, and, in more recent generations, photographs, audiotapes, and videos. **Artifacts** (like the cave drawing) are yet another type of nonwritten primary source. Artifacts are objects made and used by people in the past: houses, public buildings, tools, clothing, and much more. (Museum exhibits are often displays of artifacts.) Figures 3.1 (a slave contract from 1848) and 3.2 (a Red Cross poster from 1918), as well as Figures 3.4 through 3.16, are all examples of primary sources.

Primary source websites are abundant. For example, UCLA has an online archive of Mexican and Mexican American audio recordings; Vanderbilt University has a TV news archive; Alexander Street has an archive of women's letters. To get an idea of the size and variety of primary source websites, visit the largest of them all: "American Memory" hosted by the U.S. Library of Congress (**memory.loc.gov/ammem/browse**).

SECONDARY SOURCES

Secondary sources are the findings of writers who were not participants in a historical episode but have investigated primary evidence of it, as historians do when they conduct their research. When historians publish the results of

Historians played a central role in producing the *Final Report of the National Commission on Terrorist Attacks upon the United States*, otherwise known as *The 9/11 Commission Report*. The 9/11 Commission was established in November 2002 to investigate the facts and circumstances relating to the events of September 11, 2001. It was an initiative that came not from the White House or Congress, but rather at the insistence of the families of those who died in the attacks and who wanted a full accounting of what happened and why. Based on reviewing more than 2.5 million pages of documents and 1,200 interviews in 10 countries, as well as numerous public hearings,[1] the *9/11 Report* was a combination of fast-paced narrative chronicling the events of the separate hijackings and the personal history of the attackers, the story of the response and the responders, as well as recommendations for prevention of future terrorist attacks and for reorganization of the U.S. government to that end. As the Commission's senior advisor Ernest May put it, the report provided the "long background."[2]

[1] Thomas Kean, chair; Lee Hamilton, vice chair. *The 9/11 Commission Report*, authorized edition (Washington, DC: Government Printing Office, 2004), preface, xv–xviii.

[2] Ernest R. May, "When Government Writes History: A Memory of the 9/11 Commission," *The New Republic*, May 23, 2005: 30–35, especially p. 31.

FIGURE 3.3   Example of Secondary Evidence (2012)

This example is a paragraph from a scholarly article by Arnita A. Jones entitled "The Promise of Policy History in the Public History Curriculum," which appeared in the journal *Federal History* in 2012.

their research, they create secondary sources, which are read by other scholars and by students. Most history books and articles are secondary sources, and their **notes** and **bibliography** identify the primary sources that the historians examined. For example, a contemporary book about family life in fourteenth-century England would be considered a secondary source that is based on primary sources such as wills written during that period that describe the kinds of property inherited. If your own work is based on primary sources, your research paper will become a secondary source for others to read. Articles in academic journals are common secondary sources. For an example of such a secondary source, see Figure 3.3 (p. 43).

WHEN A SECONDARY SOURCE BECOMES A PRIMARY SOURCE

It is important to understand the basic differences between primary and secondary sources, and also to understand that in certain situations, a secondary source can *become* a primary one. Here are three examples:

1. In 2018, a historian is writing a book that discusses *the views* of early twentieth-century historians on the reasons for the decline of the Roman Empire. The works from the early twentieth century that the historian uses as his sources would generally be considered secondary works because they were written more than fifteen hundred years after the end of the Roman Empire. However, for the contemporary historian's study, they are considered primary sources because they provide *direct* evidence of what early twentieth-century historians thought about the decline of the Roman Empire.

2. In 1990, a U.S. senator writes an article about the background of the men in his state who signed the Declaration of Independence. The senator's article is a secondary source because it is based on primary sources from the time of the American Revolution rather than on his direct experience. However, if a historian, say in 2018, writes a biography of the senator that includes an analysis of the senator's views about the period of the Revolution, then the senator's article becomes a primary source because it represents *direct* evidence about the senator's views on the Revolution.

3. In History 101, a student is analyzing a document written in the tenth century that describes a much earlier document from the eighth century. If, as far as we know, the earlier eighth-century document no longer exists, then the tenth-century document is as close to the original event as we are likely to get. In such a case, if we trust the accuracy of the tenth-century account, that evidence would be considered primary because it is as close to the event as we are able to get.

ACCESSING SOURCES OF EVIDENCE
IN PRINT, IN PERSON, AND ONLINE

Don't be confused by the form in which you come across primary evidence. You may find it in print, in a museum, on a website, or in a database. In each case it is still a primary source. Written primary sources are often digitized to make them available on the web. If you find them there, as long as they are faithful copies, they remain primary evidence. Sound and video are often digitized as well. Here, you need to be sure that the digitized version is not taken from a performance different from the original. A sound recording of a Delta blues singer from the 1920s is very different than a cover version of it made in the 1950s. The recording made in the 1920s is a primary source. The "cover" is not. (However, remember, the secondary source can become primary if you are looking for the special 1950s sound of Delta blues.) You might, for example, view John Singer Sargent's painting *Gassed* as an illustration in a book or on a website, or you may even have the opportunity to see the actual painting at the Imperial War Museum in London, England. Sargent's painting, based on his own experiences in World War I, is in each case an example of primary evidence. The quality of the image may vary somewhat, and your own viewing experience may change depending on the environment in which you view it—a computer screen versus the real-life painting, which is twenty feet long—but the art-work itself, which Sargent painted as he witnessed soldiers during World War I, remains a primary source no matter how you access it.

As another example, a primary source book might be out of print and difficult to track down physically, but it may be available in digital format on a website such as Project Gutenberg. The important point to keep in mind is that a primary source book, such as *The Autobiography of Malcolm X*, is still a book and still a primary source whether it is accessed online or in print. The same is true for an artifact, such as the grinding stones shown in Figure 3.16 (p. 65). It is still an artifact and still a primary source whether you encounter it in person or see a photograph in a text such as this.

Secondary sources also maintain their status as secondary regardless of the way they are accessed. A scholarly journal article might be available both in print and in an electronic database such as *JSTOR*. But whether you read the print version or the electronic version, you are still reading a journal article and it is still a secondary source.

READING WRITTEN SOURCES

Reading history can be a satisfying experience, but to enjoy the landscape you must first know where you are: you must have a general sense of the subject and of the manner in which it is being presented. If you begin reading before you get your bearings, you may become lost in a forest of unfamiliar facts and interpretations. Before you begin reading any written document, look it over carefully. If you are reading a secondary source, look at the preface or **introduction**. This should tell you something about the author and his or her purpose in writing the work. For articles, read through the brief **abstract** (article summary), if there is one, to get a sense of the central **argument**. Also scan the table of contents of a book to get a sense of the way in which the author organized the subject. Next, skim the text itself, reading headings and glancing at illustrations and graphed material. If you have the time, preread the opening and concluding chapters of a book (or the opening and concluding paragraphs of an article) rapidly before reading the full work. For further advice on reading written sources, see the guidelines below.

After you've looked over the document in these ways, you will be ready to read. By this time, you should be familiar with the source's **topic** (what aspects of history the source covers), the background of the author (politician, journalist, historian, eyewitness, novelist, etc.), when the document was written (a hundred-year-old letter, the most recent book on a subject, etc.),

Guidelines for Working with Written Sources

- Find a place with very few distractions, and allot enough time to complete the reading assignment in one sitting.
- Consider the main purpose of your source in order to place it in context. How does it relate to the other readings for your course or for your research? How might it apply to or enhance your class assignments or lectures?
- Before reading a book or long article all the way through, preread it by looking over the table of contents and scan it for headings or visual matter. Skim the text to get a quick sense of what it covers.
- Look for a paragraph or two that provides information about the author. Is he or she a scholar in the field? Does he or she appear to have any particular motivation or bias in writing the piece?
- For primary texts, read through any headnotes or captions that provide background information on the source, keeping in mind that such material constitutes *secondary* source matter that was added later.
- As you read through the source, constantly interrogate it. Why does the author say that? What sources is he or she citing to support that point? Why is he or she spending so much time on a particular point?
- Read actively, taking notes on any points that strike you as particularly strange, persuasive, surprising, illuminating, or otherwise significant. If you are working from your own printout or copy of the book, mark it up and write in the margins; otherwise, take notes in a notebook or on your computer.
- For details on evaluating written primary and secondary sources, consult Chapter 4 (pp. 69–71).
- For advice on writing about assigned readings, see Chapter 5.

how it is organized (chronologically, topically, etc.), and, most important of all, its **thesis** and **conclusions**. The thesis is the principal point that an author wishes to make on a subject: this might be that the geography of Spain was a significant factor in that nation's failure to industrialize in the eighteenth and nineteenth centuries or that disagreement on moral issues between the physicists J. Robert Oppenheimer and Edward Teller delayed development of the hydrogen bomb. Most authors set out their thesis in a preface or introduction. If you understand the principal point the author is trying to make, then the organization and conclusions of the work will become clear to you. The author will be organizing evidence and drawing conclusions to support the thesis. The ability to recognize and describe a weak thesis or unsupportive evidence is part of learning history too. (For a discussion of thesis and argument, see Chapter 6, pp. 107–09, and Chapter 8, pp. 140–43.)

In many instances, a primary source, even a written one, may not have a thesis. For example, a raw primary source, such as a birth certificate or a land ownership record, will not contain a thesis. When you are assessing sources, the presence of a thesis statement is not as significant for primary sources as it is for secondary sources, which almost always should have a clear thesis statement or argument.

Primary Texts

One of your most important tasks when reading a primary source is determining its reliability. Primary sources can be fraudulent, inaccurate, or **biased**. Eyewitness accounts may have been deliberately distorted in order to avert blame or to bestow praise on a particular individual or group. Without intending to misinform, even on-the-scene judgments can be incorrect. Sometimes, the closer you are to an event, the more emotionally involved you are, and this involvement distorts your understanding of it. We can all recall events in which we completely misunderstood the feelings, actions, and words of another person. Historians have to weigh evidence carefully to see whether those who participated in an event understood it well enough to describe it accurately. Official statements present another problem—the issue of propaganda or concealment. A government, group, or institution may make statements that it wishes others to believe but that are not true. What a group says may not be what it does. This is especially true in politics.

To check the reliability of evidence, historians use the tests of consistency and corroboration: Does the evidence contradict itself, and does it disagree with evidence from other sources? Historical research always involves checking one source against another. For example, Figure 3.4 (p. 48) presents two primary documents that report the fighting at Lexington and Concord, Massachusetts, in 1775—battles that began the Revolutionary War. In what important ways do the two accounts differ? How do you think the conflicting goals of the colonists and the English soldiers biased each report of the battle? What phrases could you pull out of each document to highlight the bias? Notice that the American version talks of "some inhabitants

AMERICAN ACCOUNT OF THE BATTLE OF LEXINGTON:

Account by the Provincial Congress at Watertown Massachusetts, April 26, 1775

By the clearest depositions relative to this transaction, it will appear that on the night preceding the nineteenth of April instant, a body of the king's troops, under the command of colonel Smith, were secretly landed at Cambridge, with an apparent design to take or destroy the military and other stores, provided for the defense of this colony, and deposited at Concord—that some inhabitants of the colony, on the night aforesaid, whilst travelling peaceably on the road, between Boston and Concord, were seized and greatly abused by armed men, who appeared to be officers of general Gage's army; that the town of Lexington, by these means, was alarmed, and a company of the inhabitants mustered on the occasion—that the regular troops on their way to Concord, marched into the said town of Lexington, and the said company, on their approach, began to disperse—that, notwithstanding this, the regulars rushed on with great violence and first began hostilities, by firing on said Lexington company, whereby they killed eight, and wounded several others—that the regulars continued their fire, until those of said company, who were neither killed nor wounded, had made their escape—that colonel Smith, with the detachment then marched to Concord, where a number of provincials were again fired on by the troops, two of them killed and several wounded, before the provincials fired on them, and provincials were again fired on by the troops, produced an engagement that lasted through the day, in which many of the provincials and more of the regular troops were killed and wounded. . . .

By order,

Joseph Warren, President.

ENGLISH ACCOUNT OF THE BATTLE OF LEXINGTON:

Report of Lieutenant-Colonel Smith to Governor Gage, April 22, 1775

I think it proper to observe, that when I had got some miles on the march from Boston, I detached six light infantry companies to march with all expedition to seize the two bridges on different roads beyond Concord. On these companies' arrival at Lexington, I understand, from the report of Major Pitcairn, who was with them, and from many officers, that they found on a green close to the road a body of the country people drawn up in military order, with arms and accoutrements, and, as appeared after, loaded; and that they had posted some men in a dwelling and Meeting-house. Our troops advanced towards them, without any intention of injuring them, further than to inquire the reason of their being thus assembled, and, if not satisfactory, to have secured their arms; but they in confusion went off, principally to the left, only one of them fired before he went off, and three or four more jumped over a wall and fired from behind it among the soldiers; on which the troops returned it, and killed several of them. They likewise fired on the soldiers from the Meeting and dwelling-houses. . . . While at Concord we saw vast numbers assembling in many parts; at one of the bridges they marched down, with a very considerable body, on the light infantry posted there. On their coming pretty near, one of our men fired on them, which they returned; on which an action ensued, and some few were killed and wounded. . . . On our leaving Concord to return to Boston, they began to fire on us from behind the walls, ditches, trees, &c., which, as we marched, increased to a very great degree, and continued without intermission of five minutes altogether, for, I believe, upwards of eighteen miles. . . .

I have the honor, &c.,

F. Smith, Lieutenant-Colonel 10th Foot.

FIGURE 3.4   Two Conflicting Primary Documents

of the colony" who while "travelling peaceably" were "seized and greatly abused" by the English soldiers. The English officer, in contrast, says that the Americans were "drawn up in military order, with arms" and that his troops were "without any intention of injuring them." You should be able to find other important differences in the two reports of the fighting. Also, as you read the documents, consider what additional sources would help you decide which report is more accurate. The two accounts agree on some facts but disagree on the responsibility for the fighting. Eyewitness accounts from other English soldiers and from American colonials who were there will help in determining which description is more accurate. It might turn out, for example, that parts of *each* account are correct and other parts are distorted in some way. Sometimes there is no *one* true source for the history of an event. Still, the more primary sources you read, the closer you will come to know the event in all its details and meanings.

Scholarly Articles

One of the most important ways that historians present new scholarship in their field is through the publication of **scholarly articles**. These *secondary* sources are essays of about thirty to fifty pages that are found in academic (scholarly) journals. (For tips on how to identify scholarly articles, see the guidelines on p. 50.) Academic journals, such as the *American Historical Review*, differ from popular magazines, such as *Time*, because their articles are based on original research into primary sources. In addition, articles in most academic journals are **refereed** or **peer reviewed**, which means that other experts in the field assess the essay's quality before it is published in the journal. An excerpt from a scholarly article appears in Figure 3.3.

If provided, an abstract at the beginning of a scholarly article will tell you the gist of the essay, but you'll need to read the entire essay in order to evaluate it properly. Every article should have a clear thesis or central argument stated either explicitly or implicitly at the beginning. If there is an abstract, it is likely to summarize the thesis of the article.

To read an article most effectively, identify the thesis right away and consider whether the evidence that the author used supports it. Once you've read through the article, you should consider its wider place in the literature. In other words, you'll want to know not only what an author is saying but why he or she is saying it. Is this a case study meant to explore a theory developed elsewhere? Is the author challenging another historian's interpretation of a subject? Does the article revise a commonly accepted historical viewpoint? Take notes on the article to help you digest its main points and analyze its underlying philosophy.

NOTE: Historians commonly reserve broad philosophical questions for their footnotes or endnotes. In order to assess the larger purpose of the article, be sure to pay attention to the source's citations—footnotes, endnotes, and bibliography.

Guidelines for Identifying Scholarly Articles

- Look at the publisher of the article. Does the piece appear in a journal or in an anthology of articles published by a university press or non-profit institution (such as the Organization of American Historians)?
- Examine the author's credentials. Authors of scholarly articles typically hold academic positions.
- Read the complete title of the article. Scholarly article titles usually include a description of the article's content.
- Review the editorial apparatus surrounding the article. Is there an abstract (brief summary) at the beginning? Are there footnotes or endnotes that cite both primary and secondary sources? Is there a bibliography or a works-cited section? Your article need not have all of these elements, but if it has none of them, it lacks the methodological rigor demanded of scholarly research.
- Consider the article's physical appearance. Most scholarly articles consist of text alone and rely on few or no fancy typefaces and graphics. If the article contains images, charts, or tables, they should have citations explaining their origin. Articles published in scholarly journals will also have fewer advertisements around them than those in popular magazines.
- If you still have doubts about whether an article is scholarly, check with a reference librarian or ask your professor for help.

Monographs

One of the most common secondary sources of historical work is a **monograph**—a book-length study of one specialized topic. When you are reading a monograph, pay special attention to the point of view, for your instructor may expect you to learn not only about the topic but also about the argument and evidence presented in the work. You will need to determine the author's assumptions and values, and to understand his or her thesis and conclusions. Read this kind of work not only to absorb the facts but also to analyze, question, and criticize. If you own the book, you can do your questioning and criticizing in the margins. If the book is not yours, or if you wish to have an organized set of notes about it, summarize the contents and the author's thesis in a notebook or computer file. You can then review your notes or annotations before an exam. (For more on taking notes, see Chapter 4, "Interpreting Sources and Taking Notes," pp. 75–84.)

Anthologies

Another kind of work in history is an anthology—a collection of readings on a particular subject, usually primary documents (such as letters, diaries, and legal documents) or excerpted sections from larger primary or secondary works. All of the general suggestions concerning the reading of historical sources apply here as well, but this type of work often calls for a particular kind of reading. Each selection usually discusses a different aspect or interpretation of the subject or is a different kind of evidence about the subject. Some selections may be in serious disagreement. Instructors expect students to be able to assess the arguments of the various authors and documents and on occasion to take a position in the debate. Therefore, you should read this particular kind of collection with an eye to analyzing the different kinds of evidence or the arguments of the different authors. A good way to do this is to summarize briefly the argument or approach of each selection.

Literature

Works of fiction—novels, poems, short stories, and so on—are primary sources of evidence to anyone conducting research on a well-known author or the literature of a particular time or place. Sometimes a work of fiction is based on actual occurrences and real people. Historical fiction is often more dramatic and more personal than an article or monograph and describes the presumed feelings of individuals caught up in important historical events. Reading a historical novel gives you a feel for the times in which it is set and for the historical material it contains. A novelist who knows a historical period or event well can bring it to life in ways that scholarly works cannot, but be cautious not to treat a fictional text as historical truth.

WHAT IS A POINT OF VIEW

Authors of primary and secondary sources have a bias of some kind that is reflected in what they write. This bias does not mean that what they write is not worth reading. **Bias** is better understood as an author's **point of view**, that is, the point from which the author views the subject. A historian examining primary and secondary sources also has a point of view. This point of view is often referred to as the historian's **perspective** on the topic he or she is researching. A historian's perspective is more complex than that of the defense attorney who attempts to convince the jury that his or her client is innocent. Like the attorney, the author presents evidence and arguments to persuade the reader. But the similarity goes only so far. The jury knows in advance what the defense attorney's perspective will be, and their verdict makes clear that the argument has or has not convinced them. The historian's perspective is not set out in advance. The historian's education and research will slowly create his or her perspective and it will influence the way he or she explores the subject. A historian faces not an up-or-down verdict by his or her readers, but is part of a long discussion during which his or her point of view will gain or lose influence among historians and the readers of history. Perhaps the historian will change his or her own perspective.

By reading carefully and critically and noting the evidence presented, the author's perspective should gradually become clear. In most cases, the author will summarize the evidence and the conclusions drawn from it. The author does not claim that his or her conclusions are the only ones possible. History is not a science, and all conclusions are open to revision or even rejection. You need to consider the evidence and the conclusions, not to make a final judgment of the author's perspective but to understand how that perspective influenced his or her thinking and research.

NOTE: A point of view is much stronger than a mere opinion. What some-one thinks about strawberry ice cream, the way a friend laughs, or a sunset is a personal opinion. Next week their opinion might change.

"READING" NONWRITTEN SOURCES

Depending on the assignment, you may need to interpret maps, videos, sound recordings, artwork, photographs, statistical data, and other non-written sources. To use these kinds of resources effectively, you will need to learn how to work with them. The guidelines below provide general advice for interpreting nonwritten sources; the sections that follow provide details on how to examine specific types of nonwritten documents.

Maps

Important aspects of the historical record can be displayed in maps. The land-scape is one of history's fundamental settings. The rise and fall of empires, the course of wars, the growth of cities, the development of trade routes, and much more can be traced on maps of large areas. Figure 3.5 (p. 53) indicates the years in which parts of Africa came under European colonial rule. This map tells you which European countries controlled which parts of Africa and when this control was established. Analyzing the map, you can see that Britain and France had the largest colonial empires in Africa and that most of Africa was still free of colonial rule before the 1880s. Figure 3.6 (p. 54) indicates the dates on which the nations of Africa became independent. By comparing this map with Figure 3.5, you can determine which countries changed their names upon achieving independence. Comparing the dates on the two maps, you can figure out how long colonial rule lasted in different countries. Notice also that the first wave of independence came in the 1960s and that the dates of Namibian and Eritrean independence are in the 1990s.

Small area maps can show the layout of villages, the outcome of battles, or the location of mines, canals, and railroads. To read a map, you must understand the *key*, which translates the symbols used on the map. A line on a map may identify a road, a river, or a gas pipeline. The key tells you which it is. The *scale* of a map tells you the actual size of the area the map

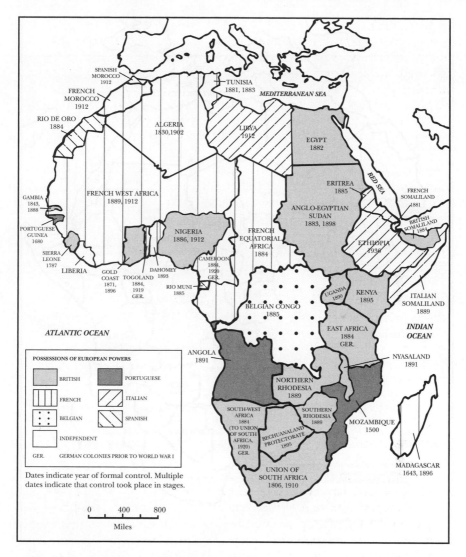

FIGURE 3.5   The March of Colonialism in Africa

represents. Maps are an important aid in understanding history because they display the physical relationships between places. Never ignore maps in a textbook or other reading. It is also wise to put a good map of the area you are studying on your wall or your laptop so that you can see the location of places mentioned in lectures and readings.

Old maps are primary documents. The way that old maps describe the territories they cover can give you clues as to what was going on in the mind of the mapmaker—an eyewitness to that era—when the map was created. A good example of the mapmaker's perspective can usually be found in the artwork around the border.

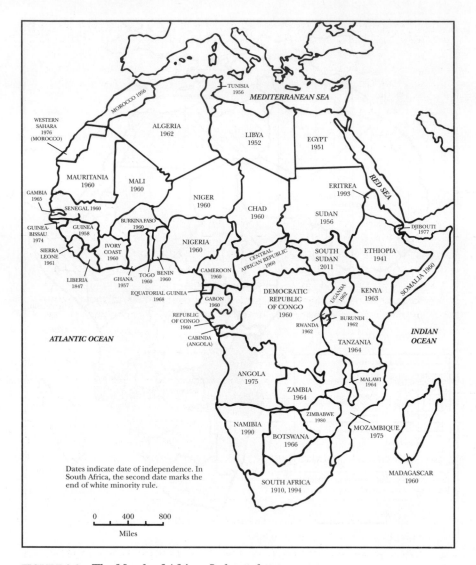

FIGURE 3.6   The March of African Independence

Statistical Data

History resources often include statistical data arranged in charts, graphs, or tables. These data describe the quantities of something (such as warships, marriages, schools, bridges, or deaths from smallpox) at a specific time in the past, and usually they compare these amounts (such as the number of marriages in relation to the number of schools) or trace changes in amounts over time (such as the number of warships in 1820, 1830, and 1840).

Figure 3.7 (p. 55) shows a tabular arrangement of statistical data with an explanation of how to read them. The table organizes population statistics from different regions and across two and a half centuries. Reading

Guidelines for Interpreting Nonwritten Sources

- If a source is accompanied by written background information, such as a caption or a headnote, read it to gain a fuller understanding of the source.
- Consider where, when, and by whom the source was created. As with written sources, understanding the historical context in which a nonwritten document was made can help you to make sense of it.
- Consider the original purpose of the source. Was it designed to inform, persuade, or entertain (or some combination of these)? Was it utilitarian in nature?
- Determine why the source still exists. Why has it been preserved or included in a collection for present-day audiences? The act of making a source available may imply a particular agenda or point of view.
- If you are dealing with a restoration or reproduction of an item, such as a reconstructed temple or a print of a cave drawing, find out if any alterations in color, size, or scope have been made.
- Make certain you know whether any audiovisual materials you are using (including photographs and sound and video recordings) have been edited from their original format.

Major area	1750	1800	1850	1900	1950	1999	2010
Africa	106	107	111	133	221	767	1,020
Asia	502	635	809	947	1,402	3,634	4,160
Europe	163	203	276	408	547	729	738
Latin America and the Caribbean	16	24	38	74	167	511	590
Northern America	2	7	26	82	172	307	345
Oceania	2	2	2	6	13	30	37

FIGURE 3.7   Estimated World Population, 1750–2010
Numbers represent millions of persons.
Data from Population Division, Department of Economic and Social Affairs, United Nations Secretariat.

across the rows allows you to trace the changes in population of a particular region at fifty-year intervals. You can note the change for each region and the rate of change. For example, the population of Africa barely increased in the fifty years between 1750 and 1800, but it grew by 800 million in the sixty years between 1950 and 2010. Reading down the columns, you can compare the populations of each region during the same period. In 1750, the population of Latin America and the Caribbean was eight times greater than the population of Northern America. In 1950, the two populations were nearly the same, and by 2010, the Latin American population had outpaced the Northern American population once again.

More complex comparisons can be made from Figure 3.7 by combining the differences between regions (reading down) and their rates of growth over time (reading across). For example, you can discover that whereas the population of Asia grew more than that of any other region in absolute terms, its *rate* of growth from 1850 to 2010 (809 million to 4,160 million, or about 500 percent) was much less than that of Africa (111 million to 1,020 million, or around 900 percent) in the same time period.

Even the cold statistics of a table can provide images of the great drama of history. The negligible increase in African population between 1750 and 1850 may tell us something of the impact of the slave trade, and the large increase in the U.S. population between 1850 and 1900 tells us something about the history of European emigration.

The information in the table can be presented differently in order to highlight different aspects of the data. In Figure 3.8, the numbers for each region are represented as percentages of the total world population. By

Major area	1750	1800	1850	1900	1950	1999	2010
Africa	13.4	10.9	8.8	8.1	8.8	12.8	14.8
Asia	63.5	64.9	64.1	57.4	55.6	60.8	60.4
Europe	20.6	20.8	21.9	24.7	21.7	12.2	10.7
Latin America and the Caribbean	2.0	2.5	3.0	4.5	6.6	8.5	8.6
Northern America	0.3	0.7	2.1	5.0	6.8	5.1	5.0
Oceania	0.3	0.2	0.2	0.4	0.5	0.5	0.5

FIGURE 3.8   Estimated World Population, 1750–2010
Numbers represent percentages of the total world population.
Data from Population Division, Department of Economic and Social Affairs, United Nations Secretariat.

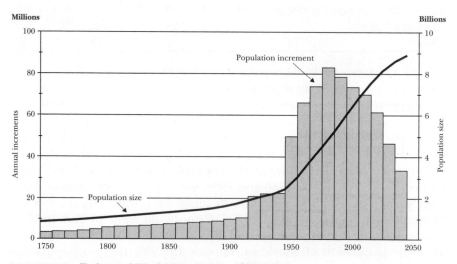

FIGURE 3.9   Estimated World Population, 1750–2050
Data from Population Division, Department of Economic and Social Affairs, United Nations Secretariat.

changing the numbers from absolute amounts to percentages, this table facilitates the comparing of populations and population growth.

Another way of presenting data is in the form of a graph. Notice that Figure 3.9 (p. 56) makes more obvious the differences between numbers and thus makes comparisons easier. However, ease of comparison is traded for loss of precision; the graph gives fewer specific numbers (along the vertical axis) than the table. A graph also often requires more space than a table to convey the same information. If Figure 3.9 included all six geographic regions listed in the table in Figure 3.8, it would be very large.

The more detailed the data and their arrangement are, the greater is the amount of historical information that can be displayed and the more intricate the comparisons that can be made. Figure 3.10 presents a table that lists the percentage of the total vote and the number of deputies elected to the German parliament (the Reichstag) by each of the major political

Party	1919	1920	1924	1928	1930	1932	1933
Communist							
# of deputies	0	4	45	54	77	89	81
% of total votes		2.1	9.0	10.6	13.1	14.3	12.3
Social Democratic							
# of deputies	165	102	131	153	143	133	120
% of total votes	37.9	21.7	26.0	29.8	24.5	21.6	18.3
Democratic							
# of deputies	75	39	32	25	20	4	5
% of total votes	18.5	8.3	6.3	4.9	3.8	1.0	0.9
Centrum							
# of deputies	91	64	69	62	68	75	74
% of total votes	19.7	13.6	13.6	12.1	11.8	12.5	11.2
Bavarian People's							
# of deputies	0	21	19	16	19	22	18
% of total votes		4.4	3.7	3.1	3.0	3.2	2.7
German People's							
# of deputies	19	65	51	45	30	7	2
% of total votes	4.4	13.9	10.1	8.7	4.5	1.2	1.1
National People's							
# of deputies	44	71	103	73	41	37	52
% of total votes	10.3	15.1	20.5	14.2	7.0	5.9	8.0
National Socialist							
# of deputies	0	0	14	12	107	230	288
% of total votes			3.0	2.6	18.3	37.3	43.9

FIGURE 3.10   Reich Elections, 1919–1933
Under the electoral system provided for in the Weimar Constitution, each party received approximately one representative for every 60,000 popular votes cast for its candidates. Various small parties, not listed here, were underrepresented in the Reichstag.
Data from E. Kolb, The Weimar Republic, *2nd ed. (New York: Routledge, 2005), 224–25.*

parties in each election from 1919 to 1933. (Notice that in a parliamentary system, elections do not come at regular intervals.)

This table allows you to follow the changing fortunes of each political party. A wealth of information on German political history is contained in these figures. Between the lines one can also find pieces of the social and economic history of Germany. For example, the strength of the Communist and Social Democratic (Socialist) Parties attests to the deep dissatisfaction of many German workers with the state of the economy during the period known as the Weimar Republic. Even more striking is the tremendous growth of the National Socialist (Nazi) Party after 1930. This development brought Adolf Hitler to power in 1933, and the results of that event would eventually reverberate around the world. As you can see, a table is more than just numbers.

Illustrations, Photographs, and Other Visual Material

Visual material also can present historical information. Gathering information from old paintings, drawings, and photographs, however, can be surprisingly difficult. First, you need to recognize the actual information that they present—what Columbus's ships looked like, how Hiroshima appeared after the explosion of the atomic bomb, and so on. Then you need to interpret them. Interpreting requires an effort to understand what the artist or photographer is "saying" in the work. When an artist draws something, and when a photographer takes a picture, he or she is not simply recording a visual image but sending a message to everyone who looks at the work. In this way, artists and photographers are like writers whose written work needs to be interpreted.

Another important aspect of a visual source is its artistic style. This refers not only to how a visual looks but also to where it fits in the history of art or photography. Is it a painting in the style of the Italian Renaissance (fifteenth century) or abstract expressionism (twentieth century)?

Figures 3.11 (p. 59) and 3.12 (p. 60) present two illustrations of the Spanish conquest of Mexico. See whether you can determine what they are saying.

Figure 3.11 is by a European artist and shows Hernán Cortés, who conquered Mexico for Spain, being offered young Indian women by a coastal tribe. The Indians seem happy to greet the Spaniards. Figure 3.12 was drawn by an Aztec Indian and shows Cortés's soldiers (having fought their way from the coast to the Aztec capital) massacring Indians in their main temple. Not all drawings have such obvious (and opposite) messages: the Spanish as friends of the Indians and the Spanish as murderers of the Indians. The interpretation of some visual material requires knowledge about the subject matter, the artist, the style, and the context in which the work appeared. Like written descriptions of past events, art does not simply "speak for itself."

FIGURE 3.11   Indian Offerings to Cortés
Kean Collection/Archive Photos/Getty Images

Now look at Figure 3.13 (p. 61), a photograph of a clash in 1968 between Chicago police and demonstrators opposing the war in Vietnam. Like the illustrations in Figures 3.11 and 3.12, it too contains information. Even a casual glance shows confusion and violence. Examining it closely, you can see the kinds of weapons used by the police and the facial expressions of some of the demonstrators. The more difficult part, again, is interpreting the photograph. Is this a scene of provocation by lawless demonstrators or an attack by the police? A careful look at the picture may help you answer this question. In any case, you need more evidence. Although an unaltered photograph does show something that actually happened, another photograph—even one of the same event—might show something very different. In most cases, the person taking the photograph has made an effort to say something, and you need to take this motive into account, as well.

Not all pictures have controversial interpretations. Figure 3.14 (p. 62) is a photograph of a city street in Ithaca, New York, in the 1890s. There is a wealth of information here about nineteenth-century town life. Notice that at this early date the town already had electric trolleys. Notice also that the horses are pulling not wagons or carriages ("buggies," as they were called) but sleighs ("cutters"). This simple fact opens up a window to farm life in winter. When roads were covered with snow and ice, the flat, smooth wheels of wagons could not navigate, but the sharp runners of the cutter dug into the ice and gave the sleigh stability.

FIGURE 3.12   Massacre of the Aztec Indians
Bridgeman-Giraudon/Art Resource, NY

FIGURE 3.13   Antiwar Demonstration at the 1968 Democratic National Convention in Chicago
Bettmann/Getty Images

Sound and Video Recordings

Electronically or digitally recorded sounds and pictures make up a large category of nonwritten primary sources. These nonwritten records of past events allow history to come alive before the researcher's eyes and ears. They provide an immediacy and sense of the past that is palpable in ways that written sources can rarely convey. Audiovisual sources, however, require special attention when being interpreted for historical research. Sound and video recordings typically do not have authors in the usual sense of the word, and their purpose can range from artistic to journalistic to persuasive. Another kind of nonwritten evidence is **oral history**. Oral history is the systematic collection of living people's testimony about their own experiences. Oral history depends upon human memory and the spoken word. The means of collection can vary from taking notes by hand to elaborate electronic sound and video recordings. To create an oral history, a historian serves as interviewer and records the conversation with another person who is the interviewee.

Like photographs, sound and video recordings need to be interpreted, particularly in terms of what they choose to place before your eyes or ears and how they do so. Although they might not have traditional authors, sound and video recordings have been created and perhaps edited by one or more individuals, usually to suit a particular political, commercial,

FIGURE 3.14   Town Life in Ithaca, New York, during the 1890s
Courtesy of The History Center in Tompkins County, Ithaca, New York,
General Photo Collection

personal, or artistic purpose. Being aware of the message behind the image or sound is critical to assessing that source's credibility. For example, sound clips might intentionally be taken out of context or edited together in such a way as to misrepresent a person's meaning. Make sure you are aware of the entire speech or interview before judging one or two sentences.

As with other types of sources, it's also important to know the actual setting of audiovisual materials so that you don't take an **ahistorical view** of them. For example, in the 1890s, there was a spiritual movement among many Native American peoples in the western United States known as "The Ghost Dance Religion." Films of the dances and recordings of the songs that are expressions of that movement are now considered important non-written primary sources of Native American history. However, the films were actually reenactments by native peoples who were part of a "Buffalo Bill Wild West Show" touring eastern cities in the 1890s. And the song recordings that exist were sung by a researcher working for the Smithsonian Institution who attempted to re-create them in an audio studio. Re-creations can be used as historical evidence, especially when no other evidence exists, but as with all evidence, you must know how they were produced.

Historians need to be very careful to distinguish between aesthetic analysis and historical analysis when examining sound or video recordings. Take, for example, the short educational film titled *Duck and Cover*, which was created in 1951 by the Federal Civil Defense Administration (see Figure 3.15, below). The film blends animation and live action in order to train young American students how to seek refuge in case of a nuclear attack. The main character, Bert the Turtle, demonstrates this technique by slipping into his shell when confronted with a lit firecracker. When a nuclear explosion occurs, the film's narrator explains, children should immediately "duck and cover" under their school desks or in the nearest ditch. If we view this source from an aesthetic standpoint, it now comes across as quaint and silly at best, and at worst as a morbid set of instructions that would provide little protection in case of a nuclear attack. But if we leave artistic merit aside and consider the historical context of the Cold War, *Duck and Cover* reveals much about the mentality of the American public in 1951. To a populace

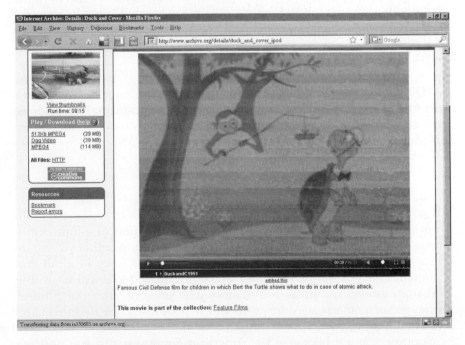

FIGURE 3.15   Short Film from 1951
A screenshot from the Federal Civil Defense Administration's 1951 film *Duck and Cover*. As silly as it looks to our eyes, what might this video tell us about everyday life in the 1950s?
Federal Civil Defense Administration

unfamiliar with the threat of direct attack or the devastation of an atomic bomb, the film would have seemed necessary and, in many cases, reassuring. Historians thus must take a serious approach to a source within its appropriate context, even when the content now appears silly or antiquated.

For a researcher, it is also important to note that establishing the authorship of modern video (and audio) productions is very problematic. Music videos, TV episodes, product and political commercials, among others, are produced by large production crews and often are assembled (mixed, dubbed, reworked, etc.) from various pieces of different kinds of media. Moreover, digitized versions of sound and video sources are easily shared, altered, or deleted. As a result, it is almost impossible to distinguish "copy" from "original." Only a very clear trail of evidence can indicate if the "original" was altered. To understand complex, modern media, you need to know their "media context"— a vital aspect of their historical context. When analyzing digital media, be sure to keep the following questions in mind:

- What is the *form* of the source: videotape, audiotape, CD, TV, digital video, web page, digitized print document, something else?
- What was the *technical process* by which the source was originally produced? (You need to know this in order to understand the way in which the source was created and thereby the ways in which it might be altered.)
- What is the *form, genre,* or *style* of the artistic aspects of the source? (This information places the source in the history of its form of art.)
- What is the social and cultural context?

NOTE: The amount of digitally recorded primary evidence is growing at a very rapid rate. The widespread use of email, digital cameras, cell phones, and social media is creating huge archives of information for future historians.

Artifacts

An artifact is an intentionally created physical object from the past: a radio from the 1920s, a rifle from the U.S. Civil War, the ruins of a fourteenth-century church in Paris, a 15,000-year-old bone needle. Whether you examine an artifact in a museum, in an attic, or in a field, keep in mind that sometimes even the simplest artifact can be interpreted to reveal surprising and sophisticated historical information. The study of "material culture" examines such objects as evidence about the people who created them and the times in which they were created.

Suppose you are hiking in the American Southwest and you notice a couple of stones that look out of the ordinary. The smaller of the two has a rectangular shape that doesn't seem natural, and the larger one is flat and has an indentation that has clearly been carved into it by human hands.

As you look around the surrounding brush, you find shards of pottery and other evidence that suggests this arid area was once inhabited by people. As you place the two stones together, you see that they fit perfectly, and when you grind them, some powdery material shakes loose from them. You've found a *mano* and a *metate*—two common tools used by American Indians to grind corn (see Figure 3.16). Once the corn is ground into a fine meal, it can be stored or made into food.

In order to place your artifacts into a wider context, consider the landscape around them. This area is arid today, but you see a few shallow ditches that seem to be arranged in a particular pattern. The crumbled stones in front of a dried-up water basin might have been a dam that once fed those ditches. Could this have been an irrigation system? The pottery shards are also important to consider. The thickness and coarse nature of their construction suggest that they were once heavy-duty containers, distinct from the more fragile decorative or ceremonial vessels that you've seen in museums. A more detailed scientific analysis of your artifacts might uncover the remnants of ground corn that was indigenous to the area and that dates back over 1,000 years. Once you've put the mano and metate into their

FIGURE 3.16   Mano and Metate
Pictured here are a mano (the smaller grinding stone) and metate (the flat grinding surface) from the southwestern United States. In a museum, these artifacts might be displayed along with a bowl of dried corn and some ground cornmeal. Would you know what the tools were for without such context? How might a museum-style presentation alter your perception of the artifacts?
Courtesy of the Arizona State Museum, the University of Arizona, photographer, Jackie Kinman

historical context, you can surmise that this area had a more cultivated landscape than it does now, and that your found artifacts might have been part of a now-defunct agricultural system.

Although field discoveries such as this will be rare in your undergraduate work, consider the benefits of exploring historical artifacts in their original setting. If you had found an image of these artifacts on the web or in a book on Native American culture, you wouldn't have had the experience of running your fingers over the mano and metate, and you wouldn't have gained the sense of how slow and difficult this work would have been and how coarse the resulting cornmeal might have felt. You also would have missed exploring the objects' immediate environment, and some of their meaning would have been lost. Fieldwork can add new dimensions to any research project.

However an artifact is initially examined, it is usually helpful to conduct additional research and consider the artifact's wider implications. The immediate suggestion might be that corn was an important part of Native American diets in the Southwest. But more research might reveal that the mano and metate were important tools in women's labor, that grinding increases the nutritional yield of cornmeal, and that cooking processed cornmeal requires less time and therefore less fuel than cooking whole kernels. This information tells us a great deal about the everyday life of the ancient residents of this land, but we can take that information a step further and glean even wider insights from the found artifacts. Many of the factors influenced by the mano and metate—a gendered division of labor, increased nutritional yields, less demand for wood fuel—allowed the population of American Indian societies like the Anasazi to expand across the arid environments of the American Southwest, which in turn resulted in the construction of sophisticated cities like Mesa Verde, in modern-day Colorado. As it turns out, the mano and metate that you found are an important link between everyday life and the grand scope of human development. Not all artifacts have such wide-reaching implications, but you never know until you explore them fully. After all, you thought you had just found some unusually shaped rocks!

NOTE: Online databases and various websites contain very large collections of digitized visual, sound, and numerical sources. These are excellent research sources. (See Appendix A for a list of some of these kinds of sites.)

CHAPTER
4

Evaluating and Interpreting Historical Evidence

EVALUATING SOURCES

Chapter 3 provided an overview of various primary and secondary sources and how to approach them most effectively. The material in this section explains how to *evaluate* sources. There are several questions you need to ask when you evaluate a book or article, a primary text, a nonwritten source, or a web-based source:

- What is the author's or creator's background, and what is his or her perspective on the subject?
- Is the source helpful in serious historical study, or was it created for a general audience?
- What is the **historical context** in which a source was created? That is, what in the author's world might have influenced what he or she wrote or created?
- Finally, what points is the author or creator trying to make?

Evaluating Secondary Sources

Most history books and articles fall into the category of **secondary sources** because they are written by someone who did not observe or participate in an event but investigated primary evidence of it. (For more on secondary sources, see Chapter 3, pp. 43–44.)

Reviewing Secondary Sources for Basic Information

Determining the background of the author will tell you much about the kind of sources you have uncovered. This kind of information is normally recorded on the cover or in the introductory pages. For more information, do an author search in your online catalog or on the web. A scholar is likely to produce a reliable and research-oriented work. Other kinds of authors—journalists, professionals with a background on the subject, a highly respected author—may also write books and articles that are valuable secondary sources. Look for notes and a bibliography as these are essential components of scholarly work. In addition, check to see who published the work. Is the publisher a university press or a commercial publisher such as Knopf or Penguin with a reputation for producing serious books?

Also consider the intended audience of the book or article. For example, scholarly journals contain scholarly articles. Popular magazines written for a general audience are not proper sources of information for historical research. (For advice on distinguishing between popular and scholarly sources, see Chapter 3, pp. 49–50.) Consider whether the source is meant to entertain or to inform. Often the title provides a clue. A scholarly book might have a title such as *Hindu Fundamentalism and the Destruction of the Mosque of Babur in Ayodya,* whereas a popular book on the same subject might be titled *Massacre at Ayodya: The True Story!* You should be able to distinguish *Changing Images of Female Beauty in Renaissance Art* from *How to Look like a Renaissance Beauty: Twelve Easy Steps.*

Examining the organization of a secondary source will tell you a lot about it. Look at the introduction or preface. It may tell you why the work was written, what aspect of its subject it explores, and perhaps some of its conclusions. The table of contents will give you a closer look at the order in which topics will be treated. The date of publication will help indicate the kinds of information used and the perspective of the author. An early work on a subject, written when very little primary evidence was available, will not

---

Guidelines for Evaluating Secondary Sources

- Is the author a scholarly writer or an expert on your topic? (If you're not sure, conduct a web search to find out more about the author.)
- To obtain an overview of the subject of the work, read the table of contents, preface, and other introductory materials. For this purpose, examine also the notes and bibliography.
- Is the intended audience scholars, serious readers, and college-level students?
- Who is the publisher? It is a good sign if the work is published by a major commercial publisher or a university press.
- Is the bias (the perspective) of the author moderate or strong? Be careful when relying upon the work of an author who uses strong language against people who disagree with him or her, or who ignores other perspectives.
- How does the date of publication affect the content of the source?

be as deep as a recent work that reflects a larger body of evidence and has the advantage of the findings of additional authors.

Reading Secondary Sources for Signs of Bias

Any **bias** on the part of an author or work will tell you a lot about a work's seriousness. Bias—an author's perspective on a topic—can be modest or very strong. Strong bias is indicated by an unwillingness to consider or acknowledge other interpretations and by the use of harsh language to characterize authors with different perspectives. A book with a strong bias is unlikely to be a useful source, unless your research requires an examination of biased works, as would a paper on the anti-Semitism expressed in nineteenth-century French accounts of the Dreyfus trial.

Moderate bias, however, is a characteristic of all authors. Every author, including scholars, has a perspective on the subject that influences his or her work. For example, two economic historians with different perspectives on the role of government in the economy are likely to draw different conclusions about the causes of the U.S. economic depression of the 1930s. Many historical developments and their interpretation are topics of profound controversy, and it is almost impossible for a historian to investigate one of these controversial areas without being affected by his or her own biases. A particular attitude toward a topic is to be expected. Historical problems are highly complex, and without a sense of which aspects of a problem are most important, a historian will be unable to develop a thesis. It is important for you to become familiar with the biases and perspectives of the authors you read so that you do not unknowingly accept their viewpoints. If you agree with someone's point of view, it is natural for you to favor his or her work. If you do not understand the points of view of the authors whose work you read, you will not know why you agree with some authors more than with others. Furthermore, you will not be able to make a clear presentation of these points of view in your own work. (See "What Is a Point of View" in Chapter 3, pp. 51–52).

Evaluating Primary Sources

As described in Chapter 3, a primary source is direct evidence of some part of the history of the time when it was created. It may be in the form of a handwritten document, it may be a typeset version published at a later date, or it may have been converted to a digital format. Or it might be art in some form. It could be recorded sound or music, or it could be an **artifact**, a physical object (building, pot, old camera, ancient coin, etc.) that has survived into the present.

Whether written or nonwritten, primary sources cannot simply be taken at face value. You must look behind them, so to speak. Be sure to take the time to learn about the historical context in which the **primary source** was created and the impact that it had on its original audience. In addition,

---

Guidelines for Evaluating Written Primary Sources

- If the author is known, check his or her background to see whether his or her political, religious, or cultural beliefs or position in society may suggest a particular point of view.
- If the author is unknown, determine when and where the source came from in order to consider who might have written it.
- Read very carefully, especially if the handwriting, spelling, grammar, or vocabulary is unfamiliar.
- Compare the source to other documents from the same period in order to determine reliability. Also consider what other scholars conclude about the source.
- Why and for whom was the document written?
- Why and how was the document preserved?
- Check for serious problems such as factual error, deception, or fabrication.

---

primary sources, just like secondary sources, must be carefully evaluated to determine their reliability.

Written Primary Sources

Written primary sources were created at the time of the events that they describe. The author of a primary source is someone who took part in or who witnessed those events. The journal written by Ibn Battuta in the fourteenth century, in which he describes his travels from North Africa to India and China, is an example of a primary document. Written primary sources record the reaction of someone who lived through a particular event and felt its effects. Be aware, however, that recorded memories can be faulty.

Primary texts are as varied as newspaper articles, written interviews, diaries, and letters. Official documents such as speeches, political platforms, statistics, and laws are also primary sources. When studied as evidence from a particular time period in history, literary works such as novels, poems, and stories are primary sources that can be particularly useful for understanding social or cultural history.

As with secondary sources, you need to become aware of the historical and cultural context: these are the circumstances surrounding an author at the time a particular document was written. For example, to understand an American woman's diary from the nineteenth century, you need to know something about the world in which the writer lived. Was she an urban or a rural resident? How old was she? Was she married, divorced, or single? Was her family rich or poor? What was her religion, her attitude toward the subjects she mentioned in her diary, and so on? Understanding the meaning of her diary entries rests on knowing something about this woman, the society she lived in, and her position in that society.

As explained in Chapter 3, written primary evidence is not always reliable (see pp. 47–49). The views of participants or observers (like the views of any author) may be biased; the writers may have misunderstood what they saw or experienced. Ancient eyewitness testimony may claim that the god of war spread great flames across the valley in what was actually the eruption of a volcano. Primary evidence can also be intentionally deceptive. The edict of a Chinese emperor may have been intended to hide the truth from his subjects. Of course, a historian may want to study the influence of the emperor's edict even if it was intended to deceive. Primary sources may also be outright fabrications. *The Protocols of the Elders of Zion*, for example, were fabricated documents created in the early twentieth century to further an anti-Semitic agenda, yet many dubious works of history cite them as real primary sources.

Nonwritten Primary Sources

Nonwritten primary sources—such as physical objects, paintings, photographs, and sound or video recordings—raise additional evaluation issues. For these kinds of primary sources, you need to know something about the technical process by which they were produced as well as the intent of the maker. Changes in the size and weight of cameras and in the time it took to develop a picture in the nineteenth century affected the subject matter of photographs, for example. (The earliest photographs required long exposure times and it took many minutes—not fractions of a second—for a camera to capture an image.) Nonwritten primary sources require kinds of interpretation that are different from those used to evaluate written sources, whether primary or secondary. Nonwritten primary sources are quite varied. Physical objects—artifacts—can take many forms. Some—such as clothing,

---

Guidelines for Evaluating Nonwritten Primary Sources

- Who created the source? What impact might the creator's political, religious, or cultural beliefs have had on the source?
- What was the creator trying to "say"? All artists, builders, performers, craftspeople, and so on, express something of themselves in their creations.
- When and where was the source created?
- How was the source created? By what technical, artistic, or natural process? (For modern chemical, electronic, or digital sources, it may also be necessary to know how sources were *reproduced*.)
- For what intended audience, if any, was the source created?
- If the source is a consciously artistic creation (whether "pure" or "commercial" art), what is its style, design, school, genre, and so on? What place does it have in the history of the art form?

See also "Guidelines for Interpreting Nonwritten Sources" in Chapter 3 (p. 55).

jewelry, furniture, and tools—were made for personal use. Others are art objects such as paintings, drawings, and sculpture. Recorded pictures and sounds (photographs, films, records) constitute one of the major categories of nonwritten primary sources. Until the last century or so, many people did not know how to write. Nonwritten primary sources are a way that we can hear them speak.

Audio and video recordings are most often treated as primary sources in the sense that they convey artistic expressions—as paintings or sculptures do. The popular movie *Gone with the Wind* is not a serious historical source, but it could be a proper primary source for anyone studying Hollywood films of the 1930s.

Nonwritten sources have to be analyzed for what they "say" even though many of them do not use words. (For more information, see "'Reading' Nonwritten Sources" in Chapter 3, pp. 52–66.) The creator—architect, photographer, potter, designer, composer—and the historical context in which the source was created need to be examined. For example, a jazz recording from the 1920s needs to be understood from a variety of perspectives: Who is playing? How, where, and when was it recorded? How popular was it? What style of jazz is it? How does it compare to other jazz styles in other periods? Any product of art or of popular culture needs to be examined in these kinds of ways.

Special Problems of Evaluating Web-Based Sources

Before we discuss the evaluation of material you might access on the internet, some advice is in order about the evaluation of websites themselves. Sites recommended by your instructor or accessed from your college library's home page (as well as those listed in Appendix A) will for the most part contain sources appropriate for serious research. A great number of institutions with educational missions (museums, research libraries, colleges, universities, private and public archives, states, cities, organizations, etc.), either on their own or as part of consortia that combine access to their collections, have created websites available to the general public. These kinds of sites offer an enormous number of resources for serious academic research.

However, if your search for historic evidence takes you to websites outside the "walls" of your school or public library or outside of the trustworthy "open" sites of major institutions, you need to be very careful in determining the quality of the information presented to you. The following guidelines point out ways of testing this information.

NOTE: Some online reference sources, most notably Wikipedia, allow anyone with internet access to anonymously edit entries. These sites should not be considered authoritative sources for a research paper; in fact, many instructors specifically forbid them. (See pp. 129–30 in Chapter 7 for details about Wikipedia.)

Evaluating Material Found Online

Certain aspects of evaluating digital sources and printed sources are similar, but some special characteristics of web-based documents make their evaluation more difficult. Authors of scholarly books and journal articles have had their work reviewed by editors and by experts in the field. Because of this process, much of what gets into print is of high quality. For the most part, the internet is unedited. *Anyone* can become the author of a website. This accessibility is one of the marvels of the internet, but it makes separating serious authors from less informed ones difficult. Nevertheless, if you take care to conduct your research in stable, scholarly sites, as explained above, you can minimize the problems noted below.

Before you download or print a possible source from a website, find out as much as you can about the author, either from the site itself or by conducting further research. If you cannot figure out who wrote the material you are interested in or how it got to the site, you would be wise not to use it.

If you can identify an author of the web-based material, you then need to ascertain the author's bias. Examine the document and the site at which you found it to determine the author's perspective on your topic. Some sites and the authors whose work they include are as serious as any university publisher or scholarly journal, but many sites are created to disseminate the viewpoint of a particular group. In the latter case, all of the documents on the site as well as those on any linked sites are likely to share a similar perspective, and you will need to be aware of this bias.

You should also be aware of potential problems concerning the accuracy and authenticity of web-based sources. Sometimes the fact that only part of a document is included on a site is not made clear. If a document has been

---

Guidelines for Evaluating Websites

- Most sites sponsored by universities, libraries, museums, governmental bodies, and research organizations are reliable ones. (Most of the URLs for these sites end with .gov, .org, or .edu.)
- Reliable sites have serious, documented content and reliable links, and they are regularly updated.
- A site for serious researchers does not have distracting visuals or advertisements. Links to the parts of the site where scholarly material is available should be clearly marked.
- To determine the degree of bias of a site, look for a formal statement by the sponsor. Note if the sources seem one-sided, are not documented, or do not indicate who wrote them and where they originated.
- If you decide to reproduce the source, be sure that you can properly document it.

Guidelines for Evaluating Material Found Online

- Try to identify the author of the source. Do an internet search for any author or sponsor name that is on the site or on the source that interests you.
- Look for signs of bias on the site or in the document: dramatic presentation, one-sided arguments, lack of documentation for statements made.
- Check reliable resources such as the online library catalog to see whether there are more recent versions or translations of a source that may be more accurate than the version or translation you found online.
- Try to ascertain whether any nonwritten materials—still photographs, sound recordings, films—that you found online were altered in any way.
- If you cannot determine the seriousness of an author or a site sponsor, or the quality of a document, do not rely on such a source until you discuss these issues with your instructor.

---

translated, the translation may not be accurate. If a document is an early version of something that was later revised, you may be missing important changes made by the author. The text of a written document may have been altered. Similarly, a photograph can be altered, and sound or video recordings may be edited. The quality of a digital source needs to be assessed with care. Your best assurance of accuracy is to confine your research to sites about whose seriousness you feel confident and to inform your instructor about any questionable web-based sources.

Documenting Web-Based Sources

Sometimes print documents are reformatted to fit the needs of the web, in which case the "pages" of the electronic version are different from the pages of the original. If you wish to cite such a source, you need to know which set of page numbers to record. If you cannot obtain the original printed source, you should record the page numbers that appear in the digital document, taking care to make that fact clear in any notes you take from the document and in the notes to the document that you may create for your written work.

Because of the unstable nature of web-based documents, you must carefully record the site a document came from (including its URL) and the title of the document. Your instructor may also ask you to include the date that you accessed the material on the site. (For information on documenting sources from the internet, see pp. 206–10 in Chapter 10.)

INTERPRETING SOURCES
AND TAKING NOTES

As you gather reputable sources that are relevant to your topic, you need to carefully read them and interpret their meaning. When you interpret a source, you make judgments about its content. To make such judgments, you need to understand what you are reading. You also need to have a clear view of your topic so that you can take notes efficiently and effectively. In order to avoid **plagiarism**, your notes need to make clear when the words you are recording are those of your source and when they are your own.

Reading Your Sources

When you first read scholarly books, journal articles, and digital documents, it can be challenging. Until you gain experience in reading serious historical studies, the going is likely to be slow. Some of the vocabulary may be new to you. A work on the French Revolution will contain words such as *Jacobin*, *Thermidor*, and *Girondin*. A study of the atom bomb will talk about *implosion* and *fission*, and it may refer to places such as Tinian and Eniwetok. Be sure to use a print or online dictionary and encyclopedia whenever you come across a word or reference that is new to you. Another challenge is the academic or scholarly style of writing found in specialized works. Ease into your topic by reading the most general works first. Read difficult sentences slowly, and, as already mentioned, look up any unfamiliar words. As you become familiar with your topic, you will learn the meanings of terms that scholars use, and you will become increasingly comfortable with their style and terminology.

When you move on to more specialized sources, your main task is to understand the points an author is trying to establish. In particular, you need to identify the author's thesis. Good historical writing does more than lay out a series of historical events and then combine them into an understandable story of what occurred. Professional historians want to prove a point — a thesis — to show that a series of historical events means one thing rather than another.

A history of the rise of Adolf Hitler, for example, won't merely tell you that the National Socialist (Nazi) Party, which he led, increased the number of its representatives in the German Reichstag (parliament) from twelve to 107 in the election of 1930. It will attempt to describe the conditions that led to such an outcome and to explain the impact of the election on later events. Among the many ways of approaching the subject, the author might discuss unemployment, German nationalism, the cartelization of German industry, the Treaty of Versailles, the growth of the German Communist Party, anti-Semitism, the structure of the German family, the philosophy of Nietzsche, or the insecurity of the lower middle class. The author will emphasize one or more of these subjects and will attempt to show how the emphasized factors offer a better explanation of the subject than the others. The argument for a particular explanation of the rise of Nazism will most likely be the author's thesis. Although almost all historians will agree on the number of National Socialist members of the 1930 Reichstag, each historian will construct the causes and effects of that fact in different ways — often as a result of his or her own philosophy or historical field (see Chapter 1) — and each will argue a somewhat different thesis to explain the outcome.

If you wish to understand a particular author's interpretation of an event, you must know how the author arrived at that interpretation and what significance he or she believes it to have. Only a careful reading of the entire work and close attention to its main arguments can give you such knowledge. Remember, history works are a selection of facts and interpretations constructed to explain a particular writer's understanding of a historical subject. If your own research relies heavily on a particular book, you will need to know its perspective and its thesis. (For more on working with historical evidence, see Chapters 3 and 5.)

Summarizing and Paraphrasing without Plagiarizing

Most notes that you take on your sources will fall into two categories: **summaries** and **paraphrases**. When you *summarize* information from a source, you are drawing upon ideas that spread across several pages in the source. You are restating these ideas briefly in your own words. When you *paraphrase* information, you are capturing the meaning of just a few sentences from a source. A third form of note taking is direct **quotation**, which is covered in Chapter 4 (pp. 78–79).

Summarizing Your Sources

When you want to record an author's general arguments and conclusions, you will probably want to write a summary of particular points or even of an entire work. As stated above, a summary is a brief restatement, in your own words, of a point made by an author over the space of several pages.

Suppose an author spends several pages connecting the eighteenth-century decline in Spanish-Mexican trade to Mexican independence from Spain. You may want to summarize the findings simply by noting that the author feels that the diminishing economic tie between colony and mother country was one of the major factors leading to Mexican independence. If you wish to record some of the evidence itself, you may want to paraphrase the author's description of the decline in trade with several sentences of your own that include the main factors of this decline.

Paraphrasing Your Sources

A paraphrase directly reflects the ideas of an author. Be sure to document any paraphrase with a footnote. Even so, paraphrasing must be done carefully.

Take care that your paraphrase does not come too close to being a loose quotation. If it does come that close to the original and is not in quotation marks, you will be guilty of plagiarism.

Examples of Ineffective and Effective Paraphrasing.   Here are examples of both effective and ineffective paraphrasing to help you learn how to avoid plagiarism. Read the passage below from the original text; then read the two versions of paraphrases that follow.

Here is a passage from J. Joseph Hutchmaker and Warren I. Sussman, eds., *Wilson's Diplomacy: An International Symposium* (Cambridge, MA: Schenkman, 1973), 13:

ORIGINAL TEXT

Wilson took personal responsibility for the conduct of the important diplomacy of the United States chiefly because he believed that it was wise, right, and necessary for him to do so. Believing as he did that the people had temporarily vested their sovereignty in foreign affairs in him, he could not delegate responsibility in this field to any individual. His scholarly training and self-disciplined habits of work made him so much more efficient than his advisors that he must have thought that the most economical way of doing important diplomatic business was for him to do it himself. Experience in dealing with subordinates who sometimes tried to defeat his purposes also led him to conclude that it was the safest method, for he, and not his subordinates, bore the responsibility to the American people and to history for the consequences of his policies.

Here is an ineffective attempt at paraphrasing, which plagiarizes the original source:

INEFFECTIVE PARAPHRASE (PLAGIARISM)

Wilson took personal responsibility for conducting diplomacy because he believed it was right for him to do so. Believing that the people had vested their sovereignty in foreign affairs in him, he couldn't delegate this responsibility. His scholarly training and self-discipline made him more efficient than his advisors. He thought that the most economical way of doing important business was to do it himself. Experience in dealing with subordinates who sometimes tried to defeat his purposes led him to conclude that it was the safest method because he bore responsibility to the American people for the consequences.

The "paraphrase" is too close to the original. The underlined phrases are almost the same as those of the source. If they were used in a paper without quotation marks, they would constitute plagiarism, even if you had included a footnote or endnote. Rather than recording the main points of the passage, this paragraph repeats much of the text word for word. It is time-consuming to take such lengthy notes, and, more seriously, the unacknowledged use of the author's wording constitutes plagiarism.

Here is an effective paraphrase, which avoids plagiarism:

EFFECTIVE PARAPHRASE

Wilson felt personally responsible for major diplomacy because he believed that the voters had entrusted him with such matters. He felt he was more capable than his advisors in this area. He, and not his advisors, was responsible to the people.

This paraphrase is effective because it records only the principal point of the passage — that Wilson decided major foreign policy issues on his own because he felt personally responsible to the people in such matters. It does not copy phrases from the original text. This type of note taking saves time and avoids plagiarism, yet conveys the central idea of the passage. Remember, however, that the effective paraphrase still needs to be footnoted in the research paper, because it incorporates ideas taken from a source.

Paraphrasing that reduces your readings to their essential points and uses your own words is not easy to do at first. But by mastering this technique, you will avoid plagiarism and produce a finished work that is truly yours.

Quoting without Plagiarizing

As you go through a source, you may find passages that you want to repeat word for word in your own research paper. Although overreliance on quotations can be a weakness, if you feel that a quote is necessary to make a very important point, be careful to copy the words exactly *and to enclose them in quotation marks.* If you quote, be sure that the meaning of the words you take from the author will be clear when they appear in your written work. Also be sure that you do not alter the author's point by quoting it out of **context**.

Suppose you wish to use a quotation to demonstrate that Robert E. Lee was an excellent military strategist — a point that is important to your thesis. The quotation "Lee was more admired by the average soldier than any other commanding officer" would not make that point because it refers to Lee's popularity, not his generalship. Moreover, if the next sentence in the text you are quoting from were "However, his strategic decisions were not usually equal to those of Union army commanders," then you would have altered the author's point by ignoring the original context.

Before you use a quotation, make sure you understand the author's meaning. Do not quote more material than is necessary to convey the desired point clearly and accurately. Never quote something in your notes simply because you find it difficult to say in your own words. You will have to express the idea in your own words when you write, and it is best to think about the meaning of your research material now, while you are taking notes.

Suppose the material you wish to quote from a source is itself a quotation from another text. You will need to make that clear in your own notes. If you think you might want to quote this material in your own paper, you should try to locate the original source that the quote comes from and quote that source directly.

Suppose a quotation is very long and some parts of it are not related to the main point or "thesis" of your essay or research paper. (For an explanation of how to formulate a thesis, see pp. 107–09 in Chapter 6.) You may omit portions of the original quote from your notes as long as you indicate the omission with an **ellipsis mark**—three spaced dots (. . .)—in the quoted material. Suppose the quotation is "Feudalism, despite later idealizations of it, was maintained by an oppressive social order." If you decide to omit "despite later idealizations of it," you must use an ellipsis mark and quote the sentence like this: "Feudalism . . . was maintained by an oppressive social order." If the portion you want to omit includes the end of a sentence, insert four dots—three to indicate the omission and the fourth to mark the end of the original sentence—and place the closing quotation mark after the fourth dot.

Never use an ellipsis mark if doing so will change the meaning of the author's words. Suppose the quoted sentence is "Feudalism in its later stages in Moravia was maintained by an oppressive social order." If you shortened it to "Feudalism . . . was maintained by an oppressive social order," the author's meaning would be seriously altered.

Organizing Your Notes

In the course of writing an essay or a research paper, you will create a large number of notes. It is important for you to organize your notes effectively as you create them so that you can find the information you need when you are ready to write your paper. Give each group or file of notes a subject heading. This heading will tell you which aspect of your paper topic it relates to. When you complete your research, you will use these headings to organize your essay or research paper. The headings will also contain the documentation for each part of your paper.

Taking Notes on Note Cards

A long-established and still effective system of note taking uses paper index cards. For an example, see Figure 4.1 (p. 80). For each source you take notes from, you create a series of cards. On the first card, called the **source card**, you record *all* of the information you will need to cite the work if you decide to use it in an essay or research paper—such as the author, title, publisher, and place and date of publication for a book. (For information about how to cite a variety of sources, see Chapter 10.) You may also want to include specific information that would help you locate the source again, if necessary, such as the library call number or the URL.

Each card in the series contains a quotation, paraphrase, or summary of information from the source that you might use, and, if helpful, any comments of your own about the source. At the top left corner of the second

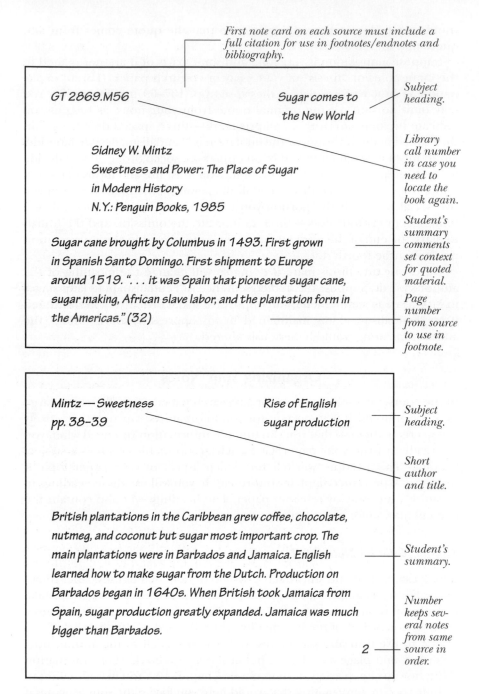

First note card on each source must include a full citation for use in footnotes/endnotes and bibliography.

GT 2869.M56   Sugar comes to
                               the New World

Subject heading.

Sidney W. Mintz
Sweetness and Power: The Place of Sugar
in Modern History
N.Y.: Penguin Books, 1985

Library call number in case you need to locate the book again.

Sugar cane brought by Columbus in 1493. First grown
in Spanish Santo Domingo. First shipment to Europe
around 1519. ". . . it was Spain that pioneered sugar cane,
sugar making, African slave labor, and the plantation form in
the Americas." (32)

Student's summary comments set context for quoted material.

Page number from source to use in footnote.

Mintz — Sweetness   Rise of English
pp. 38–39   sugar production

Subject heading.

Short author and title.

British plantations in the Caribbean grew coffee, chocolate,
nutmeg, and coconut but sugar most important crop. The
main plantations were in Barbados and Jamaica. English
learned how to make sugar from the Dutch. Production on
Barbados began in 1640s. When British took Jamaica from
Spain, sugar production greatly expanded. Jamaica was much
bigger than Barbados.

2

Student's summary.

Number keeps several notes from same source in order.

FIGURE 4.1   Example of Handwritten Note Cards for a Source

and later cards will be the author's last name, a short version of the full title (which you recorded on the source card), and the page or pages where you found the information. The top right corner will contain a word or phrase—a subject heading—that describes the aspect of your topic to which the information on the card is related. Subject headings will prove crucial when you begin the process of arranging your notes as you prepare to write your paper. (See "Organizing Your Evidence with a Writing Outline" in Chapter 8, pp. 143–47.) If a source could relate to more than one aspect of your topic, be sure to note this as well.

Taking Notes on a Computer

Note-taking programs, as you may know, allow you to write up digital note cards and create a folder for each of your sources. An example of a digital note card appears on page 82 (Figure 4.2). For an example of a digital source folder, see Figure 4.3 (p. 83). The principle is the same whether you use index cards or download a note-taking app. Be sure that each source folder has all the information you will need in order to document the source if you decide to use it in your paper. Each digital note card that you file within the source folder should indicate whether the information it records is a quotation, paraphrase, or summary. Each note card also should have a subject header that describes its content. This is the essential arranging tool that will enable you to organize your notes by content and, eventually, by the part of your essay to which they relate. If you need to reorganize your notes, the subject headers will make doing so relatively easy.

Be sure to keep all of your digital source folders and the note cards filed within them in a labeled folder separate from any folder you will create for the drafting of your paper. Be sure to give these folders different names that cannot be confused with one another so that you do not enter notes or draft text into the wrong folder.

If you copy and paste material from a digital source directly into a note card file, be sure to immediately add to the file the full source information of the pasted material. To prevent the possibility that you might later mistake the contents of this file and paste it into a draft of your paper, change the font or color of the pasted text and surround it with quotation marks.

If you download a source, do not enter this text into a note card file without including the full source information and without placing the text itself within quotation marks. Although it is likely that if you use any of the downloaded source in your paper you will change the quoted material into a paraphrase or summary, the presence of quotation marks will ensure that you never lose track of the fact that the notes contain quoted material. As with all computer files, save your notes regularly and create a backup file.

Part of an advanced note-taking program.

TOOLBAR: SEARCH OPTIONS ▾   TYPE OF SOURCE ▾   HELP ▾

To "search" and to organize notes.

SOURCE: LETTERS OF UNC STUDENTS. LETTER FROM JOHN WESLEY HALLIBURTON TO JULIET HALLIBURTON, MARCH 6, [1861].   **PAGE #** 4 (OF LETTER)

SUBJECT HEADER: Student Opinion   **CARD #** 1

Photograph / Video / Written Primary / Written Secondary/ Etc.

SOURCE TYPE: PRIMARY DOCUMENT, TRANSCRIBED LETTER

NOTE:

Written before fighting begins. He is upset at the election of Lincoln but says: "I can hate him and still love the Union." A minority opinion. Most students favor secession.

Continued on CARD #

In advanced programs these would be live links.

NOTE IS:

X QUOTATION

___ WORD-FOR-WORD TEXT BLOCK

X SUMMARY

___ PARAPHRASE

If so, describe in note box.

___ IMAGE

LINKS TO:

THIS SOURCE FOLDER

LIST OF ALL SOURCES

PREVIOUS CARD/NEXT CARD

DRAFT OUTLINE

DRAFT FOLDER OF PAPER

FIGURE 4.2 Example of a Digital Note Card
This digital note card identifies the source of the note, records the subject header the note is related to, and indicates the source type. A note from a different letter in the same collection would be filed in the same source folder. A note from a document in another part of the "Documenting the American South" collection would require a new source folder.

TOOLBAR: FOLDER NAME ▼   SORT OPTION ▼   SEARCH OPTIONS ▼ — *Part of an advanced note-taking program.*

SOURCE: University of North Carolina, "Documenting the American South," "The Lives and Writings of Antebellum Students at the University of North Carolina," Chapter 6: 1860–1869 (Primary Documents).

Be sure to use proper note style.

SHORT SOURCE NAME: Letters of UNC students.

URL & Path / Library Catalog # / Name of Database / Etc.

WHERE FOUND: http://docsouth.unc.edu/true/ (2/5/2015)

TOPIC: Anti-Secessionist Opinion in the American South, 1860–1861.

RESEARCH QUESTION: (Tentative) To what extent did Southerners oppose secession during this period?

Use "Search" and "Sort" to organize.

LIST OF SUBJECT HEADERS FOR THIS SOURCE: Student Opinion. Reaction of Secessionists to Unionists. Backgrounds of Unionists.

In advanced programs these would be live links.

COMMENTS ON THIS SOURCE:
An archive of letters by UNC students (1795–1869).

LINKS TO:
LIST OF CARDS FOR THIS SOURCE
LIST OF SOURCES
DRAFT BIBLIOGRAPHY
DRAFT OUTLINE
DRAFT FOLDER OF YOUR PAPER

2/5/15   Date Created

FIGURE 4.3   Example of a Digital Source Folder
This source folder is for a collection of digital documents containing letters by students at the University of North Carolina. Note that these letters are part of a larger collection of documents called "Documenting the American South." The source folder page includes a series of "subject headers," one of which will appear on each digital note card so that cards with similar headers can be found through a search.

Photocopying, Downloading, or Printing Sources

Whenever you come across a source that you feel may be very important to your research, photocopying it, downloading it, or printing it may seem preferable to note taking because it will save time. But don't fool yourself. At some point you will have to read and take notes on all those copied, downloaded, or printed pages. Also, don't copy, download, or print anything without reading enough of it to know that it contains material directly related to your paper topic. Finally, be sure that you have all of the source information for such documents. You may find it nearly impossible to track down the origin of an unmarked photocopy or downloaded passage of text at a later date.

AVOIDING PLAGIARISM

As a beginning researcher, you may be tempted to use the sophisticated language of the trained historians you are reading. In most cases, their expertise enables them to make their points clearly, and it is easy to fall into the dangerous habit of using *their* words instead of your own. Remember that your instructor is also a historian and can tell the difference between the language of someone who has spent years researching a topic and that of the average history student. Moreover, thinking is learning. If you substitute the simple task of copying the author's words for the more difficult but

---

Guidelines for Avoiding Plagiarism

- When taking notes from sources, rarely use the exact words of the source. If you do use them in your written work, always place the words within quotation marks. It is best to paraphrase or summarize source material. Indicate in your notes whether the words are exact quotations, paraphrases, or summaries.
- If you enter research notes directly into a computer, be sure to put your notes in a folder separate from the folder you are using for draft versions of your paper.
- If you download quoted material from a source directly into your note files, change the color or font of the quotation to avoid confusion with your own words.
- When you paraphrase a source, do not use either the sentence structure or the exact words of the author.
- When writing your paper, be certain to acknowledge your sources and to correctly document paraphrased material as well as direct quotations.

rewarding one of learning to understand the point he or she is making and then expressing it in your own words, you are doing yourself a disservice. Finally, plagiarism is cheating—a very serious violation of college rules. The penalty can be severe, sometimes leading to expulsion.

When taking notes, never copy an author's words unless you think you might need to quote them in your paper. In that case, be sure to put very clear quotation marks on your note card or digital note file at the beginning and end of each word-for-word passage. In all other instances, paraphrase or summarize the author's ideas and information *in your own words*. Moreover, your own words should not even come close to the words of the author, and all ideas taken from your sources must be documented when you write your paper, even if you are not using direct quotations. You will need to include footnotes or endnotes even for your summaries of an author's ideas in order to tell the reader where the ideas originally came from.

One of the very few times you can use information from a text without documenting it is when you are sure that the information is common knowledge. A fact is "common knowledge" when you find the fact mentioned in a wide range of sources. Proper names, dates, and other very widely known facts can generally be used without documentation. If a source says, "Isaac Newton is well known as the discoverer of the law of gravitation but he was also a serious student of biblical prophecy," you can mention Newton's scientific work without including the source. However, mention of his surprising interest in biblical prophecy would need to be documented.

Of course, the points that you record from your sources and incorporate in your paper should accurately reflect your sources. However, all of the words in your paper that are not in quotation marks must be your own, and you must document any information that you take from your sources unless it is common knowledge.

Plagiarism and Internet Sources

If you enter your research notes directly into a computer, be sure to put your notes into folders and files that are different from the folders and files that you are using (or will use) for drafts of your paper. Never cut and paste words from a source into any draft of your paper. In your note files, clearly distinguish words that you are quoting from words that you are paraphrasing or summarizing. Always put quotation marks around quoted material and fully document it. Also indicate the source of any paraphrase or summary, because you will have to acknowledge the origin of the ideas when you use them in your paper. When you create your notes, it is also wise to change the color or the font of material taken from your sources. (See "Organizing Your Notes," pp. 79–84.)

Plagiarism can be inadvertent, as described above, or deliberate, as when a student downloads an entire research paper from the web. People who are trying to make money off students who are overwhelmed by the task of conducting independent research and writing come together at websites where thousands of papers are available for sale. These websites may describe the papers only as "aids" in your research. You may even be told, in small print, not to use portions of these "aids" in your own work. Submitting such work as your own is dishonest and also foolish. Any website where you can find papers for plagiarizing can be found just as easily by your instructor. Both you and your instructor can even search the site for "your" paper. Don't play this dangerous game. It has serious consequences.

Plagiarism and Group Work

Working with other students can be an enjoyable and rewarding experience. Still, group work can lead to forms of plagiarism different from those arising from individual research. If the work of your team is evaluated as a whole, each member of the group is responsible to see to it that no part of the group's work has been taken improperly from research sources. Do not let the fact that your work is a group product lessen your concern for this vital matter.

CHAPTER
5

Writing Assignments: From Source Analysis to Comparative Critiques

Instructors give many kinds of writing assignments — including **book reviews**, papers that analyze historical sources, and **research papers**. These papers range in length from a few pages to ten or twenty. This chapter helps you understand some of the relatively short writing assignments that you are likely to encounter in history courses. (For detailed advice on writing full-length research papers, see Chapters 7, 8, and 9.)

NOTE: This chapter describes a variety of writing assignments. For specific assignments, be sure to adhere to guidelines presented to you by your instructor.

WRITING ABOUT PRIMARY SOURCES

As noted in Chapter 3, **primary sources** are the raw materials of history. **Secondary sources** — often written by professional historians — are *about* history; primary sources are *from* history. When you examine primary sources — for example, 20,000-year-old carved stone spearheads or radio commercials from the 1950s — you are handling raw materials. You may not understand much about a thirteenth-century papal decree until you become familiar with the history of thirteenth-century Europe, which will help you understand the **historical context** in which the decree was written. But even if much of the significance of a primary source is beyond your current grasp, examining it and thinking about it will lead you to a degree of familiarity with the past that can be arrived at in no other way.

Instructors often build assignments around the interpretation of primary sources. They do so to increase your interpretive abilities. You may be asked to draw connections between primary sources and some part of the historical context that you have learned about. Or you may be asked to respond to the source without much in the way of historical context. Even unsuccessful efforts to unravel the mystery of, say, a nineteenth-century love letter translated from Chinese may draw you into the past in a way that a long essay on the origins of Hindu nationalism may not.

Two typical assignments involving the study of primary sources are single-source analysis and comparative analysis. We will examine each of them.

Single-Source Analysis

When you are given a writing assignment that requires you to analyze a single primary source, read the question carefully to make sure you understand what you are expected to do. Your instructor will usually include key verbs in the assignment, such as *describe* or *explain*, that will give you a clue as to what is expected. The assignment may also include an indication of the focus your analysis should take. You may be asked to look at the economic aspects of a speech, for example, or at the political implications of a treaty. Whatever the assignment, you may find it helpful to review the sections "Primary Texts" (pp. 47–49) and "'Reading' Nonwritten Sources" (pp. 52–66) in Chapter 3 before you begin to write.

Below is an example of a single-source analysis assignment, followed by a sample student essay written in response to the assignment.

SAMPLE ASSIGNMENT: SINGLE-SOURCE ANALYSIS

As the nation awaited the Spanish Armada, Queen Elizabeth I visited the English army encamped at Tilbury on August 9, 1588. An eyewitness to the event, Dr. Leonel Sharp, transcribed her brief words to the troops years later in a 1623 letter. Although some historians doubt its complete authenticity, this speech is considered one of the great examples of English oratory. In a brief, two-page essay, consider the queen's speech (reprinted below), and describe how it reflects gender expectations in the Tudor-Stuart era.

Queen Elizabeth I's Spanish Armada Speech (1588)

My loving people, we have been persuaded by some, that are careful of our safety, to take heed how we commit ourselves to armed multitudes, for fear of treachery; but I assure you, I do not desire to live to distrust my faithful and loving people. Let tyrants fear; I have always so behaved myself that, under God, I have placed my chiefest strength and safeguard in the loyal hearts and good will of my subjects. And therefore I am come amongst you at this time, not as for my recreation or sport, but being resolved, in the midst and heat of the battle, to live or die amongst you all; to lay down, for my God, and for my kingdom, and for my people, my honor and my blood, even the dust. I know I have but the body of a weak and feeble woman; but I have the heart of a king, and of a king of England, too; and think foul scorn that Parma or Spain, or any prince of Europe, should dare to invade the borders of my realms: to which, rather than any dishonor should grow by me, I myself will take up arms; I myself will be your general, judge, and rewarder of every one of your virtues in the field. I know already, by your forwardness, that you have deserved rewards and crowns; and we do assure you, on the word of a prince, they shall be duly paid you. In the mean my lieutenant general shall be in my stead, than whom never prince commanded a more noble and worthy subject; not doubting by your obedience to my general, by your concord in the camp, and by your valor in the field, we shall shortly have a famous victory over the enemies of my God, of my kingdom, and of my people.

SAMPLE STUDENT ESSAY: SINGLE-SOURCE ANALYSIS

Eric Chin

History 100

October 15, 2018

A Woman at Tilbury

Queen Elizabeth's speech to the army at Tilbury might say a great deal about the strength of the English nation. It also speaks, however indirectly, to the limited roles designated to women in the Tudor-Stuart era and the limitations that might be applied even to a woman who ascended to the position of ruling monarch of England.

Perhaps the most obvious sign of Elizabeth's role is given when she says, "I know I have but the body of a weak and feeble woman; but I have the heart of a king, and of a king of England, too." Here, she seems to bow to contemporary beliefs that thought of women as the "weaker sex" — incapacitated by their physical makeup for anything but the simple tasks of the domestic sphere of home and family duties. She does not attempt to deny such a view of women, or excuse herself from stereotypes. Instead, she implies that her royalty, her royal blood, balances out her womanly weaknesses. She suggests that her royal heart gives her the soul and the honor of a male king — thus she can repeatedly identify herself as a "king" and a "prince." She is never merely the female equivalent, a "queen." Indeed, if it becomes necessary, she is fully capable of taking up arms herself in defense of her subjects.

What equally gives her strength is the love of her "faithful and loving people." She says that, though her advisers believe her to be in danger by presenting herself in public, perhaps because her advisers see her as a mere woman needing protection from the masses, she puts her faith and trust in her subjects. She asserts that only tyrants need fear their subjects, and, of course, she is not that. She is not, she says, a ruler who would come to speak to them only for sport or recreation; by implication, she is not a silly woman who might fail to understand the gravity of the situation or who might be there only to curry their favor. At the same time, she is not an unnatural woman, who does not care about the fate of her people or their love for her — it is their love that makes her strong, that moves her beyond the limitations of her body to be able to meet the responsibilities of a ruler. And, to prove it, she can and will take up arms if necessary to return that love; to do otherwise would only lead her to dishonor.

At the end of her speech, Elizabeth acknowledges that it is her lieutenant general — not herself — who will be leading the men into battle. But again, her words are chosen carefully. In commending her general, she equates herself with princes (men), and she calls England her "kingdom." So, in some ways, this primary source shows how even monarchs were subject to the limitations of gender roles in Tudor-Stuart England.

The student writer does a nice job of responding to the assignment, focusing on the question of gender and not simply repeating the general topics of the speech. He selects the most obvious quotes about women from the source and analyzes them, and he uses other parts of the speech to reinforce the claims he made about gender roles. The analysis is presented in a clear and logical fashion, without straying off **topic**, and it shows that the student read the source with the assignment in mind.

Comparative Analysis

Much like a single-source analysis, a comparative analysis requires close examination of primary sources. But when you are asked to compare two or more documents, you need to demonstrate that you can find and clearly explain similarities and differences between them. You must also relate the sources to their historical contexts in a way that distinguishes them from each other (or links them together). As with a single-source analysis, pay careful attention to the language used in the assignment. Look for key verbs such as *compare, contrast,* or *discuss the similarities.* Also, make sure you understand the focus of the assignment, the expected length, and the use of other sources or course material that you are expected to discuss.

Here is an example of a comparative analysis assignment, involving two contrasting images of the same political figure. Following the assignment are two sample student responses.

SAMPLE ASSIGNMENT: COMPARATIVE ANALYSIS

In a two-page essay, compare the two primary sources shown below. Describe the way each artist presents Mao Zedong. Be sure to include any aspects of the long history of China and of popular opinion of Mao in Cold War America that help to explain the less obvious aspects of these nonwritten primary sources.

IMAGE 1:   **Sun Guocheng, "Reporting to Chairman Mao," 1971**
Collection International Institute of Social History, Amsterdam

IMAGE 2:   Edmund Valtman, "The New Religion," 1966
Courtesy Estate of Ed Valtman

SAMPLE STUDENT ESSAY: EFFECTIVE COMPARATIVE ANALYSIS

Lauren Reid

History 100

December 11, 2018

Opposing Visual Images of Mao Zedong

Each of these primary sources is an example of political propaganda. They attempt to convince their audience that Mao Zedong was either a great or a terrible leader of China. We need to examine each one closely to see how it attempts to do so.

The Chinese artist portrays Mao as "father" of the nation. The readings we did on China described social hierarchy and obedience to elders as ancient aspects of Chinese civilization. The traditional Chinese ruler is not only father but also teacher. In the painting, Mao, the wise father, is surrounded by his adoring "family." His role as teacher is conveyed by the rapt attention paid by his "students" as he reads to them. The image of abundance (baskets of food, lush vegetation) in the background serves as a powerful symbol in an ancient peasant society in which food has been a precious commodity. All of these images would make a strong impression on a Chinese audience, especially a rural one.

If this painting was also distributed outside of China, it might be used for external propaganda as well. Perhaps in such a context its purpose might be to spread the image of Mao and Maoism as a way out of poverty and exploitation for Asian peasants in general. As with all propaganda, the viewer needs to be aware of the reality behind the image. This idyllic view of Mao's China was created at a time of great political upheaval, including a purge of the Communist Party leadership by Mao, an effort by military leaders to overthrow Mao, and assaults on "backward" elements by militant Red Guard youth.

The U.S. political cartoon pictures Mao as a cross between an emperor and Buddha. His brainwashed followers chant Maoist slogans as they carry him on his portable throne. Maoism, the cartoon is saying, is really a form of Eastern religious fanaticism. To make the image more threatening, the hammer and sickle — the symbol of the Soviet Union — is on the chain around Mao's neck and on top of the flags carried by the masses. The American audience is reminded that the power and ideology of the Soviet Union serve as vital support for Chinese communism. Such a strong anti-Communist statement is understandable in the historical context of mid-1960s America, which was engaged in intensifying conflict with Communist forces in Vietnam. The intended audience of this cartoon is clear: U.S. newspaper readers familiar with both Chinese government attacks on the United States as an "imperialist" power and U.S. government attacks on Chinese attempts to "enslave" the people of Asia. For this cartoon, the people of Asia are not an intended audience. Connecting Maoism to Buddhism and/or to the Soviet Union would not have been an effective way of improving the image of the United States.

This U.S. propaganda statement, like the Chinese painting, does not represent the reality of international politics in Asia. The idea that Moscow was the power behind Chinese communism is challenged by the growing ideological rift between the Soviet Union and China that had begun in the early 1960s. As we learned from our readings about the Vietnam War, Washington attempted to take advantage of that hostility to relieve its very difficult military position in Vietnam.

Note that the student writer addresses the assignment directly. She interprets what each of the artists is saying about Mao, and she provides an analysis of the wider historical contexts within which the artists did their work.

SAMPLE STUDENT ESSAY: POOR COMPARATIVE ANALYSIS

Juan Perez

History 100

December 11, 2018

These are two nonwritten, primary sources. They both show Mao Tze Tung who was the leader of the Chinese Communist Party. The first cartoon shows him reading a story to Chinese children. They are all smiling and it looks as if everything is fine in China. Our textbook had a lot of information about poverty in China but this cartoon doesn't show it. It makes it look like everybody has plenty to eat. The communists were very cruel to the Chinese people so they weren't really happy.

The other cartoon shows Mao leading a parade. It is very different from the first one. This cartoon makes him look fat and ugly. The Chinese people around him don't look happy this time. Maybe this is a communist festival and everybody has to show up. One of the essays we read said that millions of people in China believed Mao. These people look like they believe in communism.

These cartoons are not truthful. One is a very pretty painting and makes it look like everybody in China is happy. The other one tries to show that the people in China believed Communist propaganda. When you compare the two, neither one is correct.

The most serious error here is that the student fails to carry out the most basic task of the assignment, which is to "analyze" the two sources. One is a modern painting by a Chinese artist and reflects several aspects of Chinese history. The other is a cartoon in a U.S. newspaper and reflects attitudes in Cold War America. Instead, the student merely describes what he sees. The student says several times what something in the cartoon "looks like." Also, some statements contradict one another. The student says that the Chinese people in the cartoon "don't look happy" but also says that they "look like they believe in communism."

Compare this with the first sample student essay, which represents a very good response to the assignment. That student describes the historical context of each source. Understanding the historical contexts allows the student to give a richer analysis and a more effective comparison.

WRITING ABOUT SECONDARY SOURCES

A secondary source is a work of history that is based on primary sources. Having no firsthand knowledge of the subject, the author of a secondary source conducts research using primary sources to gain insights from people with such knowledge. Professor Jones writes an article on Irish immigration to Canada in the years of the Great Potato Famine. He bases his **argument**, that many passengers died because of unsanitary conditions aboard the boats, on primary sources—official immigration records, the papers of the companies whose ships carried the immigrants, and the records of the Famine Museum in Ireland. His article is a secondary source. When published in a **scholarly journal**, Professor Jones's research becomes available for study by professional historians and student researchers. Student researchers might read his article to gain background knowledge on the subject. They might compare Jones's **thesis** to that of Professor Smith, who argues that the state of semi-starvation of the passengers when they boarded the ships better explains the level of mortality aboard what were known as "coffin ships." Student researchers might test both theses by examining similar primary documents themselves. (For a more thorough explanation of secondary sources, see pp. 43–44 in Chapter 3.)

Instructors often build assignments around secondary sources. Paying close attention to these secondary sources helps you to understand how historians interpret the significance of a body of primary sources and build a thesis around them. Some assignments might require you to write short papers that identify the thesis, **summarize** the **evidence**, and assess the **conclusions** of a secondary source, or to compare one source with another.

Book reviews, article critiques, and comparative reviews and critiques are typical assignments involving the study of secondary sources. We will examine each of them.

Book Reviews

A book review is not usually a summary. Unless your instructor asks you to summarize a book's content, devote most of your review to *analyzing* its content. Identify its thesis; then describe how the thesis is presented and how well it is defended. Were you persuaded by the author's arguments? Compare the book to other course materials if doing so is part of the assignment. Be sure that your review makes it clear that you read and understood the book, and always provide the kind of analysis asked of you.

Here is a student's review of the book *Colonial Habits: Convents and the Spiritual Economy of Cuzco, Peru,* by Kathryn Burns (Duke University Press, 1999).

SAMPLE STUDENT BOOK REVIEW

Chloe Bernard

History 100

October 15, 2018

Book Review of

Kathryn Burns, *Colonial Habits: Convents and the Spiritual Economy of Cuzco, Peru* (Duke University Press, 1999).

When considering the lives of cloistered nuns, you might think that it was the deliberate choice of these women to cut themselves off from the outside world. In her book *Colonial Habits: Convents and the Spiritual Economy of Cuzco, Peru*, Kathryn Burns demonstrates that this was not always the case. She argues in her introduction that "convents were vital" to the establishment of Spanish control over the native Incas that the Spanish conquered (p. 2). The seven chapters that

---

follow trace the ways in which the nuns of Cuzco played a crucial part in the economic and political history of Spanish Peru from its founding in the 1550s through the creation of the Peruvian republic in the 1820s. The author argues that for nearly three centuries these cloistered women dwelled not at the margins but at the center of one of South America's most significant colonial societies. Although there are some additional elements of her book that are not as clear as they could be, Burns's overall thesis, that convents created a "spiritual economy" that was essential to the development of Peru, is well grounded in evidence, is clearly articulated throughout the text, and is a great example of how the hidden history of women in colonization can be revealed through meticulous research and a careful reading of the sources.

Burns begins *Colonial Habits* with a description of the founding of a convent in Cuzco called Santa Clara, less than two decades after the arrival of Europeans in Peru. Although the Spanish dominated the Inca both militarily and politically, the process of conquering them included social and cultural programs as well. One important component of this ongoing conquest, Burns argues, was the creation of monasteries and convents to provide Christian education for the children of mixed (Spanish and Inca) parentage. After the foundation of Santa Clara, the *mestiza* — the daughters of the Spanish conquistadores and Inca women — arrived there to stay "off the marriage market while it was decided exactly what role they would play in the new society" (p. 31). The new convent also helped in the colonization of Peru by holding confiscated Inca lands and leasing them out to Spanish residents. Women entering Santa Clara also gave their family dowries to the convent, which added to its wealth. By the 1600s, then, the nuns of Santa Clara held enough land and cash that they could actually lend money to Spanish colonists. Here is where Burns's idea of a "spiritual economy" really takes center stage, as she describes how the convent bypassed church laws against collecting interest in order to provide *censo al quitar* — essentially a mortgage on land — to borrowers. "The monastery did not enter into loans," she writes, "but rather contracts of purchase and sale in which the nuns purchased the right to collect an annuity" (p. 64).

After explaining how Santa Clara played such a pivotal role in early Peru, Burns explains how nuns in Cuzco could remain individually poor but collectively powerful. In the 1600s, for example, Cuzco added two more convents, Santa Catalina in 1605 and Santa Theresa in 1673, although Burns really focuses on the first of the two. These convents soon integrated themselves into the Peruvian "spiritual economy" with assets of landholdings, dowries, and *censo* arrangements similar to those of Santa Clara. But in addition to their important economic role, Burns also describes daily life in these convents, which was quite interesting. Although some cloistered women technically took vows of poverty, many of them maintained apartments and "constructed their own complex, colonial households with infants and toddlers, adolescents, maids, and slaves — perhaps all at once — inside their capacious cells" (p. 116). Since the nuns were physically separated from the material world, the residents of Cuzco would ask for prayers, loans, and other favors of them through the *locutorio*, or a receiving room with iron bars that separated the cloistered and the outsiders.

Burns sometimes seems unclear as to whether the nuns used their position to reinforce or undermine Spanish patriarchy — she claims that they did both — so it is a bit difficult to understand just where these women stood in society. Perhaps this is because the complex arrangements of *censos* and other colonial financial instruments seem so strange to modern readers. In any case, a more detailed explanation of them might have made Burns's idea of a "spiritual economy" clearer.

As Cuzco's convents entered the 1700s, their spiritual and economic influence began to wane. According to Burns, " 'enlightened' Spaniards were developing a forceful critique of the church as excessively worldly and unduly rich," and they began to fear that the Spanish economy as a whole would suffer if the church was allowed to continue acquiring property (p. 159). This shift in Spanish economic thinking, known as the *economía civil,* "threatened monastic livelihoods as far away as Cuzco" (p. 159) and weakened the "spiritual economy" just as the famous Inca rebellion led by Túpac Amaru hit Peru in 1780–1781.

Spanish authorities enlisted the convents in putting down the rebels, but this further eroded their economic standing by forcing them to reorganize their finances. Cuzco's once-prosperous nuns, whose lives were supposed to be devoted to prayer, now found themselves "scrambling for an income" (p. 182).

Political events in Europe further undermined the structure of colonial society in South America, as Napoleon's invasion of Spain in 1808 left the Viceroy of Peru short of funds and administrative support from the home country. Nuns had a difficult choice to make. Either they could prop up colonial authorities with their rapidly diminishing resources, or they could try to reconcile themselves with the growing independence movement in Peru. They tried to side with the viceroy, but the Republic of Peru nonetheless arrived on the scene by late 1824. The new republican leaders confiscated the property of convents, secularized education, and took welfare agencies out of the exclusive hands of religious institutions. "Thus by the mid-1820s," Burns concludes, "the state had placed itself right in the middle of convent business, leaving the nuns of Cuzco little room to maneuver out of their difficulties" (p. 197).

Despite the secularization brought on by independence, Cuzco's convents survive to this day. This might be enough to signal the importance of *Colonial Habits*, but there is much more here that makes Kathryn Burns's work significant. Most notably, her depiction of cloistered women at the center of a colonial economy is a far cry from the traditional notion that Spanish patriarchal traditions cast women into the margins of public life. The fact that this economic power emerged from convents is even more surprising. Who would have thought that women living out their lives in prayer and meditation would cast such a strong shadow over colonial Peru? Even though their authority waned as the colonial order fell to more secular, republican ideas, the cloistered women of Cuzco persevered. Although her explanation of the day-to-day operations of the "spiritual economy" of colonial Cuzco is at times difficult to understand, Kathryn Burns's

depiction of the influence enjoyed by the convents of Santa Clara and
Santa Catalina provides fascinating and important examples of how
women can affect history in unexpected ways that might be hidden
in traditional narratives. Even though these women individually lived
cloistered lives, Kathryn Burns successfully places their collective
presence at center stage in colonial Peru.

Reviews can vary widely in content to accommodate the different kinds
of work they discuss. Still, a good review, like this one, includes specific
elements. The book under review here is identified at the very beginning,
with all of the bibliographic data in the initial heading. Then the author's
thesis (that the economic and social influences of the Cuzco convents were
essential to the development of colonial Peru) is made clear, and the overall scope of the work (the period of Spanish colonial rule in Peru, from
the 1530s through the 1820s) is described. The **introduction** also gives the
reviewer's general assessment of the book's main argument, which in this
case is positive.

Then the review takes a more extensive look at the book's content, being
careful to include quotes that describe the author's points along with a
summary of the book's narrative scope. A student reviewer should focus on
the effectiveness of the thesis and assume that the evidence is accurate, for
students are likely not as familiar with the sources or with the wider historical literature as a professional historian would be. However, if the course
includes several related works or if students are doing primary research in
this field, the review could evaluate the primary sources as well. In this case,
the student reviewer is willing to limit the comments to the book's effectiveness as a stand-alone work.

If your instructor asks for a particular kind of review, be sure to follow
his or her directions. You might be asked to mention some of the **counterevidence** — evidence that argues against the thesis — and to assess the
author's ability to present it fairly and respond to it effectively. Or you
might be asked to comment on the author's personal or academic background and reasons for writing the book. This last point should certainly
be included if there is significant debate among historians about the thesis
of the book or if the book's preface or introduction refers to such disagreements. With a book of this kind, your instructor may ask you to comment
on the debate and perhaps also ask you how the book affects your views on
the subject.

It is usually unwise to emphasize your personal opinion in a review unless
your instructor asks you to do so. If you are asked to express it, don't write
simply, "I liked the way the author defended women's rights." Instead say,
"I was impressed by the author's use of many concrete examples of actions

> ### Guidelines for Writing a Book Review
>
> - At the top of the first page, put the name of the author, the title of the work, the publisher's name, and the date of publication.
> - State the author's topic and thesis.
> - Describe the evidence presented to support the thesis.
> - If possible, assess the arguments and evidence used. (Are they clear or unclear, strong or weak, convincing or unconvincing?)
> - If appropriate, describe the author's background and reason for writing the book.
> - If required, compare the work to related course materials. (Does it agree or disagree? Does it add a new perspective?)
> - If expected, close with your own assessment of the book's assumptions, arguments, and conclusions.

by women to dramatize their demand for the right to vote. The fact that one day they chained themselves to the White House fence made clear how strongly they felt about their cause." Show that your opinion is the result of serious thought about the arguments made in the book.

If your assignment is a review that is longer than a few pages, you might want to quote a sentence or phrase from the book to support a point you are making. But don't use too many quotations. Your review should be written in your own words rather than those of the author.

Article Critiques

An article critique assignment asks you to make a very close examination of a scholarly article — a ten- to fifty-page, heavily documented essay normally published in an academic journal. Your instructor will likely give specific instructions about the kind of critique that is expected, but you will undoubtedly need to read the source carefully before you begin writing. (For details on how to read and assess scholarly articles, see pp. 49–50 in Chapter 3 and pp. 68–69 in Chapter 4.)

In general, the goal of an article critique is similar to that of a book review, but you will be expected to treat your source in greater detail. Your assignment might also ask you to make connections between this article and related course materials. Mention any weaknesses in the author's efforts to support the thesis and any biases or unwarranted assumptions that you detect. Note any counterevidence you are aware of that the author has not mentioned.

Be sure that your critique covers the points that your instructor has asked for, and keep within assigned page limits. If you have been asked to express your own reaction to the article, do so. If not, confine your conclusions to the content of the article itself.

NOTE: As you read and take notes on the article in preparation for writing your critique, watch for any of the author's words that you might wish to quote. Leave no doubt in your notes as to whose words these are by placing them, unmistakably, within quotation marks.

Comparative Reviews and Critiques

If you have questions about writing single-source reviews and critiques, see the previous sections, "Book Reviews" and "Article Critiques." Here we take up an assignment in which you are expected to *compare* secondary sources to one another. Your instructor may point out any specific comparisons that you should make. The following is general advice about drawing comparisons.

Comparisons illustrate significant similarities and differences between the sources being examined, especially ones that are suggested in the assignment. If your instructor asks you to discuss the different views of two authors, then your comparisons are likely to be drawn from the theses and conclusions of each source. In a different kind of assignment, it may be necessary to look as well at connections between subject matter, approach to subject (social, economic, political, etc.), writing style, kind of argument (the way the thesis is supported), and primary sources drawn from, as well as theses and conclusions.

Don't begin your comparison until you have read (or reread) each of the sources. Examine each one carefully, and pay special attention to the points of comparison mentioned above. Your ability to find and explain points of comparison will rest on a careful reading of each source.

When writing comparisons, don't look only for disagreements. Authors may come to similar conclusions yet differ in the kinds of arguments they make or the evidence they use. Two different authors may agree that the religious outlook of the founders of the nation of Saudi Arabia was Wahabism. Yet one might argue that Wahabism was an authentic expression of Arabian Islam while the other might argue that it was not. To take another example, two authors may study the same subject (say, the native peoples of California in the nineteenth century) and even use similar kinds of evidence (mission records) yet draw different conclusions from their research. One may study the mission records and conclude that the native population underwent a tremendous decline, while the other concludes, from the same records, that basic cultural traits of these peoples survived well into the twentieth century. In this case, the difference between the two studies is the result of the very different kinds of information that each focused on from the same primary sources. One examined evidence of the size of populations (demographic history), while the other examined evidence of native ways of life (cultural history).

Examine each source for the basic components listed above: subject, thesis, approach, evidence, structure, sources, and conclusion. Introduce your general findings, and then build your essay around the points of similarity or difference that are most relevant to the assignment, making sure to justify any comparisons you make. Make clear to your reader not only what the similarities and differences are, but why they are important. In your conclusion, summarize your main points, and, if possible, place your findings in a wider historical context.

HOW TO ORGANIZE A SHORT ESSAY

In many history courses, you will be expected to use your analytical skills to write a short essay based upon a variety of primary and secondary sources from which you are expected to draw your conclusions. As essays become longer and the range of evidence more broad, you will need the skill to organize the evidence you gather so that it leads you toward a clear conclusion. These skills can be practiced in short essays, as well.

Let's say you are given two sets of sources about soldier's experiences on both sides of the U.S. Civil War: a secondary source of essays, "March Until You Can't" and a primary source of letters written by the soldiers. You are asked to write a three- to five-page essay responding to the question: What were the strongest emotions expressed in the letters and what do they tell you about the soldier's day-to-day experiences?

The secondary source provides context: the world in which these young men grew up and the kind of war in which they found themselves. Most of these soldiers are seventeen or eighteen years old, writing letters to their family or friends. The letters were written over 150 years ago, some in shaky handwriting. Most young men of that era would not have done much writing of any kind; they misspell words, ignore punctuation, and talk about a life very different from your own.

Read each letter carefully and more than once. What does the soldier say about his experiences and what emotions are expressed by the way he says them? At first the soldier's feelings may not seem clear, but your notes from the secondary source essays and several readings of each letter should help you recognize them.

Record each experience that the soldier describes and his feelings about it. He may write about the enemy, the experience of combat, the boredom of camp life, or his desire to be home. Organize your notes, perhaps by the kind of emotion (sad, angry, hopeful) or by its strength or by the situation that produced it. When you write your essay you will need to draw your facts from these notes. Choose your categories carefully, and label your notes clearly.

Longer essays require you to plan out your writing. How will you describe the powerful emotions and in what order? Similar planning will benefit you in a short essay. Once you have a clear idea of your conclusion; determine what evidence you need to support it, to keep from wandering away from your conclusion. Here is an outline of a well-organized essay:

1. *Introduction*: Describe the secondary source information that helped you understand what the soldiers were saying. Explain which emotions you found most powerful. Yes, your conclusion can be part of your introduction. If your instructor has asked you to state your "thesis" that is, the central point of your essay, it will need to appear in your introduction (see "Drafting a Thesis Statement" in Chapter 6).

2. Describe the strongest emotions you found and provide specific examples of each.

3. Explain how you decided which emotions were strongest.

4. Describe what this reveals about the soldiers' daily lives using examples from the documents.

5. *Conclusion*: Briefly summarize your evidence and how it supports your answer to the question.

NOTE: For information for organizing longer essays, see "Creating a Writing Outline" on page 109 in Chapter 6 and "Organizing Your Evidence with a Writing Outline" on pages 143–47 in Chapter 8.

6

Building a History Essay: From Thesis to Conclusion

WHY CLEAR WRITING IS IMPORTANT

Writing is a task of great significance. With each college writing assignment that you complete, you will be honing this important skill. Your writing skills tell the reader a lot about your ability to read critically and think clearly. A few years after graduating from college, you may no longer remember the meaning of Confucianism or when the Egyptian pharaohs of the eighteenth dynasty reigned, but if you sharpened your writing skills in history assignments, you acquired an asset that will last a lifetime.

Clear writing accomplishes two important goals. First, it demonstrates that your thinking about a subject is logical. You cannot write clearly about something that you do not understand clearly. Second, it enables you to convey to your readers in a convincing way exactly what you want them to understand. Clear writing is persuasive. The ability to write persuasively will serve you throughout your life, no matter what career path you choose.

PREPARING TO WRITE

When you are given a writing assignment in a history course, you are being asked to gain command over a group of documents—**primary** or **secondary**, print or visual. You are also being asked to turn your understanding of that material into an essay—one that responds directly to a question or **topic** and demonstrates your understanding of the topic or documents.

When confronted with a writing assignment, keep the following questions in mind:

- What is the nature of the assignment?
- What kind of writing is required?
- What kind of sources are required (and allowed)?
- What is the best way of organizing these sources?

What are you being asked to do? The question that is asked (or the topic that is assigned) helps determine the kind of writing best suited to the answer. The question "Who invented the lightbulb?" can be answered more directly and concretely than can the question "Why was electricity spoken of in spiritual as well as technical terms in the late nineteenth century?" The second question requires more background knowledge and more interpretation of **evidence**. An essay in response to the second question will be more complex and will need to be more carefully organized than a response to the first one. It will need to approach the answer in stages, and the **conclusion** will be more speculative.

The nature of the question will also help determine the kind of evidence needed to answer it. What sources are you expected to use? Are they identified for you, or do you need to find them? Even before you begin to think about writing, be sure that you have a clear idea of the kind of evidence you will need and that such evidence is available to you.

Once you understand the question and the kind of answer and sources expected of you, consider the kind of information you will need to take from those sources. As you gather that information, think about which part of it answers which part of the question. Begin to consider the organization of your essay.

The Problem of Organization

It is wise to think about the problem of organizing a longer essay at an early stage of your research. You will not solve the problem immediately, but thinking about the overall organization of your essay will help keep your research focused on your topic and help you create categories for your research notes. The following advice about organization is general only. Assignments differ in length and complexity, and therefore ideas about organization cannot be made final at an early stage. You may change your topic or your thesis or come across sources that change your ideas about your topic.

It is not at all unusual to feel uneasy about assignments that place great responsibility on you. You will choose a topic and a thesis, discover the sources needed to make a strong argument, order your notes and place them into a writing outline, and then draw all your work together in a clearly written essay. That is challenging work. Here are a few models for organizing an essay. They are general ideas to help guide you through your work. Like many other skills, your ability to give clear direction to your writing will prepare you for responsibilities of all kinds.

Narration—The writer poses a question for the reader and then tells a "story" that step by step answers the question. Here the word "story" does not refer to fiction; it is the historical evidence that tells the story.

Chronology—The evidence is presented according to the time when it occurred. More than a timeline, however, it is an explanation of how one event led to another.

Journey—The evidence may not be in chronological order; it may not be directly related to other evidence. Still, each kind of evidence joins and supports the main argument, the way creeks and streams flow into a large river. Each tributary broadens the river and adds strength to its current.

Examining Sources

In many cases, the topic of your writing assignment will be given to you, and you may even be directed to a set of particular sources to examine. For example, your assignment might be "Based on the travel reports of Marco Polo and Ibn Battuta and on the article 'Crossing Asia: Messengers and Messages,' support or challenge the view that Christians and Muslims had distinct views of Asia in the thirteenth and fourteenth centuries." In other cases, assignments may be very broad, and you will be responsible for narrowing a topic down to one manageable aspect. (Refer to p. 119 in Chapter 7 for advice on narrowing a topic.)

In either event, once you have a specific topic to write about, you will need to do some exploring. Read about your topic, using the sources assigned or, if necessary, the sources you find on your own. (See Chapter 7, pp. 124–29, for advice on tracking down sources.) As you examine a source, pay attention not only to what it says but to such questions as: When was it written, who wrote it, and for what kind of reader was it intended? As discussed throughout Chapter 3, critical thinking about the meaning of a source will lead you to your own conclusions about historical questions.

Drafting a Thesis Statement

After reading through and examining your sources, you will be ready to draft a **working thesis**. A working thesis is tentative; it helps you to organize your ideas and plan your paper. Once finalized, your **thesis** will be the *central point* of your essay; your goal as a writer is to convince your readers that your thesis is an important one. Like a lawyer before a jury, you present the evidence that your research has uncovered, and you argue that this evidence provides strong support for your thesis.

NOTE: Most, but not all, assignments will require a thesis statement. Some assignments, such as summaries, should remain neutral. See Chapter 5 for details on various types of writing assignments.

A thesis statement is not a restatement of your topic or a summary of your research; it is a specific claim that you will pursue in the essay and that the evidence that you present will support. Don't be concerned about the exact wording of your thesis statement while you are just beginning your research. You may need to refine the statement as you learn more about your subject and even as you draft your paper. (For more, see "Developing a Thesis" in Chapter 7, p. 121.)

Consider the following writing assignment: "Write an essay explaining why navigators in the time of Columbus were afraid to voyage beyond the sight of land." A paper based on such an assignment could be organized around one of several thesis statements. One essay might argue that navigators were afraid of being eaten by sea monsters. (Belief in sea monsters did exist in that era.) Another essay might argue that navigators in the fifteenth century were afraid of sailing off the edge of the (flat) earth. An examination of the relevant evidence would lead you in the direction of a particular thesis. For example, if you were impressed by the evidence about navigational instruments, your essay might begin like this, including an *effective thesis statement:*

In the fifteenth century, very few navigators believed that the earth was flat, although some did fear sea monsters. The greatest concern, however, was that the Atlantic Ocean was huge and the lack of accuracy of navigational instruments could leave a ship hopelessly lost until it was hit by a fatal storm or ran out of supplies. It was, therefore, not irrational fear but rather lack of technical knowledge that kept ships' courses in sight of land. This essay will examine the problems of shipbuilding and navigation that stood in the way of transoceanic voyages in the fifteenth century, arguing that the inadequacy of ship design and lack of precise navigational instruments made such long voyages seem so hazardous.

Here, for comparison, is an example of an opening paragraph that *would not serve as an effective thesis statement:*

Some sailors in the fifteenth century were frightened of sea monsters, but nobody thought the earth was flat. They were afraid of going out in the ocean because nobody had ever done it before. They could become lost if their navigation equipment failed. This essay says that sailors were afraid to voyage out of sight of land because they were afraid of becoming lost. It also says they were afraid of storms. The basic problem was that they didn't have the equipment they needed to sail across the ocean safely.

This paragraph is far too general (and vague) to serve as a thesis statement. It mentions several concerns of fifteenth-century navigators without clearly separating them. It does not explain to the reader which concern will serve as the thesis. In fact, it does not state *any* formal thesis.

Creating a Writing Outline

Once you have developed a thesis for your paper, you need to think about the structure of your essay. The thesis statement will help you to stay focused on the main purpose of your paper, and a writing outline will help you organize your thoughts and present your evidence. You could begin simply by listing the points you want to cover. As you work on the outline, keep in mind the length of your essay. Also think about the kinds of evidence you expect to use and the places in your essay where you will need specific kinds of evidence. Because you still have research to do, don't be concerned if your outline needs to be revised as you go along. It is normal to adjust an outline as you gather information and refine your thesis.

A sample outline, based on the writing assignment given on page 107, is shown below. Notice that the student includes a rough sketch of the thesis statement, the four main areas to cover (one with subheadings), and the conclusion. (For more on outlining, see "Organizing Your Evidence with a Writing Outline" in Chapter 8, pp. 143–47.)

EXAMPLE OF AN OUTLINE FOR A HISTORY ESSAY

Thesis: Christians and Muslims had distinct views of Asia in the 13th and
                   14th centuries.

Points to Cover: 1. Variety of travelers

                   1a. European, African, eastern Mediterranean (evidence from
                       "Crossing Asia")

                   1b. Religious; merchant; soldier (evidence from "Crossing Asia")

                   2. Views of Marco Polo (evidence from primary source)

                   3. Views of Ibn Battuta (evidence from primary source)

                   4. Comparison of views

Conclusion: Summary of evidence in support of thesis

NOTE: If, in your research, you come across information that could support a thesis very different from your own, you should address such evidence, which is known as **counterevidence**, in your outline and, eventually, in your paper. Your knowledge of opposing viewpoints, and your ability to disagree with them, indicates that your research has been thorough. No history paper can ever expect to "prove" its thesis correct. What historians claim when they defend a thesis is that the evidence presented strongly supports the thesis. It is up to other scholars, in their own research, to support, challenge, or go beyond a particular thesis.

DRAFTING YOUR ESSAY

Having examined sources, drafted a thesis, and sketched a writing outline, you have created the basic framework for your essay. Your next step is to flesh out the text into a **rough draft**. In this early stage of writing, don't worry too much about grammar or style. Get your most important ideas and the evidence that supports them down on the page. Find a place for any valuable new ideas and evidence that were not part of your original outline. If necessary, consider shortening or dropping any section that now seems less important.

Regardless of the kind of essay you are writing, the essay should open with an **introduction** that includes a clear statement of your thesis. Then, in an organized manner, the body of your essay should present the evidence supporting your thesis. Most essays should end with a conclusion that restates the thesis and summarizes how it is supported by the evidence.

NOTE: Writing is a nonlinear process. You do not have to create the introduction first. Many writers draft the body of the paper first and then write the introduction and conclusion. In addition, you probably will need to revise parts of the essay as you go. Refer to the section "Revising Your Essay" in this chapter for details (pp. 115–16).

A Clear Introduction

Your first paragraph describes your topic for the reader. It also contains your thesis statement and a brief preview of the kinds of evidence you will be using. Some other ways of looking at the topic may be mentioned as well. In a long essay, you may need two paragraphs or more to accomplish these goals.

Here is an example of an effective first paragraph of an essay on the topic "the origins of slavery in seventeenth-century Virginia":

The English settlers in the part of North America that became the United States did not arrive with the intention of creating a system of slavery. Yet, within several decades, each of the British colonies had imported African slaves. Historians have debated the reasons for this development for many years. Some emphasize the racist views of the English toward the Africans, which were quite strong well before British settlement of North America. They point out that Europeans ("whites") were never enslaved in the colonies nor were Native Americans, with a few exceptions. Other historians emphasize the growing need for labor in the colonies. With the development of tobacco agriculture in Virginia, landowners could not find enough European fieldworkers. The thesis of this paper, which is based on the diaries of seventeenth-century Virginia plantation owners, is that these landowners made a decision to solve their manpower problem by using the labor of African slaves, which they could purchase from Caribbean colonies already organized around slave labor. This paper will also argue that, without the belief that slaves were an absolute necessity for the success of the new plantations, the slave labor system might never have been established in what became the United States.

The above introductory paragraph is excellent preparation for the reader. It provides background information and briefly describes the historical debate between the "racial" and the "labor" arguments about slavery in North America. It ends with a statement of the thesis and mentions some of the documents on which it will rest.

A Cohesive Body

The main part, or body, of your essay presents the results of your research, organized in such a way as to help convince the reader of the significance and validity of the thesis. The body should consist of clear, concise sentences grouped into coherent paragraphs.

Sentences: The Building Blocks of Writing

The most effective sentences are clear and concise, and they usually employ the **active voice**. In addition, writers in history need to pay special attention to verb tense.

Clarity.   Clear writing begins with clear sentences. A clear sentence leaves no doubt about the subject of the sentence. It also leaves no doubt about what the subject is doing.

UNCLEAR

On September 1, 1939, Germany was strong and Poland was weak, and so it attacked.

The subject of the above sentence is unclear. The reader cannot tell if the subject is Germany or Poland and therefore cannot tell who attacked whom.

CLEAR

On September 1, 1939, Germany attacked Poland.

In the revised sentence, the subject (*Germany*) is placed as close as possible to the verb naming the action (*attacked*), and the meaning becomes much more clear.

Conciseness.   A phrase can add information, but the wordiness that results from the indiscriminate use of phrases can obscure a sentence's meaning.

WORDY

Although his plane was loaded down with extra fuel, Lindbergh was still able to get off the muddy runway in New Jersey despite very bad weather that rainy morning in 1927 and the fact that several other people had been killed trying to become the first person to stay awake for the thirty-three hours it took to fly solo across the Atlantic Ocean.

In the above sentence, Lindbergh's flight is surrounded by so many phrases that the main point of the sentence is lost. Never attempt to pack into one sentence every fact you have learned. If some facts are not necessary, leave them out. If they are necessary, make room for them by creating additional sentences. For example, if the weight of the fuel and the muddy runway are important but the weather conditions and the failed attempts by others are not, writing two sentences instead of one would make the additional points and make them clearly:

CONCISE

Lindbergh's plane was so heavily loaded with fuel that it almost failed to get off the muddy runway in New Jersey. Once in the air, however, Lindbergh was able to stay awake for the thirty-three hours it took to fly across the Atlantic.

Active Voice versus Passive Voice.   The subject and verb are the core of any sentence. Active voice verbs describe what the subject of the sentence is doing; **passive voice** verbs describe what is being done to the subject.

PASSIVE VOICE

A vaccination against smallpox <u>was introduced</u> in 1796.

In the above example, the verb (*was introduced*) is passive. The subject (*vaccination*) is not the actor; it doesn't do anything. As a result, the sentence is vague, and we are missing a key piece of information: Who introduced the vaccination?

ACTIVE VOICE

In 1796, Edward Jenner <u>introduced</u> a vaccination against smallpox.

In the above example, the subject—*Jenner*—is the actor. The active voice verb *introduced* clarifies the subject and its action.

NOTE: The passive voice may be needed when you want to emphasize what is being done to the subject.

PROPER USE OF THE PASSIVE VOICE

Three U.S. presidents were assassinated in the nineteenth century.

Past Tense versus Present Tense. When you are writing about historical events, use the past tense.

PAST TENSE

Thomas Jefferson wrote a draft of the Declaration of Independence.

Jefferson's action took place in the past, so it is best to use the past tense when writing about it.

When you are referring to the contents of a specific written document or to an object (such as an old building or a work of art) *that still exists*, use the present tense.

PRESENT TENSE

The Constitution guarantees equal protection under the law.

Cohesive, Connected Paragraphs

A paragraph consists of sentences that all relate to the topic of the paragraph. In a well-constructed paragraph, the topic of the paragraph is clearly expressed in a *topic sentence*, and every other sentence in the paragraph sheds light on that topic. For example, if you are writing a paragraph about Islamic architecture, every sentence in your paragraph should say something about that subject. If you have something to say about Chinese architecture, those comments probably belong in a separate paragraph.

Each paragraph in an essay should provide new information or explanation and take your essay one step closer to the substantiation of your thesis. Each paragraph should flow logically from the one that precedes it and lead smoothly into the one that follows it. As you begin each paragraph, consider how it supplements the previous one and whether it supports your thesis. A new paragraph that does not accomplish these goals needs to be rewritten or perhaps placed elsewhere in your essay.

Sometimes you will need to help your reader see the **continuity** or connection between paragraphs. A **linking sentence** at the end of one paragraph or at the beginning of the next one will inform the reader that your essay is moving from one important point to a new but related one.

LINKING SENTENCE

Therefore, changes in printing technology made newspapers cheaper and more available. But new technology alone does not explain rising readership. As immigrants poured into the country from Europe, it was the new look of the newspaper, especially the use of large illustrations and photographs, that attracted these new "readers."

The linking sentence indicates that a paragraph dealing with technological change is going to be followed by a discussion of a new topic: how changes in the look of newspapers attracted new readers.

In a long essay in which extended arguments are developed in support of the thesis, a **linking paragraph** might be needed to tell readers where your essay is heading, and why. Keep your readers in mind: if you think they might not be able to follow your line of thought, tighten the connections between paragraphs.

A Meaningful Conclusion

How do you know when to end your essay? You must not go over the page limit, of course. It is best to stop when you have made all of the points needed to support your thesis. You don't need to keep writing until you have included every point in your outline or noted every document you have read. Review the most important parts of your outline. Check your essay to see if each has been included.

How long should your conclusion be? The length of the paper determines the length of the conclusion: for a shorter paper (three to six pages), write a conclusion of one or two paragraphs; write three or four paragraphs for a longer paper (seven or more pages).

What should you say in the conclusion? Reread your introductory paragraph. What did you tell the reader you intended to do? Summarize briefly the major points that took the reader from the statement of your thesis to this conclusion. A conclusion is also the place to remind the reader of the significance of the topic and of the way your thesis has examined it.

Here is the *successful concluding paragraph* of the essay on slavery in Virginia:

> While race was a factor in the origins of slavery in Virginia, the enslavement of African Americans did not occur at the founding of the colony or even with the arrival of the first Africans. The experience of African landowners such as Anthony Johnson demonstrated that no group (white, black, or Native American) was enslaved while the tobacco economy was in its earliest stage. Not until a half century or so later were laws established that defined slavery as the status of African Americans. By that time, however, a mature tobacco economy was under the control of wealthy, white landowners. The white workers were unwilling to accept the harsh conditions of labor, so the landowners turned to blacks. The rights of blacks could (and would) be denied, and thousands of them were already enslaved in English colonies in the Caribbean. While race was clearly a factor in *who* was enslaved, the need for enslaved labor of *any* kind was a result of the perceived

economic requirements of the growing tobacco plantations. If Virginia had had a different economic base, the history of slavery in this colony, and perhaps of the entire country, might have been very different.

REVISING YOUR ESSAY

Once you have written a rough draft, you may decide to make additions to your research or changes to your writing outline. You should account for these changes by creating a revised draft. If there are no major changes to make to either your thesis statement or the supporting research, your task is to read your rough draft carefully to be sure that it has a proper thesis statement, a clear direction, adequate documentation, well-crafted paragraphs, and a meaningful conclusion. If you are asked to review a peer's paper, you should keep these same considerations in mind. For a list of questions to ask when revising a draft, see "Guidelines for Revising Your

Guidelines for Revising Your Essay

ORGANIZATION
- Does the introductory paragraph give context for the topic? Does it contain a clear thesis statement?
- Is the thesis adequately supported in the body of the essay? Is more evidence needed?
- Is any counterevidence introduced and addressed?
- Is the supporting evidence arranged in a logical order?
- Is each paragraph focused around a single main point? Does any existing material need to be removed?
- Is the direction of the essay made clear by tight, linked paragraphs? Are linking sentences used when needed for transitions?
- Does the conclusion effectively summarize the thesis and its supporting evidence?
- Are all major points documented with the proper format? (See Chapter 10.)

CLARITY
- Does each sentence clearly name its subject and state what the subject is doing (or saying, feeling, etc.)?
- Are any sentences too wordy? Is each sentence clear and concise?
- Are active verbs used whenever possible?
- Is the past tense used to describe past historical events? Is the present tense used only to describe documents or objects that still exist?

Essay" (p. 115). For a list of revision guidelines for long research papers, see "Guidelines for Revising and Rewriting" in Chapter 8 (p. 154).

PROOFREADING YOUR ESSAY

The last step in preparing a writing assignment is **proofreading**. Carefully read your entire paper and review it line by line, looking for misspellings, missing or incorrect punctuation, and layout issues (that is, how the text looks on the page). It is helpful to print out the paper; reading your work in a hard-copy format may help you catch errors that you previously missed. Read slowly to catch as many typos as you can. It may be helpful to read the paper out loud. You may hear a problem (a missing word, for example) that you haven't been able to see. A spell-checker is a terrific help in avoiding incorrect spellings, and you should always make use of one before turning in a paper. However, don't expect the spell-checker to catch every misspelled or misused word. It will not catch misspelled words that it reads as other words. For example, if you write "him" instead of "his," or "no" for "know," the spell-checker will not read it as a mistake. You must catch these kinds of errors yourself when you proofread your paper. Also, the spell-checker flags any word that it does not recognize, including correctly spelled words not in its electronic dictionary.

Grammar-checkers are even less reliable. When you use a grammar-checker, consider its advice as a suggestion for revision. If the grammar-checker questions the way you have said something, think twice before deciding to make any changes to your original sentence, phrase, or word. Keep in mind that you, not your computer, are the author of your paper.

THE DANGER OF PLAGIARISM

When you prepare a written assignment from notes that you have taken from books or other course materials, be careful how you use those notes. Otherwise, you run the risk of including in your paper sentences or extended phrases that you copied word for word from your sources. Even if you do this copying accidentally, you are guilty of **plagiarism**. Unless the phrases or sentences written by other authors are placed in quotation marks and their sources are identified in **citations**, you have committed a very serious breach of academic honesty. Plagiarism can lead to failing a course and even to expulsion from school. Be sure to read the section "Avoiding Plagiarism" in Chapter 4 (pp. 84–86).

CHAPTER
7

Conducting Research in History

The assignment to write a **research paper** requires you to select your own sources of information and draw your own **conclusions**. It is one of the most creative tasks you will do as a history student; the paper you write is uniquely your own. Because a lot of independent work is involved, research is often the most challenging history assignment. The skills you gain from this kind of project (gathering, evaluating, and organizing **evidence**) are invaluable. They will be of use to you in any career you pursue. The subjects of your research may fade from your memory in years to come, but the ability to investigate a complex **topic** is a skill you will always be able to call on.

This chapter surveys sources of historical information and explains how to use these sources most profitably. It will help you decide on a suitable topic, formulate a meaningful **research question**, and do the research necessary to propose an answer to your question, which will be the basis for the **thesis** of your paper. (See Chapter 8, "Why Your Paper Needs a Thesis," on p. 141.) This chapter will help you navigate your school library as well as the internet in your quest for relevant sources, and it will help you evaluate those sources for relevance and reliability once you have tracked them down. Finally, it will explain how to record and organize information from your sources so that you will be ready to draft your paper. (For details on writing a research paper, see Chapter 8.)

BEGINNING THE RESEARCH PROCESS

A lengthy research paper takes many weeks of research and writing. If your instructor sets interim deadlines, make a point of meeting them. Otherwise, break up the assignment into segments like those listed in the guidelines below, and set a reasonable deadline for each segment.

Choosing a Topic

Most instructors offer a list of possible research topics. Choose carefully; work on a topic that raises your curiosity or builds on your established interests. Weeks of research and writing will seem much longer if your curiosity about the topic wanes. If, early in your research, you discover that you misjudged your interest in the topic, choose another.

Read through the course materials on a topic that seems of interest. Carry out some research in generalized **reference sources** to be sure of your interest in the topic. (For a list of useful reference works, see Appendix A, or check with your school's reference librarian.) As you explore, take on the role of

---

Guidelines for the Research Process

- Browse the course materials and historical bibliographies, and find a topic that interests you.
- Do some initial reading to narrow your topic into one aspect that is manageable for the scope of your project.
- Come up with a debatable research question that is relevant to your topic and worthy of examination.
- Conduct initial research to explore possible answers to your question.
- Create a research strategy that helps you to determine which kinds of sources to read and in what order.
- Do research to gather reliable and relevant sources, interpreting them and taking notes as you go.
- Settle on a tentative thesis that proposes an answer to your research question.
- Create a writing outline for your paper, and begin to organize your research in accordance with this outline.
- Conduct further research to fill out supporting evidence for your thesis. (Be sure that you do not ignore counterevidence.)
- Write a rough draft that organizes the evidence in support of your thesis and documents your sources (see Chapter 8).
- Revise your draft to make sure it is well organized, clearly written, and properly formatted (see Chapter 8).
- Proofread your final draft for spelling mistakes and other typos.

an investigator. Ask yourself why this happened or how that happened. Most questions have more than one answer, and some answers may surprise you.

Also, carry out broader research on your tentative topic. Your goal is to become familiar with the **historical context** surrounding your topic. Some aspects of your topic will not be clear to you if you begin your research without this kind of knowledge.

Narrowing Your Topic

Once you have settled on a general topic, begin to narrow it to meet the needs of the assignment, especially those concerning form, length, and time limits. Within these constraints, look for some aspect of the topic that stimulates your curiosity—one that raises interesting questions in your mind. If your topic is Native Americans of the western United States, you may wish to explore some part of Native American life such as the practices of medicine men or the conflict between a particular tribe and European settlers. Further investigation might lead to an even more specific subject area, such as "the practice of magic among the Cheyenne" or "efforts of the Nez Percé to protect their native lands in Oregon."

If you know very little about your topic, conduct preliminary research. For example, if your topic is the Mexican Revolution of 1910, read a brief history of the subject in a good **historical dictionary** or **historical encyclopedia**. An encyclopedia article on the Mexican Revolution will mention its principal leaders—Francisco Madero, Pancho Villa, Emiliano Zapata, and Venustiano Carranza. From there, your interest in the Mexican Revolution might begin to focus on Zapata. Turn now to a **biographical dictionary**, where you will discover that Zapata led a peasant guerrilla army whose aim was to recover village lands seized by the owners of expanding sugar plantations. As you continue your initial research on this larger-than-life figure, you will find that Zapata was a highly respected military leader and a campaigner for land reform who even today inspires the Mexican peasantry. If Zapata's role in the Mexican Revolution of 1910 seems of interest, if it raises questions in your mind that you would like to pursue, then you have successfully narrowed your topic.

NOTE: Your narrowed-down topic will need to match the sources available to you. You cannot read sources in a language unfamiliar to you or sources that are located in an **archive** far from your school.

Formulating a Research Question

You have narrowed your topic and done enough broad research to become familiar with its historical context. The next step is to take your narrow topic—the role of land reform in the Mexican Revolution of 1910—and focus it more tightly by turning it into a research question. This question will serve to direct your research toward the kinds of sources that will provide an answer to it. The research question "What caused the failure of

Zapata's land reform program?" will enable you to write a paper tightly connected to this specific question. Rather than haphazardly examining several unrelated aspects of Mexican land reform, your research and your paper will focus on the reasons for its failure.

In order to guide your research effectively and pave the way for a successful, analytical paper, a research question must be *debatable* (not factual), *narrow* (not broad), *significant* (not unimportant), and *researchable* (not vague).

Debatable Questions

An effective research question is debatable rather than factual. It is not a simple "yes or no" question, but a question that can be answered in more than one way.

TOO FACTUAL

Who was the first person to sign the Declaration of Independence?

DEBATABLE

What factors might explain the historical inaccuracies in John Trumbull's famous painting *The Declaration of Independence*?

Narrow Questions

An effective research question is narrow rather than broad. A question that is too broad is unmanageable and cannot be answered adequately in an undergraduate research paper. A narrow question has boundaries; it asks about aspects of history that can be investigated and answered with a reasonable expenditure of time and effort.

TOO BROAD

Why did the Roman Empire fall?

NARROW

What aspects of the political system of the Roman Republic survived the rise of dictatorship and empire?

Significant Questions

An effective research question is significant rather than unimportant. The question has to be one that historians would take seriously, one whose answer would provide increased historical knowledge.

UNIMPORTANT

Why are Ping-Pong tables green?

SIGNIFICANT

What was the importance of "Ping-Pong diplomacy" to the relations between China and the United States?

Researchable Questions

An effective research question is researchable rather than vague. A question that is vague or aimless gives no clue as to how it might be answered. A researchable question makes clear what aspects of a historical topic need to be pursued.

TOO VAGUE

Why did Mexico have so many revolutions?

RESEARCHABLE

In the decade prior to the Mexican Revolution of 1910, in what ways were the buttresses of the Porfirio Díaz dictatorship undermined?

Developing a Thesis

A good research question will enable you to create a strong thesis for your paper. The thesis is the central **argument** of your research paper; it is the point you will be trying to convince the reader of. (For further explanation of "Why Your Paper Needs a Thesis," see Chapter 8, p. 141.) You can think of your thesis as the answer to your research question. Suppose your research is directed by the following question:

In the decade prior to the Mexican Revolution of 1910, in what ways were the buttresses of the Porfirio Díaz dictatorship undermined?

This is a debatable, narrow, significant, and researchable question. Your research could provide an answer to the question that could lead to an effective paper with the following thesis:

The dictatorship of Porfirio Díaz rested, to a great extent, on the support of the large landowners. The declining authority of landowners over peasant farmers seriously weakened the dictatorship in the years before the 1910 revolution.

Planning a Research Strategy

A **research strategy** is a plan for organizing your research tasks: what kind of sources to look for, which to read, and in what order.

Your early research helps you test the quality and availability of the evidence needed to answer your research question. It also helps you assess the amount and range of material you may need to examine. If advised by your instructor as to the number and kind of sources needed, be sure that they are available. Be sure, as well, to allow enough time to read and take notes from these materials. In assessing the time needed for specific tasks, keep in mind that there will be time lost pursuing false starts and coming upon dead ends.

Budgeting Your Time and Staying Focused

Plan ahead to manage your time and stay focused on your research question. If you are interested in the topic of Zapata's land reform program, you might come up with this research question: "To what extent was Zapata's land reform program a factor in the success of the Mexican Revolution?" Your first research task will be to learn about the historical context of the 1910 revolution. You might divide your preliminary research tasks into the following broad subject areas:

- Background on the Mexican Revolution—historical encyclopedias, textbooks, websites (approximately 3 hours)
- Overview of prerevolution land reform efforts—historical encyclopedia or general history of nineteenth-century Mexico (approximately 3 hours)
- Zapata's life—biographies and books or articles on his home state of Morelos (approximately 8 hours)

After you have done some initial reading, you will need to do more in-depth research on more specific subject areas such as land reform in Mexico. Tracking down and working with these more specific sources are covered in the remainder of this chapter and will require a significant amount of time. To continue with the Zapata example, you might break down your remaining research tasks as follows:

- Information about land reform efforts in Morelos—books, articles, and documents, perhaps from online sources (approximately 8 hours)
- Zapata's role in the effort to regain village lands—various primary and secondary sources (approximately 8 hours)
- Zapata's role in the larger revolution—various sources (approximately 10 hours)
- Zapata's specific land reform proposals—**primary sources** (approximately 6 hours)
- The fate of Zapata, the revolution, and the land reform efforts—various **secondary sources** (approximately 6 hours)

Of course, a research strategy and timeline must be flexible. Certain tasks will take more time and others less than expected. Nevertheless, a research strategy will keep your research focused and will warn you if you begin to fall behind.

NOTE: Estimates for research tasks should include the time needed to find a source, read it, and take notes from it. When searching the library's online catalog (see pp. 125–29), be sure to find out whether the material you want is readily available. Some hard-copy items may be in special collections in the library. Other items may be cataloged in a database and available only as abstracts, or in less than the full text. If so, you will need to determine, with the help of a reference librarian, how to access the full text of a book, journal article, or primary source. You may need time to discover another library that can offer you access to what you need. In general, libraries cooperate with one another in the **interlibrary loan** process.

Keeping an Open Mind

In the early stages of your research, you may become aware that there is not enough information available to answer your proposed research question and that it has to be changed. Also bear in mind that you may find an answer to your question that is quite different from what you anticipated. Should this happen, of course, your research question and thesis will have to be revised.

In addition, as you begin uncovering the evidence that relates to your research question, be aware of **counterevidence**—any respectable source that answers your research question in a way very different from yours. Don't ignore such evidence! Even if you decide that many more sources support your way of answering your question, you must acknowledge the challenging arguments in your research notes and in your written paper. Addressing counterevidence effectively will strengthen, not weaken, your paper. Don't expect to convince your reader that your argument is true and the other false. Rather, your goal is to convince your reader that, despite the counterevidence, your thesis remains strong and persuasive.

For example, you may find evidence from a reliable source or sources that the dictatorship of Porfirio Díaz was *not* weakened by the declining power of the large landowners. You must examine these sources carefully and weigh them against sources that support your original assumption. As a result, you may need to direct your research toward a different answer to your research question. If not, be prepared to explain to your reader why, in your opinion, the counterevidence is not as strong as the supporting evidence.

Maintaining a Working Bibliography

A **working bibliography** is a list of all the relevant sources you discover in the course of your research. These may be sources you read and take notes from, sources you skim and deem worthy of full examination, and sources that you see only references to but want to be able to find in case you decide you need to examine them. Of course, all of them should be (or be likely to be) relevant, available, and scholarly. Copy down the source information and enter it into your working bibliography. (If you have questions about what source information to include, see Chapter 10.)

Creating a working bibliography serves two important purposes. First, it provides the information about a source that you will need if you eventually use that source in your research paper. Second, it enables you to find the source if at a later point you wish to examine it again. A working bibliography is a valuable time-saver and organizational tool.

NOTE: There are many internet applications available that can help you to keep track of your research and create a working bibliography. If you create your working bibliography using one of these apps, be sure you understand how its tools work so you can avoid possibly misplacing any valuable information or having to re-research it.

CONDUCTING RESEARCH

Begin your research efforts by becoming familiar with your school library — both its online and physical layout. No other place brings together all of the connections between your research project and the sources you will need to carry it out. To discover the resources available in the physical library, take a formal tour, look at a "how to" video, or ask a librarian to explain the layout to you. Find out, for example, where the **library stacks** are — the shelves where bound books and journals (and audio and video materials) are stored. You also should find the periodical and reference sections and any "special collection" the library might have.

Take some time to browse the library's home page, and explore its most important links. You can follow the links to search the library's collection and research databases, as well as other useful research resources. If you learn your way around the library's online environment, you will save time in the long run and be able to find all of the resources you need to complete your research.

Most library home pages include a variety of tools for finding books, journals, and other reliable sources. Most also include links to the library's digital collections, such as electronic databases and digital archives. Some home pages include special online help areas, such as tutorials and live chats with librarians. Find out how you can access your library's home page remotely and whether you need to register for a password or create a proxy server. Also, check for any limitations to see which resources can be used remotely and which are restricted to in-library use only. Figure 7.1 (p. 125) shows an example of a typical library home page. (As discussed in "Special Problems of Evaluating Web-Based Sources" on pp. 72–74, you need to be cautious about resources you find while surfing the web. The great advantage of searching within your library's assets is that you will be in a trustworthy environment.)

NOTE: Don't make the mistake of thinking that the immense amount of information on the internet will allow you to bypass the library. In many cases, access to the most useful online research material is possible only *through* your school library, which pays for many academic database subscriptions that are not available to the general public.

Using the Library's Online Catalog

Once you have a clear sense of how your library is organized, become familiar with its **online catalog**. In most cases, the catalog is accessed through a link on the library home page. The online catalog allows you to search all of the

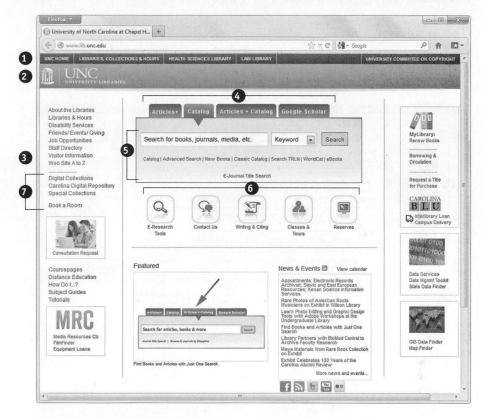

FIGURE 7.1 Example of a Library Home Page

Library home pages vary greatly in content, design, and layout, and your school's library home page will probably look quite different from this one. The numbered items listed here are some of the most common and useful features on many library home pages:

❶ Links to the university home page and to other university libraries

❷ Name of library; the sponsor of the site

❸ Searchable index of all features on the site

❹ Series of tabs that allow user to choose from popular search areas, including "Catalog" (the online catalog) and "Google Scholar"

❺ Simple search box (with "Advanced Search" option) for the online library catalog, a link to find e-journals by title and by subject

❻ Popular links for students, including online research help, a virtual librarian, and writing tips from the university writing center

❼ Links to the library's special collections

University of North Carolina at Chapel Hill Library

library's resources: books, journals, databases, and so on. When you perform a search by subject, keyword, author, or various other search parameters, you receive a list of results that match your criteria. Clicking on one of these links takes you to a catalog entry page with details about the source. For an example of a catalog entry page for a book, see Figure 7.2 below.

The Art of Searching

Knowing how to conduct an effective search of an online catalog, a database, or a website is a highly valuable skill. Each body of data and each

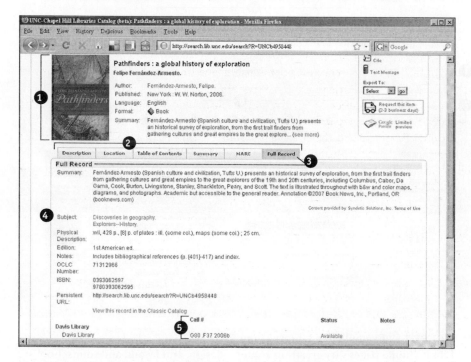

FIGURE 7.2   Example of a Catalog Entry Page for a Book

Although catalog entry pages vary from library to library, most will contain the important information listed here:

❶ Image of the cover and general information about the title.

❷ Tabs link to further details about the title, including its physical location, the table of contents, and a summary.

❸ The "Full Record" tab is highlighted, so the box below displays the complete list of details for the title.

❹ "Subject" refers to the official subject category for this title; subject categories are usually based on the system of subject headings created by the Library of Congress.

❺ The call number ("Call #") gives the title's exact location within the library stacks.

University of North Carolina at Chapel Hill Library

search engine has its own characteristics. If search "help" is available, be sure to examine it. You will save time and be more likely to find what you are searching for. In some cases, search results may be disappointing. It is possible that you could be trying to find a resource that a particular library, database, or website does not have. Or the resources may be there, but you have not mastered the search method that can uncover them. What follows is general advice on the basic kinds of searching. If you are still having trouble finding the kind of material you are looking for, ask your reference librarian or someone else familiar with the particular data set to guide you.

Searching by Subject or by Keyword

A search for resources is most commonly made by using either subject headings or keywords. **Subject headings** are the words or phrases assigned to materials in a library catalog or database so that it can be searched "hierarchically." A subject hierarchy begins with very broad terms like *History* and under that, say, *Italy* and then perhaps *Newspapers*, etc., always moving from the broader to the narrower category. **Keywords**, on the other hand, are the terms that describe a word or words that form a part of individual items in the catalog or database. For example, if you type "Italian Newspapers" and ask the search engine to return all items with these words in the title (or perhaps anywhere in the text), it will give you every item in the database with those words in the title. As you will see, you need to be wise in your choice of keywords.

Subject Searches. As noted above, searching the library catalog using a **subject search** requires that you understand its **subject hierarchy**. (A subject hierarchy is a series of subjects that moves from the broadest to the narrowest category.) The trick is to start with the broad category that is most likely to contain the narrower subject area that you are researching. For example, if you are searching for information about the construction of the Egyptian pyramids, don't start with "Pyramid." You will be presented with a long list of items about geometry or about pyramids in dozens of different places. But if you search for a too-specific term, such as "Pyramid Construction," you may get "no results." (Some newer search engines are more user friendly. They may assist you with responses such as "Are you looking for Egyptian Pyramids?" Still, it is easier for you to learn about the search engine than it is for the search engine to learn about you.)

Of course, if you are having trouble finding the proper subject headings for your search, do not hesitate to ask the advice of the reference librarian.

NOTE: One way to discover the proper subject heading for a search is to go directly (say, by title) to a book that you know is relevant to your research topic. On the catalog page for that book will be a list of "Subject" headings that are likely to include the ones you need (see Figure 7.2 on p. 126).

Keyword Searches.   In keyword searching, instead of trying to figure out which *subject* your topic is under, you ask the computer to search its records of books and other materials for certain *words*.

Suppose you are researching "women workers in the Lowell, Massachusetts, textile mills, 1820–1850." Your most promising keywords will be the nouns in your topic: *women, workers, Lowell,* and *textile mills.* Don't search by using any of these words by themselves. They are too general and will generate a long list of sources, most of them not related to your topic. It is always best to do an "advanced" or "complex" search, in which you can combine a series of keywords, asking to see only those sources that have several of the keywords in a certain order. In this case, you might use the following: *women* AND *workers* AND *textile mills.* Or, under the option "same words in same order," you might ask for *women textile workers.* The rules for advanced keyword searching are usually available through a link from the search page. As always, if you need assistance with keyword searches, ask a librarian.

Searching by Author and by Title

Author and title searches are fairly straightforward, but before you begin, you need to know the name of the author or book you are looking for. This is often not possible, especially in the early stages of research. For the most part, you will need to discover which sources by which authors are related to your topic. To do this, you must search the online catalog by subject or by keyword (see pp. 127–28).

To conduct effective author and title searches, you must spell author names and titles correctly. If you are uncertain about the spelling, ask the reference librarian for help. Sometimes the spelling of an author's name can be tricky, especially if the name is spelled differently in English than in its language of origin. Be especially careful when searching for ancient or foreign names.

Locating Materials by Using Call Numbers

You shouldn't expect to find one subject heading or keyword that will give you *everything* you want. You may need to do several different searches. Once your searches have turned up a number of promising titles, record all of the information from the catalog entry page (see Figure 7.2 on p. 126). You will need this information for your working bibliography and, eventually, for the **bibliography** for your written paper. (For information about organizing a bibliography, see Chapter 10.) If the source on your list is a book or journal on the library shelves, be sure to take down the **call number**, which indicates an item's location in the library stacks. As you look over your list of call numbers, you will probably discover that many of the books and journals you listed have call numbers that begin with the same letters or numbers. Books with similar call numbers are usually on related topics. When you get to the stacks, don't look only for the specific books you found in your computer search. Look at the books on nearby shelves as well. You are likely to find additional works related to your topic. If they seem promising, add them to your working bibliography.

NOTE: As you begin to track down sources related to your topic, be sure to mine them for clues to finding other useful sources. The **notes** and especially the bibliographies will mention the books and articles that the author relied on, and many of them will be relevant to your topic. Whenever you find a good source, check its notes and bibliography for any promising items to add to your working bibliography.

Using Print and Electronic Reference Works

Reference sources can help you define your terms, gather background information on a topic, and locate specific facts, dates, and biographical and statistical material. These reference works can be found in print form in the reference section of your library or in its online catalog. (Appendix A lists many of these sources.) Nonprint reference sources will be linked to the library home page under "Electronic Reference Sources" or a similar name. Since many reference sources are large and have special ways of organizing their content, look for the introductory section of a printed reference source or the search screen of such a source in your library's online catalog. Remember that while reference sources are good places to begin your research, no serious project can be based simply on information from them. Be sure you understand your instructor's rules about the use of reference sources.

Many electronic reference sources are also available online, but unlike those in your library, you need to judge their quality carefully. There are some excellent dictionaries and encyclopedias online, but often the best of them require password access.

The Problem of Wikipedia

The largest encyclopedia ever created is easily available online. Its tremendous size and popularity come from the fact that it is a "WIKI," a website to which users can contribute. Despite its size, it can be searched easily. Millions of people take their questions and their curiosity to this almost endless source of knowledge. As big as it is, it is still growing. Yet many instructors have strong reservations about its use for serious research.

Guidelines on the Use of Wikipedia: Possible Dangers. The authors and revisers of the articles on Wikipedia are not named. Their qualifications and their professional standards are not known. The articles they have written may be brilliant or they might be filled with error, confusion, and prejudice. There is no guarantee that the articles you read will be the brilliant ones. Some of the articles have notes to the sources on which they rest; others have few notes and refer to questionable sources. Not only is the quality of an article uncertain, its content is "unstable." Because articles can be augmented, reduced, or edited in numerous ways, there is no way to be certain that the article you read one month ago has the same content today. Overall, serious researchers find Wikipedia to be unreliable. Your instructor's opinion of Wikipedia may be more positive or more negative than the one described here. Many instructors have guidelines for the use of Wikipedia. Be sure you know what they are.

The success of Wikipedia in attracting millions of readers and contributors has been possible because of its "openness." What makes Wikipedia such an astonishing achievement also accounts for the unease of teachers and researchers. If Wikipedia had required of its authors the demonstrated level of knowledge required by academic publishers, Wikipedia would be a small, generally reliable encyclopedia rather than an enormous collection of information on an endless number of topics. Despite the fundamental difference between the Wiki world and the academic world, Wikipedia has made a serious effort to set standards for it contributors.

The people who make up the Wikipedia community consider the openness of Wikipedia to be a foundational principle. As a result, their efforts to assure the quality of their articles take the form of procedures rather than prohibitions. Though they might prefer an encyclopedia where all sorts of freedom reigns, the problem of malicious writing and revising has led them to post a few guardians at the gates. Editors and administrators have been given tools to prevent or at least minimize such intrusions. New articles and changes to existing ones are examined carefully. The first line of defense is the counter-edit; that is, a Wikipedia editor, or any public-minded reader, revises a questionable revision. If the article as a whole has problems, a "banner" is placed at the beginning drawing attention to its weaknesses such as questionable claims, lack of sources, outdated sources, and accuracy among others. Readers and contributors are encouraged to "improve" the article.

Wikipedia articles may not always be reliable, but there is a level of transparency about them that is admirable. Each article has links that take you behind the scenes. The "History" link opens a page that displays a list of every change, however minor, to that article. A brief explanation of each change is also provided. The "Edit" link spells out the rules and procedures for making changes to the article. There are a few hurdles to jump over, but openness to revision is maintained. The "Talk" link allows you to "chat" about the article, its problems, and their resolution. It is unfortunate, but the open structure of Wikipedia makes it unlikely that its content will be as identifiable, stable, and reliable as the academic community would wish it to be.

NOTE: When it comes to course assignments, you must follow your instructor's rules on the use of Wikipedia. Remember also, plagiarism from Wikipedia is no different than plagiarism from any other source. (See pp. 84–86.)

Atlases, Dictionaries, and Encyclopedias

Atlases are collections of maps. Some atlases are very specialized, showing highly detailed maps of specific regions, towns, and so on. Some of these maps lay out topography (mountains, valleys, rivers, etc.); others display the economic, ethnic, weather, or navigational features of an area. Historical atlases display changes that have occurred in nations, regions, communities, and so on, over time. For example, a historical atlas of transportation might display the expansion of different railroad lines over a period of many decades. An important development in online map collections is the ability to compare different kinds of maps or even to overlay maps.

You are already familiar with general dictionaries, but various historical dictionaries (in print or electronic form) should also be available in your school library. They define terms of historical importance not usually found in a general dictionary. Suppose your research requires that you know a particular term from the history of China. A dictionary explaining this term (such as *China: A Historical and Cultural Dictionary*) might be available in your library. Important in the study of history are biographical dictionaries, which give brief descriptions of the lives of important individuals. Information about a Canadian explorer might be found in a source such as the *Dictionary of Canadian Biography*.

Some **encyclopedias**, such as *Encyclopaedia Britannica*, are general; others focus on historical topics. You could find, for example, a historical encyclopedia of slavery or of the French Revolution. Such an encyclopedia, whose entries might run from a few paragraphs to several pages, is a good place to begin research on a historical topic.

Subject Bibliographies

Subject bibliographies list various research materials—including books, book reviews, and journal articles—by subject. They may be available in print form in the reference section of your library, or in electronic form in the library's online catalog. Some subject bibliographies are available online. A large number of print and electronic subject bibliographies are included in Appendix A.

Subject bibliographies are almost always the best sources to use when you are in the early stages of your research. Once you determine your research topic, seek out the subject bibliography that best fits your needs. If you narrow your topic to an aspect such as "the role of journalists in the Vietnam War," the print subject bibliography *The Wars in Vietnam, Cambodia and Laos, 1945–1982: A Bibliographical Guide* might lead you to many useful sources. When using a subject bibliography, keep in mind that the sources it lists will be only as up-to-date as the bibliography itself. For print bibliographies, check the publication date; for online bibliographies, check the date of the most recent update.

Using Print and Electronic Periodical Databases

A **periodical** is a publication that appears on a regular basis—daily, weekly, monthly, quarterly. For example, newspapers usually appear daily, popular magazines weekly or monthly, and **scholarly journals** quarterly (don't overlook this valuable category of periodicals in your research).

Some "directories" of periodicals can be found in print form in the library's reference section, but in most cases, the best way to search for periodicals is through the library's electronic **periodical databases**. Most of these databases are searchable by author, title, or keyword. A list of periodical databases can be found in Appendix A.

Locating Articles in Scholarly Journals

The periodicals most useful for historical research are scholarly journals. Although the articles in these journals are written for scholars, most are accessible to students. These articles are often based on primary sources, and they usually have a clear thesis or argument.

The articles in scholarly journals are **refereed** or **peer reviewed**, which means that one or more scholars in the appropriate field read each article *before* it was accepted for publication. The process of refereeing provides a kind of quality control, helping to ensure that articles in scholarly journals can serve as reliable sources for scholarly research.

There are a great number of scholarly history journals, covering many areas, such as *China Quarterly, Film and History, History of Religions, Journal of Environmental History*, and *Russian History*. Your library may have scholarly journals in its stacks, and its subscriptions to online databases such as *JSTOR, Project Muse, America: History and Life*, and *Historical Abstracts* will give you access to many others. Searching these databases is similar to searching the online catalog. Choose one of the **journal databases** that include a large number of history journals (or, if possible, search many simultaneously). Search these journals by subject or by keyword, paying attention to search rules, which may vary from database to database. For sample screens from an online database, see Figure 7.3 and Figure 7.4 (pp. 133–34).

Some journal databases contain "full text," which means that the entire article is available on the database. Other databases are "annotated" or "abstracted." Those databases do not have the articles themselves but contain summaries of their content that will help you decide whether or not to seek out the full text. Still other databases, often called "indexes," list only the basic information: author, title, journal, and date. Journal indexes usually organize articles by subject and period, and most indexes list articles from a very large number of journals, including many not covered by databases with abstracts or full texts.

NOTE: Even databases with the word *Abstracts* or *Index* in their title may lead you to full-text articles. Depending on your library's subscription, a database such as *Historical Abstracts* may be able to provide you with links to full-text articles. See, for example, the top image in Figure 7.4, which shows a list of search results in the *Historical Abstracts* database at Ithaca College.

If your library has no full-text electronic access to the particular journal articles you want, the full text may be available in the library stacks or

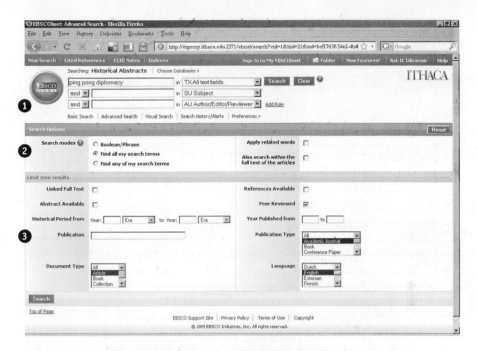

FIGURE 7.3   Advanced Search Screen in a Periodical Database

As in online catalogs, the page design and layout of the electronic databases you use will vary significantly depending on which ones your library subscribes to. However, similar search fields, options, and limiters will appear on the "Advanced Search" pages for most electronic databases. This example shows an advanced search screen for the *Historical Abstracts* database at Ithaca College. The search screen is divided into three main areas:

❶ The top section of the search screen allows the user to type in search terms for various search fields—such as text, subject, author, and others. The student decided to search the words "ping pong diplomacy" in the text fields only.

❷ The second area provides options to qualify the search. "Boolean" searches allow the user to combine search terms with the directions "and," "or," and "not"; the other checkboxes allow the user to clarify how the search terms should be used. The student checked "Find all my search terms," which means the search will return only documents with all three words—"ping," "pong," and "diplomacy."

❸ The third area of the screen provides options to limit the search by factors such as date range, language, and document type. The student decided to search only for peer-reviewed articles in academic journals available in English. The "Linked Full Text" box would allow the student to search only for articles in the *Historical Abstracts* database that can be electronically accessed in full. The student decided not to select this feature because some relevant articles may not be available in that form in the library's databases.

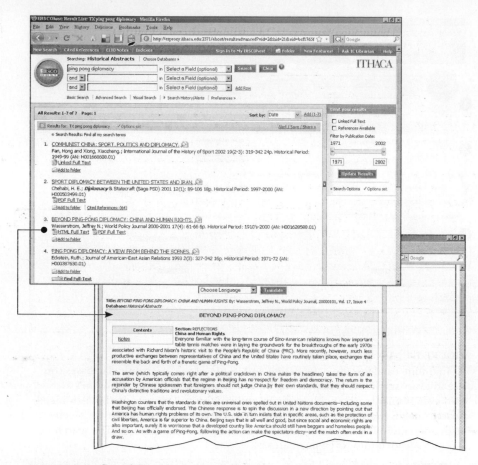

FIGURE 7.4   Search Results from a Database

Different databases display their lists of search results in different ways, but most provide a list of article titles with links to additional information, as in the top screenshot here. A link such as "Linked Full Text" (as shown under the first article in the list) typically leads to the full text of an article in a different database. A "PDF Full Text" link (as shown under the second article) usually opens the article in a format that displays actual images of print article pages, including page numbering. "HTML Full Text" links (as shown under the third article) typically lead to the complete text of the article within the same database, as shown in the bottom screenshot. Note that "HTML" links generally do not include original page numbering.

> ### Guidelines for Using Periodical Databases
>
> - Choose a database that includes a large number of history journals that deal with the general topic you are working within. For example, for the topic "apartheid in South Africa," choose a database that includes the *Journal of African History.*
> - Determine the content and range of your chosen database. What years of the journals you are interested in does it cover? Date ranges that change regularly are called "moving walls."
> - Carefully choose two or three keywords that express the most important aspects of your topic. To search by subject, choose the large category that includes your topic.
> - Scan the list of articles generated in response to your search. If the article titles do not seem close enough, refine your search terms.
> - If an abstract accompanies an article, be sure to read it.
> - If an abstract seems promising, take down *all* the information about the article so that you can find the full text.
> - If the full text of the article is contained in the database, read enough of it to be sure it is related to your topic. Don't waste time and money downloading or printing it until you have done this.

through interlibrary loan. Always seek out all the articles that you think will be most useful in your research. Don't discount articles that aren't immediately available, and don't download or print out articles simply because they are available in full text.

Even very large databases that allow you to search for articles in hundreds of journals have limitations you should be aware of. Some have articles only from *recent* issues of the journals they contain. Others have articles published only in *older* issues. In history research, the **date range** of a database is important to know; it can tell you what is *not* there and save you a lot of searching time.

Locating Articles in Magazines and Newspapers

Search for magazine articles and newspaper articles in databases and indexes dedicated to magazines and newspapers, such as *Index to Early American Periodicals* and *Reader's Guide Retrospective.* Some magazine and newspaper databases are full text and contain every page, including advertisements; others list articles by title or by subject.

Popular magazines (such as *People, Time,* and *National Geographic*) and newspapers rarely contain serious historical studies. However, if you have access to magazines and newspapers *from the period of your topic,* these can be valuable sources. For example, an 1830s newspaper article in the *Lowell Courier* that reports on women workers in the textile mills could prove to be a valuable primary source (see "Primary Sources" in Chapter 3, pp. 40–43). If you are seeking old issues of magazines and newspapers, make sure that the print copies or databases go back to the years encompassed by your topic. If your library does not have the particular newspaper or magazine you are looking for, try to find it online or borrow it—via interlibrary loan—from another library.

Searching for Primary Sources

Primary sources are as close to the past as you can get. Such sources help you to imagine what the past was like for those who lived it. Primary sources can be written, such as letters and laws, or nonwritten, such as photographs, artifacts, and audiovisual recordings. (For more details about the nature of primary sources, see Chapter 3.) To track down primary sources related to your topic, you can search in three main venues: published texts or collections, museum or library archives, and the immense number of primary sources gathered in databases and websites.

Primary Sources in Published Collections

Print collections of both written and nonwritten primary sources are available in most libraries. Each book gathers together a group of primary sources about an important topic such as Italian City States or German Colonies in Africa. The writings of important historical figures such as Socrates or Frederick Douglass may be gathered together. Often these primary documents are abridged; that is, the full document has been shortened because of space limitations. The editor should make this clear. The collection will most likely have an introduction that explains the importance of the authors and the subject. There may be notes at the bottom of the pages explaining the meaning of a word or phrase. Be sure to take advantage of these explanations.

NOTE: Illustrations, maps, photographs, and other nonwritten primary sources may be cropped to save space or they may not print clearly. The editor should make you aware of these changes to the originals.

Primary Sources in Museum Archives

Primary sources themselves, rather than print or digitized copies of them, are available in archives such as museums, historical societies, specialized libraries, and the private records of an institution or corporation, including the film and audiotape libraries of television and radio studios. Major university libraries also have large primary source collections. The experience of standing just a few feet away from the U.S. Constitution, a uniform worn by Napoleon, or a sculpture of a lion from an ancient African civilization is unforgettable. (It may surprise you to learn that most colleges, perhaps including your own, have archives of documents and artifacts that chronicle the history of the school. Could these materials serve as primary documents for your research?)

Primary Sources on the Web

A great number of archives of primary sources can be found online. Entire sites are dedicated to making primary documents widely available. These sites include not only printed and handwritten documents but visual and audio materials such as sound recordings, historical maps, artwork, photographs, and motion pictures. The largest such site for U.S. primary sources is American Memory at **memory.loc.gov/ammem/index.html**. (A large number of primary source websites are included in the lists of general and specialized resources in Appendix A.) To assist you in finding such sources, your instructors may provide links to important websites in the course syllabus. If so, be sure to follow their advice.

In many cases, access to websites for primary sources is free. This is one instance in which using the internet for research is highly recommended. Of course, you will need to know the names of these sites and how to search them. Your school library also has numerous databases of primary sources. To see an example of this kind of database, examine *Alexander Street Press* at **alexanderst.com**. This site has a well-organized collection of letters, diaries, speeches, interviews, and so on.

Certain organizations and corporations have digitized great numbers of older printed books and articles as well as many other sources (primary and secondary) of great value to researchers. Among the most important for historians are Bartleby, Project Gutenberg, Perseus Digital Library, America's Historical Newspapers, Historical Text Archive, Eighteenth Century Collections Online, Music Online (Alexander Street Press), David Rumsey Historical Map Collection, The Nineteenth Century in Print, American Memory, and ACLS Humanities E-Book. (Additional websites like these are listed throughout Appendix A.) Moreover, some of the largest companies that own powerful search engines, huge databases, and excellent search facilities have created sites where you can access (usually at no cost) a mass of digitized resources. At these sites you can often find full-text and searchable versions of these resources. Some sites have tens of thousands or even millions of such documents. Some of the biggest are Google Books, Google Scholar, Microsoft Academic Search, Yahoo!, and Amazon. However, some of the resources on these very large sites are only partially available. For more complete access, you may be directed to a publisher's site where the source may be available for purchase. Nevertheless, these sites can be a useful resource.

Interviews as Primary Sources

If your topic concerns events that occurred within the last seventy or eighty years, you might be able to interview someone who lived through them. Members of your community or your own family can be sources of historical information. You might be able to gain access to people who have been leaders in local or national affairs and have personal knowledge of important historical events. Perhaps you can prepare a list of questions about past events in which they were participants. You can write to these individuals or perhaps speak with them. They may have personal papers they are willing to show you. This kind of historical research is exciting and satisfying, and it may enable you to use primary historical material that no other historian has uncovered.

Older adults can recall their years in another country (if they are immigrants) or describe the America in which they grew up. They may not have been important historical figures, but they reflect the experiences of countless others and are thus the stuff of which history is made. Their recollections of how they felt and of what they and others did and said when Pearl Harbor was attacked, when they first saw television, when John F. Kennedy was assassinated, or when the Berlin Wall came down are priceless pieces of the historical puzzle. For information about how to conduct interviews with older people, see "How to Research Your Family History" in Appendix B.

Using Internet Search Tools

As we've discussed, the internet offers countless sites with information for historical researchers. If you know how to explore it wisely, you can find primary and secondary sources as well as trustworthy references online. In order to find the most useful and reliable sources, begin with your course website, or ask your instructor for any good sites related to your topic. Next, you can check your school or public library's home page and look for links to reputable history sites. In addition, you can find many online sources on a wide variety of historical subjects in Appendix A.

NOTE: When you track down a source online, you should use extra caution when evaluating it. See "Special Problems of Evaluating Web-Based Sources" in Chapter 4 (pp. 72–74).

Searching Efficiently

If you are not looking for a specific site but are setting out to search the vast expanse of the internet, good search skills are a necessity. Unlike an online library catalog or a periodical database, the internet isn't necessarily organized for the purpose of scholarly research, and many unreliable sites can get in the way of your finding the reliable ones. But with a little persistence, you can use the internet to your advantage.

Searching Subject.   Most search engines, such as Google and Yahoo!, allow you to search by subject just as you would in an online library catalog. As noted earlier, a subject hierarchy is a long list of information sources that begins with the broadest subject category and allows you to narrow the choices on the screen until you reach a subject category that is close to your topic. For example, to get to information about Joan of Arc, the narrowing of subjects might go like this: *Humanities> History> Europe> France> Fifteenth Century.* The goal is to choose the most promising link or links at each stage. If your choices move away from your topic, backtrack and try a different route. Using the example of Joan of Arc, if you chose "Religion" after "France" instead of "Fifteenth Century," you might be led to sites about the building of cathedrals.

Searching by Keywords.   If you search by keywords, the keywords must be chosen carefully. Poorly chosen keywords may yield tens of thousands of results that are difficult to wade through. Moreover, a high percentage of them will be nonscholarly commercial or personal sites that aren't considered credible research sources. If you do conduct a keyword search online, use "advanced search" and follow the same advice as that given for keyword searching in online library catalogs.

Previewing Search Results

If the result of a subject search or a keyword search brings to the screen a very large number of options, narrow your search terms. Use "advanced search" whenever it is offered. In that way you can combine your keywords. Doing so should significantly reduce the number of sites listed. It should also screen out sites that are not relevant. To choose the best sites for your history research, look for the following characteristics:

- Check search results for ".edu" or ".gov" domains, which are restricted to educational and governmental institutions. Also, look for site names that include the name of a major library, museum, or historical organization. Some of these sites may have the ".org" domain.
- Avoid results listed under "sponsored results" or others that are commercial in nature.
- If the brief description in the search results list sounds promising, go to the site to see if it is of an educational, noncommercial nature.
- When you reach a site, look for links to such areas as "digital archives," "electronic resources," or "research." Explore the site to see if it contains historical resources.
- If a site provides no links to relevant historical materials, abandon it and return to your search results list.
- Bookmark any promising sites or keep a file of the best sites (including URLs and brief descriptions) so you can easily find them again later.

CHAPTER

8

Writing a Research Paper

Here are three requirements to keep in mind as you approach the writing stage of your research project: (1) The **introduction** of your paper should contain a clear statement of your **thesis**, (2) the body of your paper should support your thesis with a series of logically connected, well-documented sections, and (3) the **conclusion** of your paper should summarize the principal **arguments** in support of your thesis. Chapter 6 provides basic advice on writing historical essays, from drafting a thesis to creating a writing outline to writing the paper. Here in Chapter 8, we focus on specific requirements of full-length research papers and the challenges they represent.

ASSERTING YOUR THESIS

In Chapter 7 we discussed how to choose and narrow a **topic** and then formulate a **research question** about the topic. After carefully choosing your research question and after doing the initial research to seek an answer to the question, you now should be ready to state your thesis—a formal answer to your research question. This statement should take the form of an assertion that will be sustained by the **evidence** you present.

NOTE: Before you begin to write, examine your research notes closely. If they don't provide enough support for your thesis, more research is necessary. Or if your notes point to a conclusion that is different from your original thesis, you need to alter your thesis or come up with a new one.

Why Your Paper Needs a Thesis

Good history research papers always take a stand on an issue. Rather than meandering aimlessly among interesting pieces of information, a college-level research paper makes a serious argument based on evidence. Though not intolerant of other views, the writer makes his or her own point of view quite clear. That point of view, stated at the beginning of the paper, is the thesis.

Writing a paper is like presenting a case to a jury; that is why it is often referred to as "making an argument." You organize your evidence to demonstrate to your reader that your thesis is well documented. You don't claim that your thesis is the *only* correct one; you argue that the evidence for it is strong.

Here is an example of how one student might arrive at her thesis. Having read documents on the origins of slavery in Virginia, a novice history student might be tempted to write a paper about "What I learned about slavery in Virginia." However, such a paper would be merely a **summary** and wouldn't draw any meaningful conclusion based on the evidence. After discussing the research topic with her instructor, the student realizes she has to orient her research around a serious research question, such as "Was English racial prejudice against Africans the source of slavery in Virginia?" The evidence she uncovers, however, seems to point toward a negative answer to the question. Rather, the evidence seems to indicate that the origin of slavery in Virginia was primarily the result of the need for a large, controlled labor force to work the rapidly expanding tobacco plantations. She finds the documents contain many complaints by plantation owners that European workers were too few and would not accept forced labor. She finds that there is evidence that only then did the plantation owners turn to Africans as a potential captive labor force and build the legal basis for slavery to secure their unpaid labor. Now the student can organize the evidence to support her thesis: "The need for a large, controlled labor force on tobacco plantations led to the establishment of slavery in Virginia."

What Makes a Thesis Effective

Building your research around a specific question helps keep you focused on the aspect of the topic you wish to study in depth. An effective question is debatable, narrow, significant, and researchable (see Chapter 7, pp. 118–21). Such a question will lead to a thesis statement that takes a stand on a worthwhile issue. In the example that follows, you will see the steps that a student named Sarah takes to formulate an *effective thesis* for a research paper in her current course in U.S. history.

Like many Americans back in December 1941, present-day student Sarah finds it difficult to understand the reasons for the Japanese attack on Pearl Harbor. (U.S. congressional committees, by the way, also were puzzled and held lengthy hearings, which Sarah will use as a **primary source**.)

> ## Guidelines for Developing an Effective Thesis
>
> - Begin with a topic that is appropriate to the assignment, attracts your interest, is of manageable proportions, and is one about which you can find a significant amount of evidence.
> - Focus your research on a worthwhile question that is *debatable* (more than one answer is possible), *narrow* (answerable within the scope of the assignment), *significant* (worthy of serious investigation), and *researchable* (has enough serious evidence to answer it).
> - Choose the answer to your question for which there is the strongest evidence.
> - Rephrase this answer as a formal statement of the argument you intend to make in your paper. This formal statement of your argument is your thesis.
> - Include a clear statement of your thesis at the beginning of your research paper. (Until you have organized your paper and written a rough draft, your thesis will remain in tentative form.)

Sarah's curiosity about why the attack took place leads her to make this "why" question the topic of her research paper assignment.

Initial research gives Sarah enough familiarity with the **historical context** so that she is able to formulate a possible research question. Using the criteria set forth in Chapter 7, Sarah takes one of the points she is most curious about and poses this question: Since relations between Japan and the United States were clearly heading for a confrontation by 1941, why had Washington done so little to prepare Pearl Harbor for a possible Japanese attack?

Sarah's background research makes it clear that issues surrounding her question have been debated in the scholarly literature — in **secondary sources**. Historians, she discovers, have examined various answers to the question about the inadequacy of Pearl Harbor's defenses. For this reason, Sarah feels confident that her question is serious and is worthy of debate.

Armed with her research question, Sarah conducts further research and finds sources that examine various aspects of U.S.–Japanese relations in the years leading up to the attack. From some of these sources, she is surprised to learn that what most concerned U.S. leaders during this period was not Japan but Germany. Quite a few sources, both primary and secondary, emphasize Washington's concern over the military successes of German forces beginning in September 1939. In 1940–1941, the Roosevelt administration was deeply involved in the effort to supply British forces (Britain was one of the few allies of the United States still able to resist the German attack). After examining primary documents concerning U.S. relations with Britain, Sarah feels confident that she can explain why the U.S. government considered Japan less menacing than Germany. She now has an answer to her question, and she states the answer in formal terms: "Concern about a growing threat from Germany was a major factor in the failure of the United States to adequately prepare Pearl Harbor for a possible Japanese attack." This statement is her thesis. Sarah begins her paper with the following paragraph (the thesis statement has been underlined):

> On December 7, 1941, Japan carried out a devastating surprise attack on the U.S. Naval Base at Pearl Harbor in Hawaii. A large number of U.S. ships were sunk or heavily damaged. This disaster led to a major investigation by the U.S. Congress and has long been a source of debate among historians. While my research examined several possible explanations for the disaster, it eventually led me to the conclusion that <u>failure to adequately defend Pearl Harbor against possible Japanese attack was due principally to intense concern in Washington over the growing threat from Nazi Germany.</u> This paper will present the principal evidence for this thesis.

Sarah's thesis satisfies all of the criteria of an effective thesis. Her original question results from significant research on a topic of interest to her. Further research enables her to answer that question. She states that answer in the form of her thesis at the beginning of her paper.

ORGANIZING YOUR EVIDENCE WITH A WRITING OUTLINE

Your main goal in writing a research paper is to arrange the material you have found so that it supports your thesis. If, as you begin to organize your evidence, you find that it doesn't entirely support your thesis, then you need to change your thesis or seek other evidence to support it.

Once you are satisfied that your research has uncovered sufficient evidence for your thesis, you need to present the evidence in a manner that clearly shows that the conclusion you've drawn is a proper one. If you uncover any **counterevidence**—evidence that leads to other conclusions—you have a responsibility to mention it. In doing so, you must explain why the evidence in support of your thesis outweighs the nonsupporting evidence. There are many ways to organize evidence in support of a conclusion. The pages that follow describe some possible approaches.

During the research process, your **research strategy** helped you to decide what sources to seek first and in which order to read them (see "Planning a Research Strategy" in Chapter 7, pp. 121–24). Now that your reading is mostly finished, it is time to prepare a writing outline to give yourself an overall plan for your paper. Creating this outline helps you decide the order in which to present your evidence and how each section will build toward a conclusion that supports your thesis. The outline will keep your writing headed in the proper direction.

In the course of your research, you compiled a number of notes about the sources that you found. You created headings that identified similar kinds of evidence. For a relatively simple paper, you might have organized your notes chronologically, or by major characters or events. For a complex topic, such as the impact of the sixteenth-century revolution in print technology, your note categories might reflect the various impacts of the new technology that you examined in your readings—on universities, monasteries, libraries, literacy, bookbinding, and so on.

Here is a description of one way to organize your notes for a paper on the role of Great Britain in the Middle East after World War II. Your research question asks about Britain's motives in giving up its control of Palestine in 1947. Your research leads you to a tentative thesis arguing that *domestic* political and economic factors (rather than international ones) best explain British withdrawal. Your research also leads you to create note categories concerning the post–World War II future of Palestine for Arabs, Jews, and Britain. Within these large categories you create smaller ones: Arab nationalism, Zionism, British colonial policy. Those three topics present natural sections of your writing outline. You also read many sources that deal with the role of the United Nations and the role of the United States. Those two subjects become note categories and also should be sections of your outline. Because your research question asks about Britain's motives, your notes should have a lot of evidence in this area. It makes sense, then, to create an outline section for each of the British motives that you explain.

Of course no two outlines will be alike. Still, there are general frameworks for outlines of similar kinds of topics. If you are making an argument about a person, you might choose a chronological organization. There are many variations of this form. If you build your argument around a significant aspect of someone's life, each heading might describe the influences and events that led up to the point in that person's life that your thesis deals with. For example, an argument about some aspect of George Washington's career might have sections in chronological order. These might include sections about his work as a surveyor, as an officer in the British army, as commander of the Continental forces fighting for independence from the British, and so on.

In a different example, suppose your research leads you to a question about Washington's role in the War for Independence. Your question and your research have brought you to the thesis: "Washington's status as a wealthy planter best explains his decision to support the rebellion against British rule." When your chronologically ordered outline arrives at the point when Washington's role as a planter becomes significant, your outline will become more detailed. Here you'll make room in the outline for the large body of evidence that you have gathered on this subject so you can examine this part of his life in detail.

Most research papers examine complex topics that cannot be reduced to a chronological timeline. The argument here needs to be made from a variety of angles. An outline with a topical organization—sections drawn from a wide variety of factors—may or may not present its parts in chronological order. Its goal is not to narrate a life or to focus on the "what" of history but to explain the "why" of its topic. To argue that African Americans were ignored by New Deal legislation in the Great Depression of the 1930s, you might create note categories about economic discrimination, physical separation, and southern Democratic Party politics, as well as the legislation itself. Each of these areas would deserve its own section of an outline. You might begin each section at a different point in time. For example, you would likely begin the section on physical separation, a phenomenon known as "segregation" that arose late in the nineteenth century, at an earlier point in time than the section on New Deal legislation, which was not passed until the 1930s.

Arguments of an even broader kind require outlines of an analytical (that is, explanatory) nature. This kind of outline includes categories of evidence that can account for the ways in which one strand of history becomes entwined around another—as when Arab nationalism, Eastern European Zionism, and British imperialism encounter one another in a place called Palestine. Returning to the example of the research question "Why did Great Britain decide to end its control over Palestine in 1947?" your outline would need to examine each of the three strands. As a result, you might create sections of your writing outline for (1) Arab nationalism, (2) Zionism, and (3) British colonialism. The section on Great Britain would need to be the most detailed. There, you might have sub-categories for (A) International factors, (B) Domestic influences, and (C) The situation in Palestine. If your research led you toward a thesis that emphasizes domestic influences, then section 3B (British colonialism; Domestic influences) would need to be broken down even further.

NOTE: Different *kinds* of outlines can be most effective for different *parts* of the same paper. Chronological sections can be followed by analytical ones, and so on.

No particular format for an outline is best. Some students prefer a "down-the-stairs" model, in which each heading and each subheading is indented more than the one above. Such a format is easily expandable. If you think of a new point, you enter a new heading and put it in the proper place. Changing one heading, however, may require changing others. A firm outline is very difficult to create before you begin to write. (If, however, such an outline is a required stage of a research assignment, follow your instructor's guidance.) What many students need as they begin to write is merely a list of the major sections of the paper and a commonsense order in which to put them. This "list-type" outline is illustrated in Figure 8.1. The best outline is one that gives you enough guidance about organizing the evidence for your thesis yet allows you enough flexibility to change your mind about what should come next. Some writers need write-by-outline assistance; others require only gentle reminders. Choose the format that works best for you.

Tentative Thesis: In the early years of the English colony in Virginia (1607-1665), Africans living there were not slaves. They were enslaved (only) when control over their labor was needed due to the growth of tobacco plantations. English racism was not the reason.

Will be put in final form when paper is written.

Context: (1530-1630) Idea of rights in England; treatment of Irish; treatment of Native Americans; view of Africans; religious justifications; English colonies in the Caribbean.

Background reading by student; will become introductory section of paper.

Evidence:

1. No slavery in England.

2. No slavery in English colonies in the Caribbean until rise of plantations.

The evidence the student will use to support the thesis. Also, the tentative order in which it will appear.

3. In Virginia laborers were not slaves but indentured servants.
    3a. Blacks and whites treated the same
    3b. Some evidence of friendships of blacks and whites

4. Evidence of black landowners.
    4a. Anthony Johnson
    4b. Others

5. Rise of large tobacco plantations.
    5a. White indentured servants less available as laborers
    5b. Whites want to be landowners

6. Need for a dependable labor force.
    6a. Reasons why Native Americans were not enslaved
    6b. Reasons why Africans begin to be enslaved

7. First slave laws in the colony.

Ideas encountered by the student that challenge the thesis. The student must be sure to address these.

Counterevidence:
1. English were early participants in slave trade.
2. English believe in social hierarchy; treatment of Irish.
3. Harsher penalties for black servants? (weak evidence)
4. English had a negative view of nonwhite peoples.

Summary of the main evidence in support of thesis; still in rough form.

Conclusion: Absence of slave laws; evidence of black landowners; changes in colony's economy and in its sources of labor.

FIGURE 8.1   List-Type Outline

Make sure you have enough evidence to flesh out the elements of your outline. If you discover a mismatch between a part of your outline and the evidence you need for it, alter that section or, if necessary, return to your sources to see if you can find such evidence. Notes and outline are rarely in perfect harmony at the outset, but don't wait until your paper is half written before you realize that an important part lacks the evidence it requires.

You must also make room in your outline for counterevidence — evidence that differs strongly with any argument you intend to make. Counterevidence should not be ignored. Rather than claiming that your views are the *only* valid ones, tell your reader about the counterevidence and explain why you have confidence in your thesis.

To summarize, a writing outline helps you organize your evidence and determine the order in which you will write about it. Note that the process of creating an outline works two ways: while your outline helps bring order to your evidence, that evidence helps bring order to your outline. In either case, your goal is to organize your evidence in the way that best supports your thesis.

WRITING THE TEXT

As you prepare your paper, you may find it helpful to review the section "Drafting Your Essay" in Chapter 6 (pp. 110–15). Also, keep the following basic points in mind: Don't let parts of your paper drift away from your topic. Stick to your outline and stay focused on the central arguments that support your thesis. Be sure that you can provide evidence for the points you are making.

The Rough Draft

Your **rough draft** will change, perhaps several times, so don't worry too much about the exact wording when you begin to write it. Your thesis statement, too, may change. Many a thesis needs fine-tuning before a rough draft is finished. Nevertheless, even at this early stage, you need a direction for your writing, and that direction should be indicated in your writing outline. The introduction should help set the direction for your writing as well. Your introductory paragraphs will state your thesis and any historical context that might be of interest to your reader.

Suppose the rough draft you are writing is about the independence of Texas, and your research question is "What was the role of Sam Houston in Texas independence?" You will of course need to focus tightly on Houston's role. If your thesis is that Houston's actions were vital to the success of Texas independence, you need to state this in your introduction. Of course, other people will appear in your paper (the Mexican general Antonio López de Santa Anna, e.g.), but a clear focus on Houston and his leadership role in your introduction will keep you from writing a long section on Santa Anna or saying too much about the defense of the Alamo (Houston was not there). As your writing proceeds, always use the test of relevance to the thesis so that you maintain the direction set out in your introduction.

Writing the central sections of your draft raises the practical question of how long each section should be. There is no correct length, of course, but each section should be long enough to present the evidence for one aspect of your thesis. Don't, however, feel obliged to include *all* of your evidence surrounding each claim. When you have made the case you intended to make, stop. Then begin the next section. Be sure to write a **linking sentence**—either at the end of one section or at the beginning of the next—that introduces the next claim you intend to make. Repeat the process in the next section of your paper, and in the next, until you reach your conclusion.

Keep the overall length of the paper in mind as well. If your paper is limited to twenty-five pages and your outline has seven main points, don't start out with ten pages of evidence on the first point. Of course, sections may be of unequal length; some claims are more important than others, and some evidence takes more space to document. Here is a very general guide: For a paper of about twenty-five pages, it is best to have no more than six to eight sections. You will need about two or three pages in each section to properly lay out your argument. You also need to leave about one page at the beginning for your introduction and another at the end for your conclusion. **Notes** and **bibliography** are not usually counted as part of page length, but it is best to clarify this point with your instructor.

The last section of your paper is, of course, the conclusion. Any fine-tuning of your thesis or **revising** of the central sections will necessitate fresh thinking about your conclusion. Keep in mind that the purpose of your conclusion is to summarize the arguments you have made concerning your thesis. In the paper about Sam Houston's leadership, for example, you would briefly refer to the evidence (both supporting and countering your thesis) about his leadership and explain why you concluded that it was vital to Texas independence.

Clear Writing: A Matter of Continuity

To achieve **continuity** in your paper, follow your outline and keep in mind the arguments you wish to make and the evidence you wish to include. Your principal concerns as you construct each section of your paper should be: Does this argument follow logically from the one preceding it? Does it adequately support and develop the thesis? Does it establish the necessary background for the argument that follows? Suppose your thesis is that "German aid to the forces of General Franco in the Spanish civil war was essential to victory over the Spanish republic." Your first section might focus on the reasons for German support. Here, you would explain in some detail Hitler's strategic and economic considerations as well as ideological and diplomatic factors, and you would conclude by relating these reasons to the evidence of later sections, such as the actual aid given and its effect on the course of the war.

Each section in your paper should mirror the overall structure of the paper by containing an introduction, a main body, and a transition to the next section; each paragraph within a section also contains a similar structure. A well-constructed paragraph begins with a sentence that introduces the evidence to be presented and concludes with a sentence that leads logically to the next paragraph. If each paragraph is developed in this way, and if sentences making clear the relationship between paragraphs appear where they are needed, then the paper as a whole becomes a tightly knit series of related statements. The key to tight construction is for each sentence to (1) be related to the one preceding it and (2) advance the development of the thesis to which it is related. The closer you can come to this kind of organization, the better your paper will be.

What is the best way to ensure that there are no gaps in logic between your sentences? As you construct each paragraph, take into account the knowledge of the average person likely to read your paper. Very often, a set of sentences that seems clear to you because of your familiarity with your topic will raise questions in the mind of your reader, who probably is not familiar with your thesis and is entirely dependent on the words you write. If those words do not make your point clearly, you must revise until they do. Refer to Chapter 6 for detailed help on clear writing.

Quotations: When and How to Use Them

Paraphrasing and summarizing are usually the preferred methods of integrating information from your sources (see "Summarizing and Paraphrasing without Plagiarizing" in Chapter 4, pp. 76–78). However, there are instances in which a **quotation** will best serve the purpose of supporting your thesis. The following ground rules will help you determine when to quote.

When to Quote Sources Directly

Three general rules are (1) don't quote too often, (2) don't quote too much from any one source, and (3) use your own words unless there is a good reason for quoting those of your source. When is it appropriate to quote a source directly? There are really only a few special instances that call for direct quotation:

- *When a particularly authoritative source says something very important.* If an important figure in your research makes an important and relevant comment, it may make sense to quote his or her exact words:

    It is significant that a scholar as important as Professor Smith told the conference, "After my second trip to the site, I became convinced that Professor Rodriguez's claim of its pre-Roman origins was correct."[1]

- *When an author uses especially striking language that may be lost in a para-phrase.* If an author uses vivid language that you would have difficulty putting into your own words, a quotation may make sense:

  > In an unusually strong remark, the leader of the sugar worker's union, his head still in bandages, referred to the president as "a wriggling insect."[2]

- *When an author makes a controversial claim.* If you want to make it perfectly clear to the reader that a controversial statement is that of your source, and is not a misinterpretation on your part, you may wish to use a quotation:

  > Despite the French bishop's vigorous campaign to root out heresy, Professor Georgevsky insisted that "Jews fleeing Spain were actually welcomed."[3]

In those instances, direct quotation may be useful. When you quote, be sure to include enough of the original statement to make its meaning clear, but don't make a quote any longer than is necessary.

Finally, be sure that quotations actually support the point you intend to make. Suppose your thesis is that early European settlers in the Americas got along with the Native Americans. Notice that the first quotation below does *not* support the point but the second quotation does:

IMPROPER QUOTATION

The early settlers were not hostile to the Native Americans. As pointed out by the *Claxton Banner* in 1836: "Our Sioux neighbors are peaceable but only when they are penned up in closely guarded reservations."[1]

PROPER QUOTATION

The early settlers were not hostile to the Native Americans. As pointed out by the *Claxton Banner* in 1836: "We have always respected our Sioux neighbors. There has never been warfare between us."[2]

How to Format Quotations

Introduce every quotation by clearly identifying the speaker. The reader will always want to know who is speaking and in what **context**. Don't write: "The strikers were 'a dangerous mob.'" Instead, tell the reader whose words you are repeating: "According to D. H. Dyson, the plant manager, the strikers were 'a dangerous mob.'"

If you do not wish to quote a whole statement, be sure to insert an **ellipsis mark** — three spaced dots (. . .) — wherever words are omitted. You must always let your reader know when you leave out part of a quotation. Compare the two "short quotation" examples. Of course, never omit part of a quotation if doing so would change its meaning. (See Chapter 4, "Quoting without Plagiarizing," pp. 78–79.) If a quotation is brief, taking up no more than two or three lines in your paper, then it should appear within a paragraph of your text and be enclosed in quotation marks:

SHORT QUOTATION

The early settlers were not hostile to the Native Americans. As pointed out by the *Claxton Banner* in 1836: "Our Sioux neighbors, despite their fierce reputation, are a friendly and peaceable people."[3]

SHORT QUOTATION WITH ELLIPSIS MARK

As pointed out by the *Claxton Banner* in 1836: "Our Sioux neighbors . . . are a friendly and peaceable people."[4]

If your quotation will take up more than two or three lines in your paper, it should be set off from the sentences that precede and follow it. It should be indented ten spaces from the left margin and be single-spaced. Do not put quotation marks around a long, displayed quotation, even though you are quoting. Indenting identifies the words as a quotation, as in this example:

LONG QUOTATION

The early settlers were not hostile to the Native Americans. As pointed out by the *Claxton Banner* in 1836:

> Our Sioux neighbors, despite their fierce reputation, are a friendly and peaceable people. No livestock have been disturbed, and the outermost cabins are unmolested. We trust in God that our two peoples may live in harmony in this territory.[5]

Finally, remember that the source of every quotation must be cited in a note (either a footnote or endnote) and in your bibliography (see Chapter 10). In the examples of quotations included above, the writer has used superscript numbers to indicate notes, just as you would in an essay.

Incorporating Visual Materials into Your Paper

Ask your instructor about the usefulness of visual material. Be sure to find out if the space taken up by visuals will be counted as part of the assigned length of the paper or if it will be an addition to this limit. Also ask your instructor about the quantity that is appropriate; you do not want to pad your paper with too many visuals.

If visuals are acceptable, try to find ways to include them. Illustrating important points with maps, charts, tables, drawings, and photographs can strengthen your argument. Some points—the way something looks, a very important comparison between numbers (as in a chart)—can best be made by *showing* your reader a visual of it. Be sure that any visual you use will reproduce clearly.

You can place each visual on or near the page containing the text it illustrates, or you can group all visuals together at the end of the paper

---

Guidelines for Incorporating Visuals

- Look for visual materials on your topic when you do your research. They can strengthen your argument.
- Be sure that the visual actually is what you say it is and means what you say it means. You can misinterpret a visual just as you can misinterpret a printed source.
- Learn about your word processing program's ability to download, store, and insert visuals into your paper.
- Do not pad your paper with visuals.
- Format your visuals correctly by clearly separating them from the surrounding text. Identify them correctly, and make sure that in the final draft of your paper the visual appears where you want it to.
- In addition to a proper identification of a visual on the page where it appears, you need to document its source as you would any other source. You need to tell the reader where the visual came from.

---

in an **appendix**. If you use an appendix, you need to place a note in the text that directs your reader to the page where the corresponding image is located—for example, "See Figure 3.2 on page 41." If your visuals are within the body of the paper, make sure that they are clearly separated (perhaps by a top and bottom line) from the surrounding text. Even more important, be sure they are formatted so that they end up where you expect them when your paper is printed out.

Each visual, regardless of its position (within the text or in an appendix), should have a title above or below it that tells readers what it refers to. And, at the bottom of each visual, except for visuals that you created, be sure to provide a source note indicating where you found the map, chart, table, drawing, or photo. Doing this is as necessary as using notes and a bibliography to document printed sources.

Be sure that each visual is accurate and that it really does illustrate and support your thesis. Don't assume that a visual is correct. Examine it as carefully as you would examine any other source used in your paper. (See pp. 52–66 in Chapter 3 and pp. 71–72 in Chapter 4 for advice on evaluating nonwritten sources.)

Again, be sure to document any visuals. (See model notes and bibliography entries for multimedia sources on pp. 206 and 208 in Chapter 10. Also see the documentation for the sample research paper on pp. 179–85 in Chapter 9.)

When to Use Footnotes and Endnotes

If you quote from, paraphrase, or closely summarize your research sources, you must include a **citation** telling your reader where the original information can be found. In this way, the reader can check the accuracy of your quotes and statements, judge the **bias** and credibility of your sources, or carry out research of his or her own.

Footnotes (which appear at the bottom of the page) or endnotes (which appear in a list at the end of the paper) are the preferred method that historians use to document their research. Footnotes and endnotes have the same format and provide the same information; they differ only in their placement. If your instructor has no preference, you can choose to put your **documentation** in either place, but you must be consistent throughout the paper. The following discussion uses the word *notes* to refer to both footnotes and endnotes. (For details on formatting notes, see "Formatting Footnotes and Endnotes" in Chapter 10, pp. 186–87. For sample endnotes, see "Sample Student Research Paper" in Chapter 9, pp. 179–82.)

The question that troubles students the most is: Which of the statements that I make in my paper needs documentation? There are only a few hard-and-fast rules to guide you. However, five types of statements must be accompanied by notes:

- Direct quotations
- Paraphrases
- Controversial facts or opinions
- Summaries of important points from your sources
- Statistics

NOTE: On occasion, you may want to use notes to make brief comments that qualify or supplement statements in your paper. These are called "explanatory" notes.

To review summarizing, paraphrasing, and quoting, see pages 76–79 in Chapter 4.

What is meant by "controversial facts or opinions"? Facts or opinions about which your sources disagree are considered to be controversial. So are facts or opinions that will surprise your readers. Suppose, in a paper on "the treatment of slaves on Mississippi plantations," you write that some slave owners were kind to their slaves. This statement may surprise some readers and thus must be documented. Suppose, while researching the topic "European discoverers of America," you find that all your sources agree that Vikings visited the New World long before Columbus. If you suspect that most of your readers believe that Columbus was the first European to see the New World, then you must include a note identifying the source of your information.

The number of notes to use is another thorny problem. If your paper goes on for several pages without any notes, you are not documenting as much as you should. If you are writing five or more notes per page, you may be overdoing it.

Here is a final point about using notes. Citing a source with a note does not give you permission to plagiarize. If the words in your paper are the same, *or very nearly the same,* as the words in your source, you have committed **plagiarism** even if you include a note. (For more on plagiarism, see "Avoiding Plagiarism" in Chapter 4, pp. 84–86.) You should not use sentences or even phrases from your sources unless you put them in quotation marks.

REVISING AND REWRITING

Leave time in your writing schedule for revising your paper. Before writing your final draft, put the paper aside for a day or two (another reason to allow extra time) and then reread it. This way, you will gain a fresh perspective, and you may spot weaknesses that you hadn't noticed before.

A rough draft always needs smoothing out. As you reread your paper, check for continuity. Look for any places where it seems to wander away from a direct focus on the thesis. Be certain that the thesis is stated clearly at the outset and that each part of the paper contains information that supports the thesis. Does each part of the paper seem clearly connected to the part that follows it? Be sure that documentation appears wherever it is needed.

While you examine the overall structure of the paper for defects, you also need to look closely at the language itself. If you repeated yourself,

---

Guidelines for Revising and Rewriting

- Revising a rough draft takes time. Be sure to include that time in your writing schedule.
- Wait a day or two after completing the rough draft to prepare the final draft. This will help you to look at your rough draft with a fresh perspective.
- Examine the overall structure of the rough draft. Is it clearly focused on your intended thesis?
- Be sure that the introduction states your thesis and that the major arguments behind your thesis are supported in the body of your paper.
- Check to see if the parts of the paper follow one another in a clear and direct way.
- Rewrite or eliminate any points that are weak, are repetitive, seem out of order, or are unrelated to your thesis.
- Examine the placement, form, and accuracy of the notes. Check the bibliography for form and accuracy as well.
- Proofread your paper carefully, looking for errors of grammar and spelling. Check the format of the paper, looking at margins, spacing, and the insertion of any visual material.

eliminate the repetition. If you included material that is unrelated to your thesis, discard it. Check the connections between paragraphs to see whether the reader will be able to follow your argument. Make sure that you have accomplished what you set out to do in your introduction, that you have sufficiently supported your thesis, and that your conclusion makes it clear that you have done so. Check the notes and bibliography entries for proper style and accuracy.

Finally, examine your writing for errors in spelling and grammar. **Proof-read** carefully and slowly. At normal reading speed your eyes can go right by major errors. You are so familiar with your paper that you may not see what is on the page. Reading your paper aloud will help you catch unclear phrases. (For more revising and editing advice, see "Revising Your Essay" in Chapter 6, pp. 115–16, and the guidelines above.)

NOTE: Spell-checkers and grammar-checkers are *not* replacements for word-by-word proofreading. They catch only those spelling errors that are not actual words. Grammar-checkers balk at some words or phrases that may be fine. Only you know what you meant to say. Use the computer's tools, but also print out and carefully read each page for yourself.

Sometimes **peer reviewing**, or reading a draft of another student's paper, is part of the work for the course. If your instructor gives specific guidelines for this assignment, follow them. (You may also find it helpful to refer to "Guidelines for Peer Reviewing" in Chapter 2, p. 37.)

9

Example of a Research Paper

A SAMPLE RESEARCH PAPER

As a final aid in preparing your research paper, this chapter contains a full-scale example. The examination of the research paper begins with a discussion of how the **topic**, **research question**, and **thesis** were chosen and then moves on to the writing outline that the student developed. Finally, there is the paper itself, including **endnotes** and a **bibliography**, all of which follow the rules and suggestions made earlier in this chapter.

This sample research paper can help you in two important ways. First, reading the sample paper as a whole *before* you write your own will give you a clear sense of what your paper should look like, how it should be developed, and what kind of **documentation** it should have. Second, referring to the sample paper *while* you are writing your own will help you answer specific questions about issues such as the **introduction**, **continuity** between paragraphs, **paraphrases** and **quotations**, the format of notes and bibliography entries, and the **conclusion**.

Annotations in the margin of the sample paper help you to see what the writer is trying to accomplish. Also in the margin is a series of explanatory phrases that identify stages in the unfolding story and are related to specific sections of the writing outline. Finally, a numbered comment in the margin of each endnote tells you what point in the paper is being supported. As you read the sample paper, ask yourself what point the author is making and whether she is accomplishing her goal. Pay special attention to the way in which the parts are put together and how each section advances the effort to describe and support the thesis. Read the endnotes to determine why a **citation** is full or shortened and to see the format used for citations.

Notice also the format of the bibliography. If anything is unclear, review the discussions of writing in Chapter 6 and the "Writing the Text" section of Chapter 8 (pp. 147–54).

How the Thesis Was Developed

The topic of this paper would fit a variety of courses: pre–Civil War U.S. history, American labor history, women's history, and the history of industrialization, among others. Within the framework of one such course, the student became curious about the lives of workers in the earliest factories. Her curiosity led to a narrower topic about industrialization in New England, where the student had grown up. Preliminary research indicated that textiles were the first goods to be made in factories, so the topic was narrowed further to workers in that industry. When the student discovered that many of the earliest workers were young women who were the same age as she was, she decided to look at their lives in particular. At this point, her broad topic, "early industrialization in New England," had been narrowed to "women workers in early industrialization in New England." The largest number of these women worked in mills in Lowell, Massachusetts, so that town was chosen. (The student's research also made it clear that there were numerous sources that discussed Lowell mill workers.) The time period to be covered was the one during which women workers were the principal workforce in Lowell. Finally, the student formulated a preliminary research question: How did American women respond to their experience with industrial labor in the early nineteenth century?

All of this background research and the eventual research question led the student to her thesis: Women workers in Lowell, though working under difficult material conditions, were able to put up with the rigors of factory work while at the same time gaining a new sense of independence in their lives. Finally, the student chose a title that introduced the reader both to her general topic, "women workers in the Lowell, Massachusetts, textile mills, 1820–1850," and to the question she intended to answer. (See the sections on coming up with a topic, a research question, and a thesis for your paper in Chapter 7, pp. 118–21.)

The Writing Outline for the Paper

During the research phase, the student uncovered several sources that gave detailed accounts of the experiences of the women workers, showing both positive and negative aspects of their working lives. It became clear that the trade-offs between hard work and independence should have an important place in the paper. Sections 4, 5, and 6 of the writing outline described below focus on this subject. Section 4 talks about work life in general, section 5 discusses social life, and section 6 explores the independent attitudes that women began to embrace as a result of their new work experiences. Having decided on the importance of the work experience, the student found it necessary to give the reader an understanding of how these women came to be mill workers in the first place. Section 3 examines this subject. Showing how the women came to be mill workers required an explanation of where the mills themselves came from. This was necessary because the mills represent the first stage of industrialization in America. Sections 1 and 2 deal with industrialization. Section 7 covers the end of the period during which women workers predominated in textile work. The other two sections, of course, are the introduction and conclusion.

The subheadings within each section are divisions of the larger subject and indicate the order in which a section will be developed. For example, section 4, "Life on their own in a mill town," examines, in order, adjusting to life in a mill town, a typical workday, the work itself, and the pay received. Look at each part of the outline to see the function it serves and how the whole of the outline fully covers the important parts of the thesis. Try to be sure that your own outline sets the stage for writing your paper the way this one does.

SAMPLE WRITING OUTLINE

Wage Slavery or True Independence:
Women Workers in the Lowell, Massachusetts,
Textile Mills, 1820-1850

Introduction (thesis statement): Women were not merely exploited laborers, but were active participants in broadening their own lives.

1. Background on industrialization
   a. Early industrialization in England
   b. Attitudes toward industrialization in the United States

2. The origins of the textile industry in eastern Massachusetts
   a. The preindustrial economy in America
   b. Slater-type mills
   c. Plans for a textile mill in Lowell, Massachusetts
   d. The choice of a female workforce

3. Recruiting women workers
   a. The prejudice against women working outside the home
   b. Building a "moral" community

4. Life on their own in a mill town
   a. Adjusting to life in the mills
   b. Typical workday
   c. Nature of work
   d. Rate of pay

5. Social life
   a. Leisure hours
   b. Female companionship

6. Independent attitude gained from mill experience
   a. The *Lowell Offering*
   b. "Turn outs"
   c. Critics of female labor
   d. Saw themselves as "Daughters of Free Men"

7. Recession and declining conditions of work in the Lowell mills
   a. Many women left by choice
   b. End of paternalism
   c. The coming of the Irish workers

Conclusion: Young women experienced independence in early industrialization.

Formatting a Research Paper

The student research paper that follows illustrates generally accepted standards for formatting. Unless your instructor requires a special format, follow these guidelines:

- Use one-inch margins on all four sides of each page.
- Include a title page (which is *not* numbered) with your name, the course name and number, the name of your instructor, the date of your paper, and the title of your paper.
- Double-space the body of the paper.
- Single-space long (indented) quotations.
- Single-space footnotes or endnotes, but double-space between notes.
- Single-space bibliography entries, but double-space between entries.
- Consecutively number all pages following the title page—including pages with illustrations, maps, graphs, and anything else.
- If you include visuals, mention them by number in your text—for example, "See Figure 6." Immediately below each visual, place the figure number, a brief description, and the source.

Sample Student Research Paper

The following sample paper is documented according to the *Chicago Manual of Style* documentation system, which is explained in Chapter 10, "Documenting Your Paper."

Unless your instructor specifies a format, your title page should resemble this one. Whatever layout you choose, be sure to include paper title, course name and number (and section, if necessary), the instructor's name, your name, and the date.

Wage Slavery or True Independence:

Women Workers in the Lowell, Massachusetts,

Textile Mills, 1820-1850

American History 200

Section 4

Professor Kumar

Julia Matthews

December 12, 2018

1

This paper will examine the development of the textile industry in Lowell, Massachusetts, and the young women who served as its principal workforce between 1820 and 1850. It will describe how these women came to accept what was for them an unusual and difficult form of labor, but it will argue that they shaped this experience to serve their own purposes. Such a story helps to explain much about early industrialization in America and particularly about the role of women in the early factory system. The paper argues that these women workers were not mere laborers exploited by the mill owners but were actively engaged in expanding the constricted opportunities for women.

In the early part of the nineteenth century, while the vast majority of Americans were living on family farms, the industrial revolution was beginning to spread across England. One of the most rapid and noticeable changes in British manufacturing was the making of cloth. As late as the 1760s, English textile merchants were still making cloth by the age-old "putting out" system. They bought raw wool and hired women to spin it at home. When the wool had been spun into yarn, the merchant then sent it to weavers who also worked in their homes. In that decade, however, new machinery (the carding cylinder, spinning jenny, and, most important, the water frame) was developed that made possible the shift of spinning and weaving from homes to what were called "factories." By 1800, many such factories had been established in England, usually employing children to do most of the work. Many of these children were orphans or "paupers" from families so poor that they could not even afford to feed them. Conditions in these factories were very bad, and stories of these dark and dangerous mills (some accurate, some exaggerated) filtered back to America.[1]

Rural Americans felt certain that the dark and dreary factory towns now dotting the English countryside should not arise in America. Political leaders Thomas Jefferson and James Madison both warned that large-scale manufacturing would lead to a class of propertyless wage

Introduction.

Statement of thesis.

Background information.

Superscript numbers refer to endnotes.

2

Attitudes toward industrialization in the United States.

earners and would threaten the survival of republican government. New Englanders watched the rise of industrialization in England with special concern. In New England, which had been at the forefront of the struggle against British rule, people were especially proud of their independence and suspicious of anything that seemed to copy the ways of the English. How could New England's men, let alone its women, be expected to work in factories?[2]

The reservations about factory labor persisted through the War of 1812, as Americans had little need for large factories to produce items like textiles. While great changes in the production of textiles were taking place in England, most New Englanders still spun yarn at home and some also wove their own cloth. In most cases they were simply making clothes for their families. Much of this work was done by women. A spinning wheel was a possession of almost every household.[3] Despite their anti-industrial prejudice, however, New England farmers witnessed, in the first two decades of the nineteenth century, a slow shift in the

The origins of the textile industry in eastern Massachusetts.

way cloth was made in America. Farm families began to adapt the old English system of "putting out" — weaving prespun yarn at home for sale in the market. Historian Thomas Dublin notes that young girls could keep up with their duties such as watching over younger siblings, preparing food, and cleaning house in addition to weaving yarn, and thus "fit the demands of such work into the rhythms of their daily lives."[4] Even though the girls were staying at home to perform this work, known as "outwork," they were beginning to develop industrial-type skills, and home production of textiles would gradually be replaced by factory production.

Samuel Slater and Francis Cabot Lowell, two leading New England merchants, were impressed by the mechanization of English textile production and began to think about an American textile industry. Men like these noted the massive increase in productivity in the English textile industry. At first, Slater, and others who followed his lead, built

3

small mills in rural villages and employed not children as in England but whole families. The building of Slater-type mills did not directly challenge the New England way of living. Most villages already contained small mills run by water power (streams pushing paddle wheels) that ground corn or wheat. Since the textile mills hired whole families who already lived in the villages, family and village life was not greatly altered. Early mills therefore did not really challenge the traditional division of labor in homes any more than outwork did.[5]

One new development in textile production, however, did raise troublesome questions about the impact of industrialization on America's rural way of life. This change came from a new type of mill. The first of its type was built in Waltham, Massachusetts, in 1813 by Francis Lowell and a small group of wealthy Boston merchants.[6] Three years earlier, Lowell had returned from a long trip to England. The British government would not allow the plans for the new power looms to be taken out of the country, but Lowell had paid close attention to their construction on his many tours of English mills and returned to America with enough knowledge in his head to eventually reproduce a machine comparable to the English power loom.[7]

In Waltham, Francis Lowell built a large mill that carried out both the spinning and the weaving processes. In fact, every step of the production process was done in a series of connected steps. Waltham was not a village with a textile mill in it; it was a "mill town" in which the factory dominated the economic life of a rapidly growing city. Most significantly, Lowell's system of production brought important changes in the lives of his workers. He hired them as individuals, not as families, and many came from great distances to live and work in the new mill town. When Lowell died in 1817, the small group of Boston businessmen who had invested in his mill at Waltham spread the new factory system to other places. Their biggest investment was in the small village of East Chelmsford about twenty-seven miles from Boston

Transition sentence introduces discussion of new type of mill.

4

and lying along the swift-flowing Concord and Merrimack Rivers. There they built what was soon the biggest mill town in the nation, with more than a dozen large integrated mills based upon mechanical looms. In honor of their friend, they called the new town Lowell. (See Figure 1, a map of Lowell in 1845.)[8]

The growth of Lowell between 1821 and 1840 was unprecedented.[9] A rapidly developing textile industry like the one at Lowell needed larger and larger numbers of people to work the mechanical looms and other machines in the factories. Given the prejudice against factory work in New England, how could large numbers of natives be drawn to work in the mills? Could they draw upon female labor for their factories? If so, would they pay them cash wages, or would they try to bring them to Lowell as "servants"? These questions were carefully pondered by the wealthy men who built the big textile mills at Lowell, Massachusetts.

Recruiting women workers.

The mill owners, aware of the negative view of English mill towns, decided to confront the problem by creating a *planned* community where workers would live in solid, clean housing rather than slums. Their source of workers would also be different. The rapidly running rivers that ran their mills were not near the major coastal cities. No large pool of potential laborers lived near their new town. The mill owners had to find a large group of people whose labor was not absolutely necessary to the farm economy. The solution to their labor problem came in the form of hundreds (later thousands) of young women who lived on the farms of the region.[10]

Several developments in the social and economic history of New England tended to make this group of workers available. Population growth was making it more and more difficult for farmers to find land close by for their sons (and their sons' families). Generations of the

Problems of the farm community.

same family had hoped to live near one another. By the 1820s, however, many farms in New England, especially those on the less productive land of Maine and New Hampshire, had run out of good land and had to

5

Visual documentation of location of mills and boarding houses.

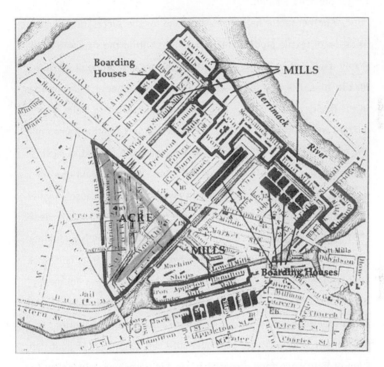

Figure 1.   Adapted from Map of Lowell, Massachusetts, ca. 1845. *Lowell Historical Society*

6

find sources of income outside of agriculture. While some farmers went
west to find more fertile land and a less harsh climate, others sent
their sons to work on neighboring farms, or as apprentices to craftsmen
(shoemakers, blacksmiths, or leather workers). Extra cash was something that most farm families were in great need of, and outwork no
longer provided enough.[11]

Another factor helped set the stage for the successful industrialization of textile production. This one was within the structure of the
family itself and worked in favor of producing a new group of workers
Subordinate status for the mills. The position of women (wives and, especially, daughters)
of women. in the family was an inferior one. Adult, property-holding males were
citizens with full civil rights, but the same was not true for women *of
any age*. The father of the family had the legal right to control most
aspects of the lives of his wife and daughters. His wife could own no
property. Her signature on a document meant nothing because only her
husband could transact business. Daughters had even less independence.
They were bound by social conventions to obey their fathers and rarely
were able to earn money of their own. Even travel away from home was
unusual. The idea that a woman's place was in the home was not merely
a powerful concept; it was, with rare exceptions, a rule binding a woman's
behavior. Although the work of daughters and wives was important to
the family economy (it literally could not have functioned without their
labor at field work, food preparation, cleaning, washing, etc.), they
gained no independent income or freedom as a result. In fact, so strong
was the belief that daughters' lives would be bound by decisions made
by their fathers, their older brothers, and, eventually, their husbands,
that many could not imagine for themselves a life of active, public
involvement of the kind expected of men. For some women, however,
their inferior position in family and society gave them an incentive to
take hold of any opportunity to weaken their bonds of inferiority. So,
when the opportunity knocked, many young and single New England

7

women chose to answer by going willingly to work in the textile factories.[12]

Women's motives were economic as well as social. Very few opportunities for employment outside the home existed; teaching in a local school was one of the most common, but that was very poorly paid and lasted for only a few months a year. The new mill work was steady work, and it paid more than any alternative available to women.[13] Young girls could thus contribute to their family's welfare by sending home a portion of their pay. This economic motive added to their desire to move outside the traditional sphere of the family. For many of them, the chance to live away from home and with other young women like themselves offered an independence that was otherwise impossible.[14]

Hiring young women, of course, ran up against strong Yankee resistance. As noted above, fathers rarely allowed their daughters to leave home when they were young. According to the prejudices of the period, young women were unprepared for a life among adult, male strangers. Their "innocence" and "purity" had to be protected by their family. The goal held out for these girls (almost the only respectable one) was eventual marriage. To prepare for that, they had to learn wifely duties and practical household skills. God-fearing New England fathers were very reluctant to let their daughters leave the farm to live and work among strangers in a faraway town.[15]

Prejudice against women working outside the home.

To confront this prejudice, the mill owners created boarding houses around the mills where groups of girls would live and take their meals under the care of a boarding housekeeper who was usually an older woman, perhaps a widow. Strict boarding-house rules were laid down by the company — rules that served the company's purposes but also reassured parents that their daughters' behavior would still be monitored even though they were away from home. For example, the young women could not have visitors in the late evening. (See Figure 2, a reproduction of boarding-house regulations.) Moreover, the girls would never grow

8

*Visual documen-
tation of boarding-
house life.*

REGULATIONS
FOR THE
BOARDING HOUSES
OF THE
MIDDLESEX COMPANY.

THE tenants of the Boarding Houses are not to board, or permit any part of their houses to be occupied by any person except those in the employ of the Company.

They will be considered answerable for any improper conduct in their houses, and are not to permit their boarders to have company at unseasonable hours.

The doors must be closed at ten o'clock in the evening, and no one admitted after that time without some reasonable excuse.

The keepers of the Boarding Houses must give an account of the number, names, and employment of their boarders, when required; and report the names of such as are guilty of any improper conduct, or are not in the regular habit of attending public worship.

The buildings and yards about them must be kept clean and in good order, and if they are injured otherwise than from ordinary use, all necessary repairs will be made, and charged to the occupant.

It is indispensable that all persons in the employ of the Middlesex Company should be vaccinated who have not been, as also the families with whom they board; which will be done at the expense of the Company.

SAMUEL LAWRENCE, Agent.

JOEL TAYLOR, PRINTER, Daily Courier Office.

Figure 2.   Rules for boarding houses where mill girls stayed.
Lowell Historical Society

9

into a permanent working class — something that no one wished to see — as it was expected that they would return to their homes for visits and after a year or two would go back to their villages. While they stayed in Lowell, their reputations (and thus their opportunity for marriage) would be protected by the town fathers.[16]

The mill owners did not advertise for help. They sent recruiters into the countryside to explain the special nature of Lowell and to soothe parents' fears. Because of the farmers' need for extra income, and the women's desire for independence, this effort was often success-ful.[17] Over the years, thousands of young women took the long trip by stagecoach or wagon from their rural homes to mill towns like Lowell.

Upon first arriving in Lowell, the young girls were naturally nervous. They had not lived away from home or ever worked in a factory. They were not used to the atmosphere of a city. The boarding house was new also. Living with a strange woman (and probably her family), who might or might not be a caring mother-substitute, also required adjustment. The girls shared the home with a dozen or more other girls and usually roomed with three or four of them. While all this was happening, of course, the girls had to make the difficult adjustment to the rigorous rules and long hours at the mill. Making the transition from rural to industrial rhythms wore on these girls.[18] As Harriet Robinson wrote in her memoir entitled *Loom and Spindle*,

Life in a mill town.

> And sorrowful enough they looked, even to the fun-loving child who has lived to tell the story; for they had all left their pleasant country homes to try their fortunes in a great manufacturing town, and they were homesick before they landed at the doors of their boarding-houses.[19]

Indented quotation.

Mill work was not only an opportunity; like so much of early factory labor, it was hard work. These girls were used to hard work on the farm, but industrial labor created an entirely new pattern of life. The typical workday began at five a.m. and did not end until seven in the evening, or later. Thus the women worked an average of twelve hours a

Mill work and the workday.

day. (See Figure 3, an image of a bobbin girl.) They were given only thirty minutes for lunch and forty-five for dinner. Since they took their meals at the boarding house, the thirty minutes for lunch had to include a quick walk (perhaps a run) to and from the house, leaving only fifteen or twenty minutes for the meal.[20] The mills operated six days a week so that the only day off was Sunday, part of which was usually spent at church. Thus free time was confined to two or three hours in the evening (boarding-house rules required them to go to bed at ten) and to Sunday afternoon.[21] For many, however, this was still more leisure (and more freedom) than they would have had at home.

Despite a workday that, including meals, took up fourteen hours, most of the young women did not find the work very strenuous or particularly dangerous. As the mill owners had claimed, Lowell did not resemble the grimy, packed mill towns of England.[22] Still, the work was tedious and confining — doing the same operation over and over again and under the watchful eye of the overseer. In the ideal plan for Lowell, the overseer was to take the place of the absent father (just as the boarding-house widow was to be the substitute mother), someone responsible for seeing to the safety and welfare of the girls on the job. Of course, the overseer was also hired by the company to ensure that the mill ran smoothly and efficiently. He saw to it that the women worked steadily and recorded their hours of labor; any possibility of time off required his approval.[23]

The young women earned an average of three to four dollars a week, from which their board of $1.25 a week was deducted.[24] At that time no other jobs open to women paid as well. As noted above, rural schoolteachers earned less than one dollar a week and taught for only three months of the year.[25] Three or four dollars a week was enough to pay their board, send badly needed money home, and still have enough left over for new clothes once in a while. Many women workers even established savings accounts, and some eventually left work with

11

Visual of a mill girl.

Figure 3.   Image of a girl winding a shuttle bobbin, by Winslow Homer, 1871.
Lowell National Historical Park

12

several hundred dollars, something that they could never have done at home.[26]

Social life.   In Lowell the women became part of a growing city that had shops, social events, and camaraderie that were absent in their rural villages and farms. Most felt responsible to send part of their earnings home, but enough was left over to give them consumer choices unavailable to their rural sisters, cousins, and friends. Also, unlike farm and family chores, mill work offered free time on Sundays and in the evenings.[27]

Leisure hours.   Even though their free time was very limited, the women engaged in a wide variety of activities. In the evening they wrote letters home, entertained visitors (though there was little privacy), repaired their clothing, and talked among themselves. They talked of friends and relatives and also of conditions in the mill. They could go out to the shops, especially clothing shops. The mill girls at Lowell prided themselves on a wardrobe that, at least on Sunday, was not inferior to that of the wives of prosperous citizens.[28] One of the most surprising uses of their free time was the number of meetings attended by mill girls. There were evening courses that enabled the young women to extend their education beyond the few years of schooling they had received in the countryside. They could also attend lectures by prominent speakers. It was not unusual for the audience at serious presentations to be composed mostly of mill girls. In their spare time, they also read novels and essays. So strong was the girls' interest in reading that many mills put up signs warning "No reading in the mills."[29] Perhaps the most unusual pursuit of at least some mill girls was writing. Determined to challenge the idea that mill girls were mindless drones of the factory and lacked the refinement necessary to make them good wives, about seventy-five mill girls and women contributed in the 1840s to a series of publications that featured stories and essays by the workers themselves. Indeed, much of the editorial work was done by these women as well.[30]

13

The most well known of these publications was the *Lowell Offering*, which consisted exclusively of articles written and edited by women in the factories. Although many of the articles in the *Offering* reinforced traditional ideas and focused on noncontroversial subjects such as family, courtship, fashion, morality, and nature,[31] some writers used the publication to express a newfound sense of worldliness and independent thought. For example, one factory worker explains in a letter to the editor in 1840 that her boarding house is not like a domestic home at all, but is comprised of about a dozen young women of different backgrounds, faiths, and ideas. Of herself and her colleagues, she says, "we *need* not be ignorant upon the subjects which are agitating the world around us, nor of the transactions which excite the interest of others besides 'factory girls.'"[32]

Although they stayed away from outright criticism of working conditions, the women did manage to find a voice of opposition to factory life in their writings. According to historian Chad Montrie, the young writers typically expressed their disillusionment with factory life by "embrac[ing] a romantic version of nature, which they identified with the homes and the landscapes they had lost."[33] One writer in the *Lowell Offering*, for example, wrote in 1841:

> Those who have for any length of time been pent up in a cotton-mill and factory boarding-house...can appreciate the pleasures of a journey through the country, when the earth is dressed in her richest robes of green, bedecked with flowers, and all smiling with sunlight.[34]

During the early years of the mill towns, the owners had tried to keep up the image of the factory as a pleasant place. Buildings had many windows and much sunlight. The town had large green spaces and the atmosphere of a country village.[35] As time went on, however, the mill companies became more interested in profits and less concerned about their role as protectors of their young workers. By the 1830s, tensions in the mills had begun to rise. Factory owners, observing a

The Lowell Offering.

Example of a quotation with an ellipsis mark.

14

Women workers' resistance to factory discipline.

decline in the price of their cloth and the growth of unsold inventories, decided to lower their workers' wages.[36] When the reduction was announced in February 1834, the women workers circulated petitions among themselves pledging to stop work ("turn out") if wages were lowered.[37] When the leader of the petition drive at one mill was fired, many of the women protested. They left work and marched to the other mills to call out their workers. It is estimated that one-sixth of all women mill workers walked out as a result. The strikers wrote another petition, stating that "we will not go back into the mills to work until our wages are continued . . . as they have been."[38] In 1836, another effort to lower wages led to an ever larger "turn out."[39]

Some critics of the Lowell system argued that girls could not serve as successful factory operatives and that industrial labor would deprive them of both their independence and their womanly virtue. One critic, for example, wrote to the *New York Herald* in 1843 that the Lowell factory girls earned "a very low position in society and very little weight in the scale of virtue and the female ornaments" in the opinion of many observers. After all, he argued, very few girls actually contributed to the *Lowell Offering*, thus creating a "splendid illusion" of factory life that was "got up by a clergyman on speculation and sustained by the companies for effect."[40] Some southern newspapers, alert to challenge northern claims of the superiority of free labor, doubted that the Lowell girls could compare themselves favorably to African American slaves. One Kentucky critic argued they were "in point of morals on a level with the wretched females of a southern plantation — defencelessly exposed and subjected to the brutality of master and overseer,"[41] and a correspondent for the *Vicksburg Sentinel* argued, "The negroes of the South could not be driven to do what those poor creatures are compelled to submit to, to procure a subsistence."[42]

The preponderance of evidence, however, suggests that the Lowell girls retained their moral and economic standing despite the rigors of

15

factory life and the stresses caused by strikes. They were not any less feminine, nor were they slaves. Although "turn outs" were brief and did not achieve their purposes, they demonstrated not only the independent attitude of many of the women workers but also their unique status among American workers. They did not accept the owners' view that they were minors under their benevolent care; nor did they consider themselves to be members of a permanent working class. The petitions prepared by the strikers indicate that they thought of themselves as the equal of their employers. The sense of independence gained by factory work and cash wages led them to reject the idea that they were mere factory hands. Petitions referred to their "unquestionable rights," and to "the spirit of our patriotic ancestors, who preferred privation to bondage. . . ." One petition ended, "we are free, we would remain in possession of what kind providence has bestowed upon us, and remain *daughters of free men still.*"[43] This language indicates that the women did not think of themselves as laborers complaining about low wages. They were free citizens of a republic and deserved respect as such. Because many of the women had relatives who had fought in the Revolutionary War, they felt that they were protecting not only their jobs but also their independence.

Example of a quotation with emphasis added.

Although the strikes failed and these women did not really have complete "independence," this issue was so important to them that many left the mills and went home when it became clear that mill work would require a lessening of their status. As Harriet Robinson recalled, "the best portion of the girls left and went to their homes, or to the other employments that were fast opening to women, until there were very few of the old guard left."[44] They had originally accepted mill work because life away from home and good wages gave them greater freedom. When mill work came to seem less like independence and more like "slavery" (a comparison that also appeared in the petitions), many changed their minds. The willingness of these young women to challenge

16

the authority of the mill owners is a sign that their new lives had given them a feeling of mutual strength.[45]

Declining conditions of work in the Lowell mills.

Economic recession in the late 1830s and early 1840s led to the layoff of hundreds of the women workers. Many of the mills were forced to part-time schedules. In the 1840s and 1850s, the mill owners tried to maintain profits despite increased competition and lessened demand. They did so by intensifying the work process. The speed of the machinery was increased as was the number of machines tended by each worker. Historian David Zonderman argues that textile mill workers resented the so-called "speed-up and stretch out" because of "the physical toll of the intense labor, the constant reduction of piece rates, and the knowledge that their extra efforts were being exploited by the owners."[46] Paternalism was discarded. To save money, the companies stopped building boarding houses.[47] The look of Lowell changed as well. Mill buildings took up more of the green space that had been part of the original plan.

The coming of Irish workers.

By 1850, Lowell did indeed look something like an English mill town. By then, however, the desire to pacify the fears of potential workers and their families was gone. Terrible famine in Ireland in 1845 and 1846 had caused a large number of Irish to immigrate to the United States.[48] As conditions in the mills declined and more and more young Yankee women left the mills for home or other work, their places were rapidly taken up by the very poor Irish for whom work of any kind in America was an opportunity, and who did not have the option of returning to their homes. Slowly, Lowell had become just another industrial city. It was dirty and overcrowded, and its mills were beginning to look run-down.

Conclusion.

By 1850, an era had passed. By then, most of the mill workers were recruited from newly arrived immigrants with backgrounds very different from those of the young New England women. During the period from the 1820s to the 1840s, however, young women from rural

17

New England made up the majority of the textile workers in the area. At that time, an unusual era in the development of industrialization took place. Large textile mills with complex production systems were operated largely by young women who thought of themselves not as workers but as free citizens of a republic earning an independent existence for a few years before returning to their homes. These women gave the mill owners the workforce that was needed to make the U.S. textile industry large and profitable. Many fortunes were made for investors living in Boston and other major cities.[49] But the farmers' daughters profited as well. Not only did they earn more than earlier generations of women had been able to, but they did so outside the home.

Restatement of part of thesis.

A great debate had raged during the 1830s and 1840s about the impact of industrialization on American life. Because of the general belief that women were weak, it was presumed that they would be taken advantage of as workers, especially as they were away from the protection of the male members of their families. Further, it was feared that mill work would "defeminize" them and that young men would not marry them because they had not been brought up in an environment of modesty, deference to their fathers and brothers, and daily practice in domestic tasks such as cleaning, sewing, and cooking.[50] (Textile mill workers were known as "spinsters," a word that came to mean a woman who never married.) Seen from a longer perspective, however, the women showed these fears to be unfounded. Even more important, as effective workers they undermined the stereotype of women as frail and as thriving only in a domestic environment. While these young women helped make possible the industrialization of New England, at the same time they expanded their opportunities. Many women reformers and radicals in later years, as they raised the banner for equal rights for women in more and more areas of life, referred back to the example of the independent mill girls of the 1830s and 1840s who resisted

Summary.

Restatement of thesis.

18

pressures from their employers, gained both freedom and maturity by living and working on their own, and showed an intense desire for independence and learning.[51] Great fortunes were made from the textile mills of that era, but within those mills a generation of young women gained something even more precious: a sense of self-respect.

19

Endnotes

1. Barbara M. Tucker, *Samuel Slater and the Origins of the American Textile Industry: 1790-1860* (Ithaca, NY: Cornell University Press, 1984), 33-40.

2. Caroline F. Ware, *The Early New England Cotton Manufacture* (Boston: Houghton Mifflin, 1931), 4-8; Tucker, *Slater*, 38-41; Walter Licht, *Industrializing America: The Nineteenth Century* (Baltimore: Johns Hopkins University Press, 1995), 15; Robert F. Dalzell, *Enterprising Elite: The Boston Associates and the World They Made* (Cambridge, MA: Harvard University Press, 1987), 12-13; Allan Kulikoff, "The Transition to Capitalism in Rural America," *William and Mary Quarterly* 46 (1989): 129-30, 141-42.

3. Thomas Dublin, *Women at Work: The Transformation of Work and Community in Lowell, Massachusetts, 1826-1860* (New York: Columbia University Press, 1979), 14; Adrienne D. Hood, "The Gender Division of Labor in the Production of Textiles in Eighteenth-Century Rural Pennsylvania," *Journal of Social History* 27 (Spring 1994): 542, www.jstor.org.ezproxy.ithaca.edu:2048/stable/3788986.

4. Thomas Dublin, *Transforming Women's Work: New England Lives in the Industrial Revolution* (Ithaca, NY: Cornell University Press, 1994), 30.

5. Tucker, *Slater*, 79, 85, 99-100, 111; Barbara M. Tucker, "The Family and Industrial Discipline in Ante-Bellum New England," *Labor History* 21 (Winter 1979-80): 56-60.

6. Dalzell, 26-30; Tucker, *Slater*, 111-16.

7. Dalzell, 5-6.

8. Tucker, *Slater*, 116-17.

9. Dublin, *Women at Work*, 19-21, 133-35.

10. Dublin, *Women at Work*, 26, 76; Benita Eisler, ed., *The "Lowell Offering": Writings by New England Mill Women (1840-1845)* (Philadelphia: Lippincott, 1977), 15-16; Peter Temin, "The Industrialization of New England, 1830-1880," in *Engines of Enterprise: An Economic History of New England*, ed. Peter Temin (Cambridge, MA: Harvard University Press, 2000), 96-101.

11. Christopher Clark, "The Household Economy: Market Exchange and the Rise of Capitalism in the Connecticut Valley, 1800-1860,"

Endnotes begin on a new page. The numbered annotations correspond to the endnote numbers.

1. The rise of industrialization in England.

2. American attitudes toward industrialization in England and mill work in general.

3. Home spinning in America.

Citation of an article from a database.

4. The origins of industrialization in America.

5. Slater-type mills and family production.

6. The creation of Waltham mills.

7. H. C. Lowell and power loom.

8. The founding of Lowell.

9. The growth of Lowell.

10. The owners' choice of a female workforce.

11. Problems of the farm economy.

20

Journal of Social History 13 (Winter 1979): 175-76; Gail Fowler Mohanty, "Handloom Outwork and Outwork Weaving in Rural Rhode Island, 1810-1821," *American Studies* 30 (Fall 1989): 42-43.

12. Eisler, 16, 19, 62; Barbara Welter, "The Cult of True Womanhood," *American Quarterly* 18 (1966): 155, 162-65; Dublin, *Transforming Women's Work*, 89.

13. Eisler, 16, 193; Clark, 178-79; Dalzell, 33.

14. Dublin, *Women at Work*, 40; Tucker, *Slater*, 255-56; Harriet H. Robinson, *Loom and Spindle* (1898), in Leon Stein and Annette Baxter, ed., *Women of Lowell* (New York: Arno Press, 1974), 194; Eisler, 61-63, 81-82.

15. On the influence of patriarchy, see Tucker, *Slater*, 25-26; Robinson, 61; Welter, 152, 170-71. Also see *Sins of Our Mothers*, http://www.pbs.org/wgbh/americanexperience/films/SinsofOurMothers.

16. Dublin, *Women at Work*, 77-79; Eisler, 19-24.

17. Eisler, 18-19. On the decline of New England agriculture, see Clark, 176; Ware, 14.

18. Dublin, *Women at Work*, 80; Eisler, 73-74.

19. Robinson, 64.

20. Dublin, *Women at Work*, 80; Robinson, 31; Lucy Larcom, "Among Lowell Mill Girls: A Reminiscence" (1881), in *Women of Lowell*, 602; Eisler, 75-77.

21. See the table of mill hours printed in Eisler, 30. Boardinghouse curfew is listed in "Regulations for the Boarding Houses of the Middlesex Company," in Figure 2 on page 8. For a very negative view of work hours and conditions, see A Citizen of Lowell, *Corporations and Operatives: Being an Exposition of the Condition [of the] Factory Operatives . . .* (1843), in *Women of Lowell*, 15-19, 21.

22. Larcom, 599-602; Eisler, 56-66.

23. "Factory Rules from the Handbook to Lowell, 1848," *Illinois Labor History Society,* accessed September 27, 2018, illinoislaborhistory.org/education/71-curriculum-resources/239-lowell-mills-lesson-7.htm.

24. Dublin, *Women at Work*, 66, 183, 185; Ware, 239.

12. The inferior position of women.

13. Limited opportunities for women in New England.

14. Women's desire for independence.

15. Early nineteenth-century rural attitudes toward women.

Example of a film citation.

16. Early Lowell paternalism.

17. Recruiting women workers.

18. Getting used to town life and the boarding house.

19. Firsthand account of mill-girl experience.

20. The nature of mill work and the workday.

21. Work hours and free time.

22. Lowell mill girls' favorable comments on mill work.

23. Role of the overseer.

Example of a web citation.

24. Rate of women's pay.

21

25. Ware, 240-42. For teachers' pay, see Eisler, 193.

25. Low alternative pay for women.

26. Elisha Bartlett, *A Vindication of the Character and Condition of the Females Employed in the Lowell Mills . . .* (1841), in *Women of Lowell,* 21; Dublin, 188.

26. Savings accounts.

27. Larcom, 599-600.

27. Free time.

28. Eisler, 49-50.

28. Leisure time and wardrobe.

29. Robinson, 91-93; Eisler, 113-32. For mill rules concerning reading, see Eisler, 31.

29. Reading and education.

30. Robinson, 97-102.

30. Women's writing.

31. Eisler, 33-40; Dublin, *Women at Work,* 123-24, 129-30; Robinson, 114-20; Bertha Monica Stearns, "Early Factory Magazines in New England: The *Lowell Offering* and Its Contemporaries," *Journal of Economic and Business History* (August 1930): 690-91, 698.

31. The Lowell Offering.

32. H. T., "Our Household," *The Lowell Offering* (April 1841), in *The Lowell Offering: A Repository of Original Articles on Various Subjects, Written by Factory Operatives,* ser. 2, vol. 1 (Lowell, MA: Powers and Bagley, 1841-1842), 364-65.

32. Offering quote demonstrates independent thinking.

33. Chad Montrie, " 'I Think Less of the Factory Than of My Native Dell': Labor, Nature, and the Lowell 'Mill Girls,' " *Environmental History* 9, no. 2 (April 2004): 275-95, www.search.proquest.com.exproxy.ithaca .edu:2048/docview/216124138/.

33. Significance of nature writing.

Online document.

34. C. N., "Journey to Lebanon Springs," *The Lowell Offering* (September 1842), in *The Lowell Offering: A Repository of Original Articles on Various Subjects, Written by Factory Operatives,* ser. 2, vol. 2 (Lowell, MA: Powers and Bagley, 1841-1842), 221.

34. Offering quote demonstrates opposition to factory life.

35. Larcom, 598, 609; Eisler, 63-65.

35. The early Lowell setting.

36. Dublin, *Women at Work,* 87-90.

36. Tensions of the 1830s; lowered wages.

37. Dublin, *Women at Work,* 89-91.

37. The 1834 "turn out."

38. Dublin, *Women at Work,* 91.

38. Strikers' petitions.

39. Dublin, *Women at Work,* 98-99.

39. The 1836 "turn out."

40. "Lowell," *New York Herald,* November 5, 1843.

40. Criticism of female labor.

22

41. Comparison to slavery.

41. "Infamous Slander," *Boston Emancipator and Weekly Chronicle*, December 11, 1844.

42. Another comparison to slavery.

42. "White and Black Slavery," *Cleveland Daily Herald,* October 11, 1845.

43. More quotes from petitions.

43. Dublin, *Women at Work*, 93 (emphasis added).

44. Firsthand account.

44. Robinson, 86.

45. Mutual support.

45. Dublin, *Women at Work*, 44, 82-83, 103; Licht, 58-61.

46. Reasons for resistance.

46. David Zonderman, *Aspirations and Anxieties: New England Workers and the Mechanized Factory System, 1815-1860* (New York: Oxford University Press, 1992), 33.

47. Declining working conditions.

47. Dublin, *Women at Work*, 108, 134; Robinson, 204, 208-9; Eisler, 215.

48. The workforce after 1845; Irish immigration.

48. Dublin, *Women at Work*, 140, 156, 197. On the decline of Lowell, see Dalzell, 69.

49. Profits for owners.

49. Dublin, *Women at Work*, 60-61, 70-73.

50. The status of women.

50. Dublin, *Women at Work*, 32; Welter, 151-74. For the contemporary debate about the impact of factory work on women, see these pamphlets: Bartlett, *A Vindication of the Character and Condition,*and A Citizen, *Corporations and Operatives.*

51. Lowell women activists and later movements.

51. Dublin, *Women at Work*, 127-29; Ware, 292.

23

Bibliography

Books

Bartlett, Elisha. *A Vindication of the Character and Condition of the Females Employed in the Lowell Mills*. . . . 1841. Reprinted in *Women of Lowell*. New York: Arno Press, 1974.

Citizen of Lowell, A. *Corporations and Operatives: Being an Exposition of the Condition [of the] Factory Operatives*. . . . 1843. Reprinted in *Women of Lowell*. New York: Arno Press, 1974.

Dalzell, Robert F. *Enterprising Elite: The Boston Associates and the World They Made*. Cambridge, MA: Harvard University Press, 1987.

Dublin, Thomas. *Transforming Women's Work: New England Lives in the Industrial Revolution*. Ithaca, NY: Cornell University Press, 1994.

————. *Women at Work: The Transformation of Work and Community in Lowell, Massachusetts, 1826-1860*. New York: Columbia University Press, 1979.

Eisler, Benita, ed. *The "Lowell Offering": Writings by New England Mill Women (1840-1845)*. Philadelphia: Lippincott, 1977.

Licht, Walter. *Industrializing America: The Nineteenth Century*. Baltimore: Johns Hopkins University Press, 1995.

Robinson, Harriet H. *Loom and Spindle; Or, Life among the Early Mill Girls*. 1898. Reprinted in *Women of Lowell*. New York: Arno Press, 1974.

Tucker, Barbara M. *Samuel Slater and the Origins of the American Textile Industry: 1790-1860*. Ithaca, NY: Cornell University Press, 1984.

Ware, Caroline F. *The Early New England Cotton Manufacture*. Boston: Houghton Mifflin, 1931.

Zonderman, David. *Aspirations and Anxieties: New England Workers and the Mechanized Factory System, 1815-1860*. New York: Oxford University Press, 1992.

Articles

Clark, Christopher. "The Household Economy: Market Exchange and the Rise of Capitalism in the Connecticut Valley, 1800-1860." *Journal of Social History* 13 (Winter 1979): 169-89.

Bibliography begins on a new page.

Citations are listed alphabetically under each heading.

Second and following lines of each citation are indented.

Multiple sources by the same author.

Newspaper articles are not included in bibliography.

24

Hood, Adrienne D. "The Gender Division of Labor in the Production of Textiles in Eighteenth-Century Rural Pennsylvania." *Journal of Social History* 27 (Spring 1994): 537-61. www.jstor.org.ezproxy .ithaca.edu:2048/stable/3788986.

Kulikoff, Allan. "The Transition to Capitalism in Rural America."*William and Mary Quarterly* 46 (1989): 120-44.

Larcom, Lucy. "Among Lowell Mill Girls: A Reminiscence." 1881. Reprinted in *Women of Lowell*. New York: Arno Press, 1974.

Mohanty, Gail Fowler. "Handloom Outwork and Outwork Weaving in Rural Rhode Island, 1810-1821." *American Studies* 30 (Fall 1989): 41-68.

Montrie, Chad. " 'I Think Less of the Factory Than of My Native Dell': Labor, Nature, and the Lowell 'Mill Girls.' " *Environmental History* 9, no. 2 (April 2004): 275-95. www.search.proquest.com.exproxy .ithaca.edu:2048/docview/216124138/.

Stearns, Bertha Monica. "Early Factory Magazines in New England: The *Lowell Offering* and Its Contemporaries." *Journal of Economic and Business History* (August 1930): 685-705.

Temin, Peter. "The Industrialization of New England, 1830-1880." In *Engines of Enterprise: An Economic History of New England,* edited by Peter Temin, 109-52. Cambridge, MA: Harvard University Press, 2000.

Tucker, Barbara M. "The Family and Industrial Discipline in Ante-Bellum New England." *Labor History* 21 (Winter 1979-80): 55-74.

Welter, Barbara. "The Cult of True Womanhood."*American Quarterly* 18 (1966): 151-74.

Documents

"Factory Rules from the Handbook to Lowell, 1848." *Illinois Labor History Society*. Accessed September 27, 2018. illinoislaborhistory .org/education/71-curriculum-resources/239-lowell-mills- lesson-7.htm.

The Lowell Offering: A Repository of Original Articles on Various Subjects, Written by Factory Operatives. Ser. 2. 2 vols. Lowell, MA: Powers and Bagley, 1841-1842.

25

Regulations for the Boarding Houses of the Middlesex Company.
      ca. 1850. American Textile History Museum, Lowell, MA.Sign.

Nonwritten Sources

Homer, Winslow. Image of a girl winding a shuttle bobbin. 1871.
      Lowell National Historical Park. http://library.uml.edu/clh/all/
      mgi04.htm.

"Map of Lowell, showing the location of mills and boarding houses."
      In *So Far from Home*, by Barry Denenberg, 164b. New York:
      Scholastic, 1997.

Sins of Our Mothers. Boston: http://www.pbs.org/wgbh/
      americanexperience/films/SinsofOurMothers.

CHAPTER

10

Documenting Your Paper: How to Cite Sources in *Chicago* Style

Documentation tells your reader where you found the material in your paper. Most undergraduate history professors require students to follow what is known as "*Chicago* style": documentation as described in *The Chicago Manual of Style*, 17th ed. (Chicago: University of Chicago Press, 2017), or Turabian's *A Manual for Writers of Research Papers, Theses, and Dissertations*, 9th ed. (Chicago: University of Chicago Press, 2018). *Chicago*-style documentation for history papers usually includes both **notes** (numbered footnotes or endnotes) and a **bibliography** that lists sources alphabetically.

The pages that follow include dozens of documentation models for a wide variety of sources, as well as detailed guidelines showing how to document some of the most common types of sources. For ease of reference, the model note and bibliography entries are displayed as paired examples in the "Documentation Models" (pages 189–213). An "**N**" in the margin signifies "note" examples, and a "**B**" indicates "bibliography entry" examples. A directory of models can be found on page 188.

FORMATTING FOOTNOTES AND ENDNOTES

The section "When to Use Footnotes and Endnotes" in Chapter 8 (pp. 152–54) explains the circumstances in which **citations** are required. If a note is necessary, place a raised (superscript) numeral at the end of the sentence that contains the information to be documented. Do not enclose the superscript note number in parentheses, and be sure to insert it *after* any punctuation except a dash.

According to Diamond, "Different rates of development on different continents, from 11,000 B.C. to A.D. 1500, were what led to the technological and political inequalities of A.D. 1500."[1]

---

1. Jared Diamond, *Guns, Germs, and Steel: The Fates of Human Societies* (New York: Norton, 1999), 16.

If you are documenting a general idea or opinion, place the number at the end of the paragraph or paragraphs in which you discuss it.

Footnotes are placed at the bottom of the page containing the text to which they refer (as is shown above). Endnotes are gathered together in numerical order in an "Endnotes" section, which is placed after the text of the paper. (See the "Endnotes" section of the sample student paper in Chapter 9, pp. 179–82.)

The example above shows the correct format for a note. The first line is indented five spaces or one-half inch; the other lines begin at the left margin. Both footnotes and endnotes are single-spaced, and an extra line of space separates individual notes. Notes should be numbered consecutively throughout your paper.

ORGANIZING A BIBLIOGRAPHY

A bibliography is an alphabetical listing of nearly all of the sources that appear in the notes in your paper. (Some sources, such as personal interviews, are cited in notes but are not included in bibliographies. See individual models for details.)

Entries in a bibliography that is long may be arranged by category, such as books, articles, documents, and nonwritten sources (maps, photographs, audio and video recordings, etc.). See "Sample Student Research Paper" in Chapter 9, pp. 183–85. Each section is alphabetized according to the *last* name of the author. If a work has more than one author, alphabetize according to the last name of the first author mentioned on the title page of the book or article. That name should be followed by the names of all of the other authors listed with their *first* names first. A work that has no author (or editor or translator) is alphabetized according to the first word of its title, excluding *A, An,* and *The.*

Begin each entry at the left margin, and indent any subsequent lines five spaces or one-half inch. Each entry in a bibliography is single-spaced, with an extra line of space between entries. You should notice that the parts of a note generally are separated by *commas,* but the parts of a bibliography entry usually are separated by *periods.* For further details, see the documentation models that follow.

Directory of Documentation Models for Notes and Bibliography Entries

DOCUMENTATION MODELS

Overview of Notes

1. FIRST REFERENCE TO A SOURCE

The first time you document any source in a note, include the author's full name, followed by a comma; the full title of the work; the publication information; and the page number or numbers that you cited (followed by a period).

N   1. Robert Darnton, *George Washington's False Teeth: An Unconventional Guide to the Eighteenth Century* (New York: Norton, 2003), 64.

2. SUBSEQUENT REFERENCE TO A SOURCE

If you cite the same work again in your paper, include only the author's last name and the page number in your note.

N   2. Darnton, 102.

When your sources include *more than one* work by the same author, any second or later reference to every work by that author must include a shortened form of the title so that the reader will know which work you are citing.

N   2. Darnton, *George Washington's False Teeth*, 68.

Overview of Bibliography Entries

3. TYPICAL BIBLIOGRAPHY ENTRY

Bibliography entries generally include the same information as notes, but the information is listed slightly differently. The author's last name is listed first, for the purposes of alphabetizing, and page numbers usually are not included. Also, periods (not commas) are used to separate information.

B   Darnton, Robert. *George Washington's False Teeth: An Unconventional Guide to the Eighteenth Century*. New York: Norton, 2003.

4. MULTIPLE WORKS BY THE SAME AUTHOR

If your bibliography includes more than one work by the same author, give the author's complete name in only the first entry. Replace it with three dashes in the second and any other entries. List the works in alphabetical order by title, ignoring *A*, *An*, and *The*. Be sure to check with your instructor before employing this method.

B   Darnton, Robert. *George Washington's False Teeth: An Unconventional Guide to the Eighteenth Century*. New York: Norton, 2003.

B   ———. *The Great Cat Massacre and Other Episodes in French Cultural History*. New York: Vintage Books, 1995.

Author Variations

The models below (items 5-16) indicate how to format the names of authors in your notes and bibliography. In general, author names are followed by a comma in notes, and by a period in bibliography entries. Only author names and editor names are shown here.

5. ONE AUTHOR

When a source has a single author, list the name in normal order in the note, and follow the name with a comma.

N   5. Jules Benjamin,

In the bibliography entry, list the author's name last name first, insert a comma between the last and first names, and end with a period.

B   Benjamin, Jules.

NOTE: If "Jr.," "Sr.," or a numeral appears after the author's last name, put it after the first name in the bibliography entry, preceded by a comma. In the note entry, "Jr.," "Sr.," or a numeral need not be preceded by a comma.

N   5. Harvey C. Mansfield Jr.,

B   Mansfield, Harvey C., Jr.

N   5. Joseph M. Marshall III,

B   Marshall, Joseph M., III.

6. TWO AUTHORS

When a source has two authors, both names, separated by "and," appear in the note and in the bibliography entry in the order in which they appear on the title page.

N   6. Pat Nyhan and Helen Epstein,

In the bibliography entry, invert the name of only the first author; put a comma after the first author's last name; and use a comma and "and" to separate the first author name from the second.

B   Nyhan, Pat, and Helen Epstein.

7. THREE AUTHORS

When a source has three authors, all three names, separated by commas, appear in the note and in the bibliography entry in the order in which they appear on the title page.

N   7. Ronald Inden, Jonathan Walters, and Daud Ali,

B   Inden, Ronald, Jonathan Walters, and Daud Ali.

8. FOUR OR MORE AUTHORS

When a source has more than three authors, only the name of the author listed first on the title page appears in the note, and the abbreviation "et al." (from the Latin, meaning "and others") follows that name.

N   8. Thomas G. Weiss et al.,

In the bibliography, all names are usually included.

B   Weiss, Thomas G., David P. Forsythe, Roger A. Coate, and Kelly-Kate Pease.

9. AUTHOR'S NAME IN TITLE

In some cases, such as autobiographies and edited collections, the name of the author is part of the title of the book. The note for such a book may begin with the book title.

N   9. *Personal Memoirs of Ulysses S. Grant*,

The bibliography entry should begin with the last name of the author.

B   Grant, Ulysses S. *Personal Memoirs of Ulysses S. Grant*.

10. ORGANIZATION AS AUTHOR

When documenting a source with organizational authorship, use the name of the corporation, government agency, or other organization as the author name.

N   10. League of Women Voters,

B   League of Women Voters.

11. UNKNOWN AUTHOR

If the author of a work is unknown or is listed as "Anonymous" on the title page, begin both the note and bibliography entry with the title of the work.

N   11. *Australia's Aborigines: A Dispute over Mistake Creek*,

B   *Australia's Aborigines: A Dispute over Mistake Creek*.

NOTE: In your bibliography, alphabetize anonymous works according to the title, ignoring *A*, *An*, and *The*. For example, *A Woman in Berlin* would be alphabetized under *W*.

Books

12. BASIC FORMAT FOR A BOOK

When citing a book, include the author's name; the complete book title (including subtitle after a colon), italicized; and publication information — place of publication (followed by a colon), publisher's name (followed by a comma), and date of publication.

In notes, commas separate the author name and book title, the publication information is enclosed in parentheses, and the page number or numbers you are citing are listed at the end.

N   12. Juliana Barr, *Peace Came in the Form of a Woman: Indians and Spaniards in the Texas Borderlands* (Chapel Hill: University of North Carolina Press, 2007), 112-16.

In bibliographies, the parts of the entry are separated by periods, publication information is not enclosed in parentheses, and page numbers usually are not listed.

B   Barr, Juliana. *Peace Came in the Form of a Woman: Indians and Spaniards in the Texas Borderlands*. Chapel Hill: University of North Carolina Press, 2007.

For a detailed illustration of a basic book citation, see page 193. For author variations, see items 5 through 11. For shortened forms for second and subsequent references to the same source, see item 2. For specific types of books and parts within books, see items 13 through 23.

13. ONLINE BOOK

To cite a printed book that has been digitized and stored online, list all the information as you would for a printed book, along with the title of the collection of online books in which you found it and the URL (or DOI if available).

N   13. George Rawlinson, *History of Phoenicia* (London: Longmans, Green and Co., 1889), 116, Project Gutenberg, http://www.gutenberg.org/etext/2331.

B   Rawlinson, George. *History of Phoenicia*. London: Longmans, Green and Co., 1889. Project Gutenberg. http://www.gutenberg.org/etext/2331.

NOTE: The access date is not required when citing electronic sources unless the publication or modification date cannot be determined. If your professor requests this information, it should appear before the URL or DOI.

14. E-BOOK

To cite an e-book, list all the information as you would for a printed book, along with the format for e-books downloaded from a library or bookseller and the chapter number or another locator.

N   14. Niall Ferguson, *The War of the World* (London: Penguin, 2007), chap. 8, Kindle edition.

B   Ferguson, Niall. *The War of the World*. London: Penguin, 2007. Kindle edition.

Guidelines for Citing Books

When citing a book, include the following information, found on the title page and copyright page:

1 Author
2 Title and subtitle
3 City of publication
4 Publisher

5 Date of publication
6 Page number or numbers (for notes but not bibliography entries)

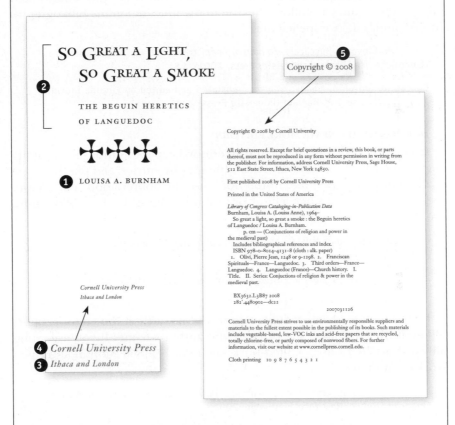

Here are a note and a bibliography entry for the book shown above:

N   1. Louisa A. Burnham, *So Great a Light, So Great a Smoke: The Beguin Heretics of Languedoc* (Ithaca, NY: Cornell University Press, 2008), 51-52.

B   Burnham, Louisa A. *So Great a Light, So Great a Smoke: The Beguin Heretics of Languedoc*. Ithaca, NY: Cornell University Press, 2008.

15. TRANSLATED BOOK

In the note, after the title of the work, put the name of the translator, preceded by the abbreviation "trans." In the bibliography, put the phrase "Translated by" before the translator's name.

N   15. Mohandas K. Gandhi, *An Autobiography: The Story of My Experiments with Truth*, rev. American ed., trans. Mahadev Desai (Boston: Beacon Press, 1993), 74.

B   Gandhi, Mohandas K. *An Autobiography: The Story of My Experiments with Truth*. Rev. American ed. Translated by Mahadev Desai. Boston: Beacon Press, 1993.

If the same person translated and edited the book, the abbreviated phrase "trans. and ed." follows the title in the note, but in the bibliography, "trans." and "ed." are spelled out.

N   15. Giovanni Boccaccio, *Famous Women*, trans. and ed. Virginia Brown (Cambridge, MA: Harvard University Press, 2001), 88.

B   Boccaccio, Giovanni. *Famous Women*. Translated and edited by Virginia Brown. Cambridge, MA: Harvard University Press, 2001.

16. BOOK WITH ONE OR MORE EDITORS

If a work has both an author and an editor, keep the author's name at the beginning of both the note and the bibliography entries, and put the name of the editor after the title. In the note, use the abbreviation "ed." before the name of either a single editor or multiple editors. In the bibliography, use the phrase "Edited by."

N   16. John Stuart Mill, *On Liberty*, ed. John Gray (Oxford: Oxford University Press, 2008), 62-63.

B   Mill, John Stuart. *On Liberty*. Edited by John Gray. Oxford: Oxford University Press, 2008.

If an edited work has a single editor and no author, the editor's name, followed by "ed.," takes the place of the author's name. If you are citing only one article from an edited work, see item 17, "Selection in an Edited Work or Anthology."

N   16. Nancy Shoemaker, ed., *Clearing a Path: Theorizing the Past in Native American Studies* (New York: Routledge, 2002), 51.

B   Shoemaker, Nancy, ed. *Clearing a Path: Theorizing the Past in Native American Studies*. New York: Routledge, 2002.

If a work has two or three editors and no author, use the format for two or three authors (see items 6 and 7), but follow the names with "eds."

N   16. Camron Michael Amin, Benjamin C. Fortna, and Elizabeth B. Frierson, eds., *The Modern Middle East: A Sourcebook for History* (Oxford: Oxford University Press, 2006), 326.

B   Amin, Camron Michael, Benjamin C. Fortna, and Elizabeth B. Frierson, eds. *The Modern Middle East: A Sourcebook for History*. Oxford: Oxford University Press, 2006.

If a work has four or more editors and no author, write the full name of only the first editor followed by "et al." to indicate the other editors, and conclude with "eds."

N   16. Esther Breitenbach et al., eds., *The Changing Politics of Gender Equality in Britain* (New York: Palgrave, 2002), 18-21.

B   Breitenbach, Esther, et al., eds. *The Changing Politics of Gender Equality in Britain.* New York: Palgrave, 2002.

17. SELECTION IN AN EDITED WORK OR ANTHOLOGY

If you are using only part of an edited work—for example, a chapter, an essay, one document—begin with the name of the author of that part, followed by the title of the selection, the title of the edited work (preceded by the word "in," which should be capitalized in bibliography entries), the name of the editor (preceded by "ed." in the note and by "edited by" in the bibliography), and publication information.

N   17. Paul R. Jones, "The Two Field System," in *Europe's First Farmers*, ed. T. Douglas Price (Chicago: University of Chicago Press, 2000), 26.

B   Jones, Paul R. "The Two Field System." In *Europe's First Farmers*, edited by T. Douglas Price, 26. Chicago: University of Chicago Press, 2000.

18. LETTER IN A PUBLISHED COLLECTION

For letters and other forms of communication in published collections, begin with the names of the sender and recipient. If available, include the place of writing and the date that the letter was written. Next, include the title of the collection, name of the editor or compiler, and the publication information. Include the page number or numbers in the note but not in the bibliography entry.

N   18. Nicola Sacco to Bartolomeo Vanzetti, Dedham Jail, June 18, 1925, in *The Letters of Sacco and Vanzetti*, ed. Marion Denman Frankfurter and Gardner Jackson (New York: Penguin, 1997), 27-28.

If your paper refers to only one letter in a collection, list it individually in your bibliography, alphabetized by the name of the letter writer.

B   Sacco, Nicola. Nicola Sacco to Bartolomeo Vanzetti, Dedham Jail, June 18, 1925. In *The Letters of Sacco and Vanzetti*, edited by Marion Denman Frankfurter and Gardner Jackson. New York: Penguin, 1997.

If your paper references more than one letter from a collection, the bibliography should include a single entry for the entire collection, beginning with the editor's name, rather than the names of the individual letter writers.

B   Frankfurter, Marion Denman, and Gardner Jackson, eds. *The Letters of Sacco and Vanzetti.* New York: Penguin, 1997.

19. EDITION OTHER THAN THE FIRST

If you are using an edition other than the first edition of a work, place the number of the edition after the title.

N   19. Jules R. Benjamin, *A Student's Guide to History*, 14th ed. (Boston: Bedford/St. Martin's, 2019), 189.

B   Benjamin, Jules R. *A Student's Guide to History*. 14th ed. Boston: Bedford/ St. Martin's, 2019.

If you are using a revised edition, use the abbreviation "rev. ed." in the note and "Rev. ed." in the bibliography.

N   19. Carlton Jackson, *Who Will Take Our Children? The British Evacuation Program of World War II*, rev. ed. (Jefferson, NC: McFarland, 2008), 127.

B   Jackson, Carlton. *Who Will Take Our Children? The British Evacuation Program of World War II*. Rev. ed. Jefferson, NC: McFarland, 2008.

20. MULTIVOLUME WORK

When a work consists of more than one volume and the volumes all have the same title and were published in the same year, the volume number, followed by a colon, goes directly before the page number or numbers in a note. Notice that "vol." is not used and no space separates the colon from the page numbers.

N   20. Michael O'Brien, *Conjectures of Order: Intellectual Life and the American South, 1810-1860* (Chapel Hill: University of North Carolina Press, 2004), 1:193-97.

In the bibliography, the volume number, preceded by "Vol.," follows the title.

B   O'Brien Michael. *Conjectures of Order: Intellectual Life and the American South, 1810-1860*. Vol. 1. Chapel Hill: University of North Carolina Press, 2004.

When each volume of a multivolume work has its own title, the title of the volume you used follows the author's name, and the number of that volume precedes the general title.

N   20. Robert A. Caro, *The Passage of Power*, vol. 4, *The Years of Lyndon Johnson* (New York: Knopf, 2012), 104.

B   Caro, Robert A. *The Passage of Power*. Vol. 4, *The Years of Lyndon Johnson*. New York: Knopf, 2012.

When your bibliographic citation is to all of the volumes of a work, be sure to indicate in the entry the total number of volumes.

B   Schama, Simon. *A History of Britain*. 2 vols. New York: Hyperion, 2000-2001.

21. ENCYCLOPEDIA OR DICTIONARY

Well-known encyclopedias and dictionaries are usually cited in the notes but not in the bibliography. The facts of publication may be omitted, but the edition number is needed unless you are citing the first edition.

Guidelines for Citing Letters in Published Collections

When citing a letter in a published collection, include the following information, found on the book's title page and copyright page as well as in the letter itself:

1 Author (sender) of the letter
2 Recipient of the letter, if given
3 Letter writer's location, if given
4 Date, if given
5 Title and subtitle of collection

6 Editor of collection
7 City of publication
8 Publisher
9 Date of publication
10 Page number or numbers (for notes but not bibliography entries)

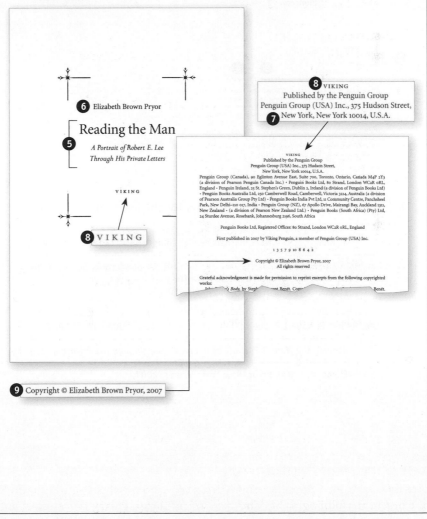

Citing Letters in Published Collections (continued)

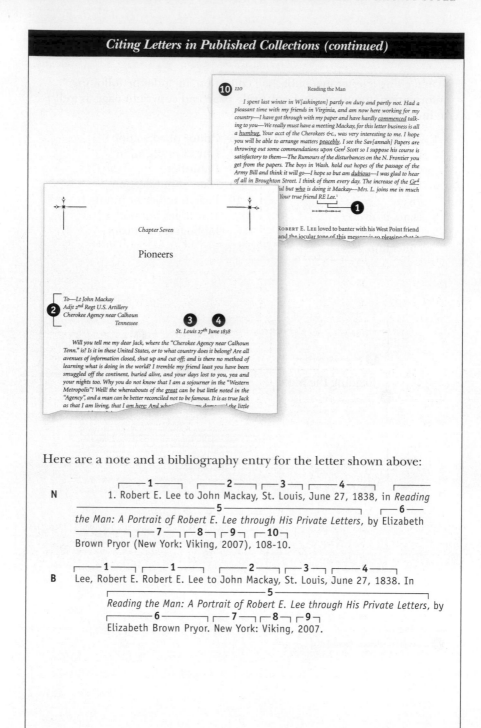

Here are a note and a bibliography entry for the letter shown above:

N   1. Robert E. Lee to John Mackay, St. Louis, June 27, 1838, in *Reading the Man: A Portrait of Robert E. Lee through His Private Letters*, by Elizabeth Brown Pryor (New York: Viking, 2007), 108-10.

B   Lee, Robert E. Robert E. Lee to John Mackay, St. Louis, June 27, 1838. In *Reading the Man: A Portrait of Robert E. Lee through His Private Letters*, by Elizabeth Brown Pryor. New York: Viking, 2007.

When a reference work is organized alphabetically, the title of the item being cited is followed by the date in parentheses and preceded by "s.v." (short for the Latin *sub verbo*, meaning "under the word"). Volume and page numbers are not needed.

N   21. *The Columbia Dictionary of Quotations* (1993), s.v. "Lincoln, Gettysburg Address."

If the author of an item in an encyclopedia is identified, list the author name at the end of your note, and include the work, alphabetized by the author's last name, in your bibliography.

N   21. *Handbook of American Women's History*, 2nd ed. (2000), s.v. "Willard, Frances E. (1839-1898)," by Anita M. Weber.

B   Weber, Anita M. "Willard, Frances E. (1839-1898)." In *Handbook of American Women's History*, 2nd ed., edited by Angela M. Howard and Frances K. Kavenik. Thousand Oaks, CA: Sage, 2000.

22. BOOK IN A SERIES

If a book you are citing is part of a series, the series title (not italicized) should be included after the book's title (and editor or editors, if applicable). Notice that the editor of the individual book is included, but not the editor of the entire series.

N   22. Sir Walter Ralegh, *The Discovery of Guiana: With Related Documents*, ed. Benjamin Schmidt, Bedford Series in History and Culture (Boston: Bedford/ St. Martin's, 2008), 27.

B   Ralegh, Sir Walter. *The Discovery of Guiana: With Related Documents*. Edited by Benjamin Schmidt. Bedford Series in History and Culture. New York: Bedford/ St. Martin's, 2008.

23. SACRED TEXT

When documenting sacred religious works such as the Bible or the Qur'an, give the chapter and verse numbers (or their equivalents), separated by a colon. For the Bible, begin with an abbreviation of the book name ("Matt.," "Gen.," etc.), and end with the version you are referencing ("Revised Standard Version," "New American Bible," etc.). Page numbers are not necessary.

N   23. Rom. 2:1-4 (Revised Standard Version).

N   23. Qur'an 17:90-93.

Sacred texts are usually not included in bibliographies.

Periodicals

24. BASIC FORMAT FOR A JOURNAL ARTICLE

In a note for a journal article, include the author's full name followed by a comma; the title of the article followed by a comma, all in quotation marks; the title of the journal, italicized or underlined; the volume number (and issue number, if given) of the journal; the date of publication in parentheses, followed by a colon; and the page or pages cited, followed by a period.

N   24. Joshua Weinstein, "The Market in Plato's *Republic*," *Classical Philology* 104
    (2009): 444.

Bibliography entries include nearly the same information but presented differently. The author's name appears last name first, periods (not commas) separate items, and inclusive page numbers for the article are listed.

B   Weinstein, Joshua. "The Market in Plato's *Republic*." *Classical Philology* 104 (2009):
         440-54.

For a detailed illustration of a print journal citation, see page 201. For author variations, see items 5 through 11 above. For shortened forms for subsequent references to the same source, see item 2 above.

25. JOURNAL ARTICLE ACCESSED FROM A DATABASE

Cite a journal article that you accessed from an electronic database as you would cite an article from a printed journal (see item 24). Then add the URL of the database (and the DOI for the article if the database provides one).

N   25. Robert Finlay, "Weaving the Rainbow: Visions of Color in World History,"
    Journal of World History 18, no. 4 (December 2007): 402-3, http://muse.jhu.edu/
    journals/journal_of_world_history/.

B   Finlay, Robert. "Weaving the Rainbow: Visions of Color in World History." *Journal
         of World History* 18, no. 4 (December 2007): 383-431. http://muse.jhu.edu/
         journals/journal_of_world_history/.

For a detailed illustration of a database article citation, see "Guidelines for Citing Articles in Electronic Databases." (See page 202).

26. ARTICLE IN AN ONLINE JOURNAL

Cite an article from an online journal as you would cite an article in a printed journal (see item 24); then also include the DOI if the article has one. If the journal was part of a database, include the title of the database, the creator of the database (if available), and the URL of the article. If you read the journal on the journal's own website, then use the URL of that site, as in the following example.

N   26. Scott Gac, "Jazz Strategy: Dizzy, Foreign Policy, and Government
    in 1956," *Journal of American Popular Culture* 4 (Spring 2005), http://www
    .americanpopularculture.com/journal/articles/spring_2005/gac.htm.

B   Gac, Scott. "Jazz Strategy: Dizzy, Foreign Policy, and Government in 1956." *Journal of
         American Popular Culture* 4 (Spring 2005). http://www.americanpopularculture
         .com/journal/articles/spring_2005/gac.htm.

27. ARTICLE IN A MAGAZINE

Reference to a popular magazine (rather than to a scholarly journal) requires author, title of article, title of magazine, date, but no volume or issue number. Include the cited page number or numbers in the note, preceded by a comma, but do not include any page numbers in the bibliography entry.

Guidelines for Citing Articles in Print Journals

When citing a journal article that you accessed in print, include the following information, found on the journal's title page as well as in the article:

1 Author
2 Title of article
3 Title of journal
4 Volume number

5 Issue number, if given
6 Date of publication
7 Page number or numbers

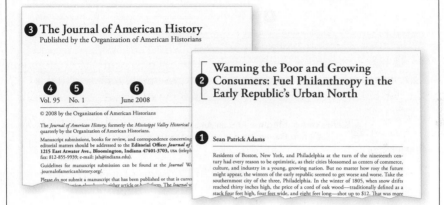

Here are a note and a bibliography entry for the article shown above:

N
     1. Sean Patrick Adams, "Warming the Poor and Growing Consumers: Fuel
Philanthropy in the Early Republic's Urban North," *Journal of American History*
95, no. 1 (June 2008): 73.

B
     Adams, Sean Patrick. "Warming the Poor and Growing Consumers: Fuel Philanthropy
in the Early Republic's Urban North." *Journal of American History* 95,
no. 1 (June 2008): 69-94.

Guidelines for Citing Articles in Electronic Databases

When citing a journal article that you accessed from an electronic database, include the following information:

1 Author
2 Title of article
3 Title of journal
4 Volume number
5 Issue number, if given

6 Date of publication
7 Page number or numbers (often visible in PDF file)
8 URL of database, or DOI* if available

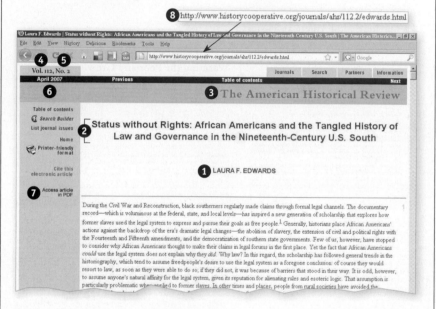

Here are a note and a bibliography entry for the article shown above:

N   1. Laura F. Edwards, "Status without Rights: African Americans and the Tangled History of Law and Governance in the Nineteenth-Century U.S. South," *American Historical Review* 112, no. 2 (April 2007): 373, http://www .historycooperative.org/journals/ahr/112.2/edwards.html.

B   Edwards, Laura F. "Status without Rights: African Americans and the Tangled History of Law and Governance in the Nineteenth-Century U.S. South." *American Historical Review* 112, no. 2 (April 2007): 365-93. http://www .historycooperative.org/journals/ahr/112.2/edwards.html.

* A digital object identifier (DOI) is a string of characters assigned to an electronic document, such as a journal article. Referring to an online document by its permanent DOI provides more stable linking than simply referring to it by its URL.

N   27. Greg Grandin, "Latin America's New Consensus," *Nation*, May 1, 2006, 24.

B   Grandin, Greg. "Latin America's New Consensus." *Nation*, May 1, 2006.

28. ARTICLE IN A NEWSPAPER

Individual articles from daily newspapers usually are not listed in a bibliography, but they are cited in notes. Reference to a newspaper article requires issue date (day, month, year), as well as author name (if available), article title, and newspaper name. If the newspaper has separate sections, add the number, letter, or name of the section in which the article begins. Use the abbreviation "sec." Page numbers can be omitted, as they may vary from one edition of a daily paper to the next.

N   28. Liz Goodwin, "Genealogy or Family Lore? A Search for Cherokee Roots," *Boston Globe*, February 23, 2018, sec. A.

29. ARTICLE FROM AN ONLINE NEWS SOURCE

Include author name (if given), article title, name of the online newspaper or service, date of publication, and URL.

N   29. Adam Nossiter, "Macron Aims to Keep Migrants, and Far Right, at Bay in France," *New York Times*, February 22, 2018, https://www.nytimes.com/2018/02/22/world/europe/france-immigration-law.html?rref=collection%2Fsectioncollection%2Fworld.

B   Nossiter, Adam. "Macron Aims to Keep Migrants, and Far Right, at Bay in France." *New York Times*, February 22, 2018. https://www.nytimes.com/2018/02/22/world/europe/france-immigration-law.html?rref=collection%2Fsectioncollection%2Fworld.

30. EDITORIAL

The editorial page of a newspaper generally has short articles written by a member of the paper's editorial board as well as by invited columnists. If the name of the writer accompanies the editorial, then cite the editorial as you would an article in a newspaper. If the editorial is unsigned, write the name of the newspaper in the position usually reserved for an author's name. Unsigned newspaper articles, such as editorials, are not included in the bibliography.

N   30. "Saving Detroit from Itself," *New York Times*, November 15, 2008, sec. A.

Editorials from magazines are listed in the bibliography. When you cite an editorial from a magazine, list the name of the editorial writer (if known), the title of the editorial, the name of the magazine, and the issue date.

B   Winfrey, Carey. "Standing Tall: Niger's Giraffes and Our 16th President." *Smithsonian* 39, no. 8 (November 2008): 8.

31. LETTER TO THE EDITOR

To cite a letter to the editor of a magazine or a journal, list the author's name, followed by the identifier "letter to the editor," then the publication information.

N   31. Andrew Morriss, letter to the editor, *Economist* 389, no. 8605 (2008): 20.

B   Morriss, Andrew. Letter to the editor. *Economist* 389, no. 8605 (2008): 20.

For notes citing letters to the editor of a newspaper, use the same identifier after the writer's name and then provide publication information. Such letters are not listed in the bibliography.

N   31. Anton Mikofsky, letter to the editor, *New York Times*, February 4, 2018, sec. B.

32. BOOK REVIEW OR FILM REVIEW

In a reference to a book review or a film review, include the author of the review, the title (if any) of the review followed by the phrase "review of," the title of the book or film being reviewed, the name of the author or director of the reviewed work, and the relevant publication information.

N   32. Harold Kinkaid, "Scientific Historiography and the Philosophy of Science," review of *Our Knowledge of the Past: A Philosophy of Historiography*, by Aviezer Tucker, *History and Theory* 45 (2006): 125.

B   Kinkaid, Harold. "Scientific Historiography and the Philosophy of Science." Review of *Our Knowledge of the Past: A Philosophy of Historiography*, by Aviezer Tucker. *History and Theory* 45 (2006): 124-33.

33. ONLINE REVIEW

For a review accessed online, include the URL (or DOI if available) and, if required by your instructor, the date you accessed the review if no publication or modification date is given.

N   33. Robert Eisen, review of *War and Peace in Jewish Tradition*, by Yigal Levin, Amnon Shapira, eds., H-Net Review, September, 2012, http://www.h-net.org/reviews/showrev.php?id=35754.

B   Eisen, Robert. Review of *War and Peace in Jewish Tradition*, by Yigal Levin, Amnon Shapira, eds. H-Net Review, September, 2012. http://www.h-net.org/reviews/showrev.php?id=35754.

Public Documents

For government publications, *Chicago* recommends following the citation guidelines found in *The Bluebook: A Uniform System of Citation*. Most federal documents are available in both print and electronic formats, and while it is preferred to use print editions, if you access a public document online, include the URL as the final element of your citation.

The following items are models for different kinds of government documents. They are intended not to be exhaustive but to give a sense of how to cite some types of public documents. Keep in mind that public documents are not typically cited in the bibliography.

34. U.S. LEGISLATIVE BRANCH COMMITTEE REPORT

Indicate whether the report is from the U.S. House of Representatives or the Senate; this is abbreviated "H.R. Rep." or "S. Rep." followed by the number of the Congress, connected to the report number with a hyphen. Any page or part information is included after the report number. Lastly, the year is included in parenthesis. If you do not mention the author or committee name in the text, it may be included in the citation (as shown below).

N   34. Select Comm. on Assassinations, Report of the Select Committee on Assassinations, H.R. Rep. No. 95-1828, pt. 2 (1979).

35. U.S. TREATY

Treaty citations should include the title of the treaty, abbreviated names of the signatories, article number, the date the treaty was signed, and the source of the treaty. Common treaty sources include the *United States Statutes at Large* (Stat.), *United States Treaties and Other International Agreements* (U.S.T.), and *Treaties and Other International Acts Series* (T.I.A.S.).

N   35. Mutual Defense Treaty between the United States and the Republic of Korea; U.S.-Kor., art. 4, October 1, 1953, U.S.T. 23602376.

36. U.S. SUPREME COURT DECISION

U.S. Supreme Court decisions are published in the *United States Supreme Court Reports* (abbreviated U.S.). Full court citations include the case name, followed by the volume number, abbreviated name of the publication, page number that indicates the beginning of the decision, and the date of the decision.

N   36. Brown v. Board of Education of Topeka, 347 U.S. 483 (1954).

37. CANADIAN LEGISLATIVE STATUTES

Canadian statutes can be found either in the *Revised Statutes of Canada* (R.S.C.) or in the *Statutes of Canada* (S.C.), depending on the year they were issued. In your citation, include the name of the act, the abbreviated name of the source, the publication date, chapter number, and section number (if applicable). You may also include "(Can.)" at the end of your citation to make it clear this is a Canadian legislative document.

N   37. Access to Information Act, R.S.C., 1985, c. A-1 (Can.)

38. ONLINE GOVERNMENT DOCUMENT

Follow the same citation guidelines for a print source, but include the URL at the end of the citation.

N   38. National Drug Policy: A Review of the Status of the Drug War, H.R. Rep. No. 108-815, at 6 (1996), http://frwebgate.access.gpo.gov/cgi-bin/getdoc .cgi?dbname=104_cong_reports&docid=f:hr486.104.pdf.

Multimedia Sources

39. MATERIAL FROM A WEBSITE

Much of the material you find online is a specific type of source (a government document, an article, a book) that you can cite by following the style for that particular item, then adding the access date (if no publication or modification is given) and the URL. When citing original material from a website, refer to the models below.

If the author is known, include his or her name, the title of the document, the title or owner of the website, the date of access (if no publication date or modification date is given), and the URL.

N   39. E. L. Skip Knox, "The Papacy," *Europe in the Late Middle Ages*, accessed October 1, 2016, http://www.boisestate.edu/courses/latemiddleages/papacy/.

B   Knox, E. L. Skip. "The Papacy." *Europe in the Late Middle Ages*. Accessed October 1, 2016. http://www.boisestate.edu/courses/latemiddleages/papacy/.

If you are citing a digital document whose authorship is unknown, begin with the owner of the site.

N   39. National Park Service, "Ancestral Puebloans and Their World," Mesa Verde National Park, accessed September 21, 2018. http://www.nps.gov/meve/forteachers/upload/ancestral_puebloans.pdf.

B   National Park Service. "Ancestral Puebloans and Their World." Accessed September 21, 2018. *Mesa Verde National Park*. http://www.nps.gov/meve/forteachers/upload/ancestral_puebloans.pdf.

For a detailed illustration of how to cite original material from a website, see page 208.

40. DVD OR VIDEOCASSETTE

The citation for a DVD or a videocassette includes the title of the film or episode, followed by the name of the series (if applicable), the type of medium, the name of the director, and the publication information.

N   40. "The Challenge of Freedom," *Slavery and the Making of America*, directed by Leslie D. Farrell (New York: Ambrose Video, 2005), DVD.

B   "The Challenge of Freedom." *Slavery and the Making of America*. Directed by Leslie D. Farrell. New York: Ambrose Video, 2005. DVD.

41. BROADCAST INTERVIEW

For a broadcast interview, include the name of the person interviewed, the title of the interview (if any), the name of the interviewer, the name of the show and network on which the interview appeared, and the date. If the broadcast was retrieved from an online archive or from some other source (such as a DVD or a museum archive), include that information as well.

N   41. Saddam Hussein, interviewed by Dan Rather, *CBS News*, CBS, February 24, 2003, http://www.cbsnews.com/htdocs/iraq/framesource_interview.html.

Broadcast interviews are not included in bibliographies. For information on citing a published transcript of an interview, see item 51. For personal interviews, see item 57.

42. RECORDED SPEECH OR READING

List the speaker, the title of the recording (italicized), the publication information, and the medium.

N   42. Martin Luther King Jr., *I Have a Dream* (London: Open Source Studios, 2005), MP3.

B   King, Martin Luther, Jr. *I Have a Dream*. London: Open Source Studios, 2005. MP3.

To cite an unrecorded lecture or public address, see item 56.

43. MUSICAL RECORDING

For a recorded musical composition, list the name of the composer, the title of the piece (italicized), the performer or performers, the recording company, the number of the recording, and the medium.

N   43. Bernard Rands, *Le Tambourin, Suites 1 and 2*, Philadelphia Orchestra, New World Records 80392, compact disc.

B   Rands, Bernard. *Le Tambourin, Suites 1 and 2*. Philadelphia Orchestra. New World Records 80392. Compact disc.

For information on citing a printed musical composition, see item 52.

44. CD-ROM

To cite a CD-ROM, list the title, the location and name of the production company, the date, and the medium.

N   44. *U.S. History: The American West* (San Jose: Fogware Publishing, 2001), CD-ROM.

B   *U.S. History: The American West*. San Jose: Fogware Publishing, 2001. CD-ROM.

45. WORK OF ART

If you found an illustration or a photograph in a printed work, begin with the name of the artist, followed by the title of the work of art, the title of the book or article in which you found it, and the publication information. Include the page number at the end of the note.

N   45. Alexis Preller, "Hieratic Women," in *A History of Art*, rev. ed., ed. Sir Lawrence Gowing (Ann Arbor, MI: Borders Press, 2002), 973.

B   Preller, Alexis. "Hieratic Women." In *A History of Art*. Rev. ed. Edited by Sir Lawrence Gowing. Ann Arbor, MI: Borders Press, 2002.

If the artist is unknown, begin with the title or description of the work.

Guidelines for Citing Information from Websites

When citing original material that you found on a websites, include as much of the following information as possible:

1   Author or sponsoring institution
2   Title of the document or selection
3   Title of the site
4   Access date
5   URL

Arctic Studies Center, Smithsonian Institution

Here are a note and a bibliography entry for the article shown above:

N   1. Smithsonian Institution, "Indigenous Whaling Traditions: Northern Whaling Traditions," *Alaska Native Collections: Sharing Knowledge*, accessed October 4, 2015, http://alaska.si.edu/tours.asp?page=1&tour_id=1.

B   Smithsonian Institution. "Indigenous Whaling Traditions: Northern Whaling Traditions." *Alaska Native Collections: Sharing Knowledge*, accessed October 4, 2015, http://alaska.si.edu/tours.asp?page=1&tour_id=1.

N   45. "A Chavin Hammered Gold Plaque," in *A History of Art*, rev. ed., ed. Sir
Lawrence Gowing (Ann Arbor, MI: Borders Press, 2002), 479.

B   "A Chavin Hammered Gold Plaque." In *A History of Art*. Rev. ed. Edited by Sir
        Lawrence Gowing. Ann Arbor, MI: Borders Press, 2002.

If you saw the photograph, painting, or sculpture in a museum, an
archive, or a private collection, tell the reader where you saw it. Include the
name of the artist, the title of the work, the type of medium, the date the
work was created, and where it can be found.

N   45. Ansel Adams, *The Golden Gate before the Bridge, San Francisco, California*,
1980, gelatin silver print, National Gallery of Art, Washington, DC.

B   Adams, Ansel. *The Golden Gate before the Bridge, San Francisco, California*. 1980.
        Gelatin silver print. National Gallery of Art, Washington, DC.

If you cite an image found online, include all the information that you
would for an image found in a print book, but also add the URL.

N   "Mummy Case Lid." Egypt: 1085-730 B.C. Wood wrapped in linen and then
painted. Museum of the University of Pennsylvania, http://www.penn.museum/
collections/object/316885.

B   "Mummy Case Lid." Egypt: 1085-730 B.C. Wood wrapped in linen and then painted.
        Museum of the University of Pennsylvania. http://www.penn.museum/
        collections/object/316885.

46. SLIDE

A citation for slides should include the compiler of the collection, the
title of the collection, the name of the editor (if any), the publication information, and the identifier "slides."

N   46. Elizabeth Hammer, *The Arts of Korea: A Resource for Educators*, ed. Judith
G. Smith (New York: Metropolitan Museum of Art, 2002), slides.

B   Hammer, Elizabeth. *The Arts of Korea: A Resource for Educators*. Edited by Judith
        G. Smith. New York: Metropolitan Museum of Art, 2002. Slides.

47. MAP OR ILLUSTRATION

Treat a map or an illustration that you found in a printed work as you
would treat any other printed visual. Include the name of the map designer
or illustrator (if one is recorded), the title of the map or illustration followed by "in," then the title of the work in which the visual was found,
the author or editor of the work, and the usual publication information.
Include the page number at the end of the note.

N   47. "Francophone France in 1863," in *The Discovery of France: A Historical
Geography from the Revolution to the First World War*, by Graham Robb (New York:
Norton, 2007), 54.

B   "Francophone France in 1863." In *The Discovery of France: A Historical Geography from
        the Revolution to the First World War*, by Graham Robb. New York: Norton, 2007.

48. CHART, GRAPH, OR TABLE

If a chart is in a printed work, treat it as you would a map or an illustration. Include the title of the chart, graph, or table, usually found beneath it, and the publication information for the work in which it appeared. Include the page number at the end of the note.

N   48. "Reich Elections, 1919-1933," in *The Weimar Republic*, 2nd ed., by Eberhard Kolb (New York: Routledge, 2005), 224-25.

B   "Reich Elections, 1919-1933." In *The Weimar Republic*, 2nd ed., by Eberhard Kolb. New York: Routledge, 2005.

Other Published Sources

49. PAMPHLET

Cite a pamphlet as you would a book.

N   49. United Nations, *Report of the United Nations High Commissioner for Refugees* (New York: United Nations Press, 2008), 25.

B   United Nations. *Report of the United Nations High Commissioner for Refugees*. New York: United Nations Press, 2008.

50. DISSERTATION ABSTRACT

To cite a dissertation abstract, list the work as you would list a dissertation (see item 54), but indicate where you found the abstract, including volume number and date (if applicable) before the page number.

N   50. David Charles Engerman, "America, Russia and the Romance of Economic Development" (PhD diss., University of California, Berkeley, 1999), abstract in *America since 1607* 678 (1999): 308t.

B   Engerman, David Charles. "America, Russia and the Romance of Economic Development." PhD diss., University of California, Berkeley, 1999. Abstract in *America since 1607* 678 (1999): 308t.

If you accessed the abstract in an electronic database, include the name of the database and the URL.

N   50. William Kessler Jackson, "A Subcontinent's Sunni Schism: The Deobandi-Barelvi Rivalry and the Creation of Modern South Asia" (PhD diss., Syracuse University, 2013), abstract in *Syracuse University Research Facility and Collaborative Environment*, http://surface.syr.edu/hst_etd/102.

B   Jackson, William Kessler. "A Subcontinent's Sunni Schism: The Deobandi-Barelvi Rivalry and the Creation of Modern South Asia." PhD diss., Syracuse University, 2013. Abstract in *Syracuse University Research Facility and Collaborative Environment*. http://surface.syr.edu/hst_etd/102.

51. PUBLISHED INTERVIEW OR TRANSCRIPT

If an interview has been published, cite it by listing the person interviewed, the title of the interview, the name of the interviewer, the name of the publication, the date, and the page number.

N   51. Herman J. Viola, "Viola Records the View of the American Indian," interview by Stephen Goode, *Insight on the News*, January 3, 2000, 37.

B   Viola, Herman J. "Viola Records the View of the American Indian." Interview by Stephen Goode. *Insight on the News*, January 3, 2000.

For personal interviews that you conducted yourself, see item 57. For broadcast interviews, see item 41.

52. MUSICAL COMPOSITION

To cite a printed musical score, list the composer, the title of the piece, the editor or arranger (if applicable), and the publication information. If the score is part of a series, list the volume number and title of the series after the title of the score.

N   52. Luciano Berio, *Alternatim: per clarinetto, viola e orchestra* (Vienna: Universal Edition, 2001).

B   Berio, Luciano. *Alternatim: per clarinetto, viola e orchestra*. Vienna: Universal Edition, 2001.

If you are citing a musical recording rather than a score, see item 43.

53. SOURCE QUOTED IN ANOTHER SOURCE

You should try to track down every original source you wish to cite, but you may not always be able to do so. When citing a source (such as a long quotation) that you discovered in another person's work, begin with the information about the original source, and then provide details of the secondary source where you found it.

N   53. *Baltimore Herald*, July 3, 1903, quoted in Edmund Morris, *Theodore Rex* (New York: Random House, 2002), 257.

B   *Baltimore Herald*, July 3, 1903. Quoted in Edmund Morris, *Theodore Rex*. New York: Random House, 2002.

Unpublished Sources

54. UNPUBLISHED THESIS OR DISSERTATION

After the name of the author, give the title of the dissertation in quotation marks. For a note, indicate within parentheses the type of thesis ("master's thesis," "PhD diss.," etc.), the university at which the paper was written, and the date, all separated by commas, and provide the page number or numbers outside the parentheses.

N   54. Daniel R. Magaziner, "From Students to Prophets: Writing a Political Faith in South Africa, 1968-1977" (PhD diss., University of Wisconsin-Madison, 2007), 143-48.

B   Magaziner, Daniel R. "From Students to Prophets: Writing a Political Faith in South Africa, 1968-1977." PhD diss., University of Wisconsin-Madison, 2007.

55. UNPUBLISHED LETTER IN A MANUSCRIPT COLLECTION

As with published letters (see item 18), begin with names of the sender and recipient, followed by the place of writing and the date the letter was written (if available). Also include identifying information about the manuscript collection, such as the name and location of the collection and the number of the file, box, or container where the letter reposes.

N   55. John Potts to Robert E. Hobard, December 5, 1805, Alexandria, Virginia, letter box 1, folder 1, John Potts Business Papers, Hagley Museum and Library, Greenville, DE.

If your paper refers to only one letter in a collection, list it individually in your bibliography, alphabetized by the name of the letter writer.

B   Potts, John. John Potts to Robert E. Hobard. December 5, 1805. John Potts Business Papers. Hagley Museum and Library, Greenville, DE.

If your paper references more than one letter from a collection, your bibliography should list the entire collection rather than the individual letters.

B   Potts, John. Business Papers. Hagley Museum and Library, Greenville, DE.

56. UNPUBLISHED LECTURE, PAPER, OR PUBLIC ADDRESS

To cite a lecture, paper, or public address that has not been published, list the name of the speaker and the title of the presentation. Then, in parentheses, identify the type of program, the sponsoring organization, the location, and the date.

N   56. Eva Bremner, "From Heldenkaiser to Hausvater: Wilhelm I as the King of Christmas" (paper presented at Young Scholars Forum, "Gender, Power, Religion: Forces in Cultural History," at the German Historical Institute, Washington, DC, March 31, 2001).

B   Bremner, Eva. "From Heldenkaiser to Hausvater: Wilhelm I as the King of Christmas." Paper presented at Young Scholars Forum, "Gender, Power, Religion: Forces in Cultural History," at the German Historical Institute, Washington, DC, March 31, 2001.

For a recorded speech or reading, see item 42. For a published lecture, follow the format for the source in which it was published (book, journal article, etc.).

57. PERSONAL INTERVIEW

To cite an interview that you conducted yourself, start with the name of the person you interviewed. Then describe the nature of the interview ("telephone interview by author"; "in-person interview by author"), the place of the interview (if applicable), and the interview date. Do not list personal interviews in your bibliography.

N   57. Sandra Thurlow, telephone interview by author, April 6, 2018.

For broadcast interviews, see item 41. For published transcripts of interviews, see item 51.

58. PERSONAL EMAIL MESSAGE OR LETTER

Be sure to obtain permission to use the content of an email message or a letter from the person who wrote it. In the citation, begin with the author's name, the type of message ("email message to author"; "letter to author"), and the date on which it was sent. Do not include the author's email address in your citation. Do not list personal letters or email messages in your bibliography.

N   58. Heidi Hood, email message to author, March 26, 2018.

59. WEB FORUM OR DISCUSSION

Give the author's name or screen name, the thread title if there is one, or the content of the post (up to 160 characters), the name of the forum or discussion, the date when it was posted, and the URL. Do not include online forum or discussion in your bibliography.

N   National Park Service (@NatlParkService), "The public comment period for the peak seasons entrance fee proposal will be open from 10/24/17 to 11/12/17 here," Twitter, October 26, 2017, https://twitter.com/NatlParkService/status/922890060860678144.

APPENDIX

A

Resources
for History Research

The resources in Appendix A will assist you in choosing a **topic**, narrowing a topic, and conducting research on a topic. Different kinds of resources lead you to different kinds of information. Some are most useful at the beginning of your research when you are choosing or refining the topic. Others are necessary later, when you are gathering the information that will support your **thesis**. **Historical dictionaries**, **historical encyclopedias**, and **historical atlases**, for example, will be especially useful in the early stages of your research. More specialized resources should be consulted once you have chosen your topic and become familiar with the basic information about it.

The categories of resources described in this appendix are as follows:

- Comprehensive reference databases (p. 215)
- Historical dictionaries, encyclopedias, and atlases (p. 215)
- Biography collections and databases (p. 220)
- Newspaper indexes and databases (p. 222)
- Periodical indexes and databases (p. 224)
- Public documents (p. 226)
- Historical statistics (p. 228)
- General resources in world history (p. 231)
- Specialized resources in world history (p. 234)
- General resources in United States history (p. 254)
- Specialized resources in United States history (p. 257)

Each category begins with a brief description of the kinds of information the listed resources contain and at what stage of your research they are likely to be most helpful. Within each category, individual items are listed alphabetically by title. In most cases, the title is followed by the name of the person or organization that compiled the resource and then by the publication or database information or the URL.

Many valuable research resources are in print form, and more are published each year. But the tremendous growth of online resources has, over the years, shifted the emphasis of this appendix. With each edition, there has been an increase in the number of databases and websites listed. As pointed out in Chapter 7, websites vary greatly in quality, and care must be taken when using them. The websites chosen for this appendix are reliable sources of high-quality research material. The databases are also of high quality. To be available to you, however, your school library must subscribe to them. If you do not have access to a particular database, use an equivalent one.

Resources on CD-ROM or **microfiche**, though now less common, should be included in your library's **online catalog**. As always, the reference librarian is the best guide to your library's information resources.

COMPREHENSIVE REFERENCE
DATABASES

The following databases cover the broad spectrum of historical research. Each contains a number of more specific databases as well; indeed, you will see references to these sub-databases throughout this bibliography. These comprehensive reference databases are a good place to start searching for a topic, and they will also be useful as you refine your project. Check with your library to see if you have access.

History Reference Center. EBSCO Publishing.

History Studies Center. Chadwyck-Healey.

Oxford Reference Online. Oxford University Press.

ProQuest Research Library. ProQuest.

Sage Reference Collection. Sage.

Gale Virtual Reference Library. Gale/Cengage.

HISTORICAL DICTIONARIES,
ENCYCLOPEDIAS, AND ATLASES

The resources included here will be most useful when you are choosing and refining a topic. Once you have begun research on a particular topic, they also may be helpful by explaining any unusual terms you may encounter.

A *historical dictionary* (in print, in a database, or online) will help you define a term such as "Austro-Hungarian Empire." The brief description of this term will tell you when the empire existed, what lands it encompassed, the names of its rulers, and several of its major characteristics. This information will let you know if the term falls within the subject area of your course, and if it seems of interest to you as a possible topic. At later stages of your research, you can use a historical dictionary to obtain a brief description of a term you came across in your reading.

In most cases a *historical encyclopedia* treats a term in greater depth than a historical dictionary. It might describe how the Austro-Hungarian Empire was formed, the forces that enabled it to expand, its alliances and conflicts with neighboring states and empires, the tensions among the different peoples who were part of the empire, and the forces that worked to break up the empire. An encyclopedia article can be of assistance in choosing a topic and in determining which aspects of the topic you wish to pursue.

A *historical atlas* contains a series of maps showing geographical changes over time or lays out in spatial form the location of different kinds of information. In the case of the Austro-Hungarian Empire, a historical atlas would likely picture the territories of the empire, when they were acquired, and what groups of people lived in those territories. A good historical atlas would include information about those peoples—for example, the population size of each group, the percentage of Catholics and Protestants in different parts of the empire, and the languages they spoke. Some interactive websites and databases have base maps on which you can overlay different kinds of data and thereby make your own contrasts and comparisons.

It is important to remember that historical dictionaries, encyclopedias, and atlases are most valuable at the beginning stages of research. They do not contain extended examinations or interpretations of historical subjects. You should not depend on them for the substance of your paper. For more highly specialized reference works, see "Specialized Resources in World History" (p. 234) and "Specialized Resources in U.S. History" (p. 257) later in this appendix.

NOTE: If your topic concerns recent history, or if important new facts and interpretations have arisen in recent years, be sure to use the latest edition of any historical dictionary, encyclopedia, or atlas that covers your topic.

Historical Dictionaries—World

The Blackwell Dictionary of Modern Social Thought. 2nd ed. Ed. William Outhwaite. Malden, MA: Blackwell, 2006.

The Cambridge Historical Dictionary of Disease. Ed. Kenneth F. Kiple. New York: Cambridge University Press, 2003.

Dictionary of Race and Ethnic Relations. 4th ed. By Ellis Cashmore. London: Routledge, 1996.

Historical Dictionary of Judaism. 3rd ed. Ed. Norman Solomon. Lanham, MD: Rowman & Littlefield Publishers, 2015.

New Dictionary of the History of Ideas. Ed. Maryanne Cline Horowitz. 6 vols. New York: Scribner, 2004.

The New Grove Dictionary of Music and Musicians. 2nd ed. Ed. Stanley Sadie and John Tyrrell. 29 vols. New York: Macmillan, 2003. Also see the online database *Grove Music Online* at **oxfordmusiconline.com/public/book/omo_gmo**.

The New Penguin Dictionary of Modern History, 1789–1945. 2nd ed. Ed. Duncan Townson. Baltimore: Penguin Books, 2001.

The Oxford Dictionary of Philosophy. 3rd rev. ed. Comp. Simon Blackburn. Oxford: Oxford University Press, 2016.

The Oxford English Dictionary. 2nd ed. 20 vols. Oxford: Clarendon Press, 1989. This is the most complete English-language dictionary. If you are tracing the historical development of the meaning of a word, it is an essential reference.

If, however, you wish to determine the contemporary spelling or definition of a term, other general dictionaries are better sources. If the term is colloquial or is a recent derivation, be sure to use the most recent edition. The *Oxford English Dictionary* is now on some databases and online by subscription.
Historical dictionaries for other regions or nations are listed separately, on pages 257–76.

Historical Dictionaries — United States

American Economic History: A Dictionary and Chronology. James Olson and Abraham O. Mendoza. Westport, CT: Greenwood Press, 2015.

Dictionary of American History. 3rd ed. Ed. Stanley I. Kutler. 10 vols. New York: Thomson Learning, 2003.

Historical Dictionaries of Diplomacy and Foreign Relations. Series Ed. Jon Woronoff. Lanham, MD: Scarecrow Press, 2005–2012.

The Penguin Dictionary of Contemporary American History, 1945 to the Present. Ed. Stanley Hochman and Eleanor Hochman. New York: Penguin Books, 1997.
Historical dictionaries for specific topics in U.S. history are listed separately, on pages 257–76.

Historical Encyclopedias — World

Bioethics. 4th ed. Ed. Bruce Jennings. 6 vols. New York: Macmillan, 2014.

Colonialism: An International Social, Cultural and Political Encyclopedia. Ed. Melvin E. Page. 3 vols. Santa Barbara, CA: ABC-CLIO, 2003.

Companion Encyclopedia of the History of Medicine. Ed. W. F. Bynum and Roy Porter. New York: Routledge, 1997.

Encyclopaedia Britannica. 15th ed. 32 vols. Chicago: Encyclopaedia Britannica Educational Corp., 2003. This is one of the best encyclopedias. It is also available online at **britannica.com**, but only by subscription.

Encyclopedia Judaica. 2nd ed. Ed. Fred Skolnik and Michael Berenbaum. 22 vols. Detroit: Macmillan Reference in association with the Keter Publishing House, 2007.

Encyclopedia of the Age of the Industrial Revolution, 1700–1920. Ed. Christine Rider. 2 vols. Westport, CT: Greenwood Press, 2007.

Encyclopedia of Children and Childhood: In History and Society. Ed. Paula S. Fass. New York: Macmillan Reference USA, 2003.

Encyclopedia of Early Cinema. Ed. Richard Abel. New York: Routledge, 2005.

Encyclopedia of the History of Science, Technology, and Medicine in Non-Western Cultures. 3rd ed. Ed. Helaine Selin. 2 vols. Berlin: Springer, 2016.

Encyclopedia of the Middle Passage: Great Milestones in African American History. Ed. Toyin Falola and Amanda Warnock. Westport, CT: Greenwood Press, 2007.

Encyclopedia of Nationalism. Ed. Alexander Motyl. 2 vols. New York: Academic Press, 2000.

Encyclopedia of Race and Ethnic Studies. Ed. Ellis Cashmore. London: Routledge, 2004.

Encyclopedia of Religion. Ed. Mircea Eliade. 16 vols. New York: Macmillan, 1993.

Encyclopedia of Religion. 2nd ed. Ed. Lindsay Jones. 15 vols. Detroit: Macmillan Reference USA, 2005.

Encyclopedia of the Scientific Revolution: From Copernicus to Newton. Ed. Wilbur Applebaum. London: Routledge, 2008.

Encyclopedia of Social History. Ed. Peter N. Stearns. New York: Garland, 1994.

Encyclopedia of World Environmental History. Ed. Shepard Krech, John R. McNeill, and Carolyn Merchant. 3 vols. New York: Routledge, 2004.

Film Encyclopedia. 7th ed. Ed. Ephraim Katz and Ronald D. Nolen. New York: Collins Reference, 2012.

Greenwood Encyclopedia of Global Medieval Life and Culture. Ed. Joyce Salisbury. 3 vols. Westport, CT: Greenwood Press, 2008.

The Harper Encyclopedia of Military History: From 3500 B.C. to the Present. Ed. Ernest R. Dupuy and Trevor N. Dupuy. New York: Harper & Row, 1993.

Historical Encyclopedia of Natural and Mathematical Sciences. Ed. Ari Ben-Menahem. 5 vols. Berlin: Springer, 2009.

The Historical Encyclopedia of World Slavery. Ed. Junius P. Rodriguez. 2 vols. Santa Barbara, CA: ABC-CLIO, 1997.

New Catholic Encyclopedia. 2nd ed. 15 vols. Detroit: Gale, 2003.

New Encyclopedia of Islam. 5th ed. Ed. Cyril Glasse. Walnut Creek, CA: Alta Mira Press, 2014.

The Oxford Companion to the History of Modern Science. Ed. J. L. Heilbron. Oxford: Oxford University Press, 2003.

Oxford Encyclopedia of the Modern World: 1750 to the Present. Ed. Peter N. Stearns. Oxford: Oxford University Press, 2008.

The Shorter Routledge Encyclopedia of Philosophy. Ed. Edward Craig. New York: Routledge, 2005.

Women's Studies Encyclopedia: History, Philosophy, and Religion. Ed. Helen Tierney. 3 vols. Westport, CT: Greenwood Press, 1999.

Specialized encyclopedias for specific regions or nations are listed separately, on pages 234–54.

Historical Encyclopedias — Europe

Ancient Europe, 8000 B.C. to A.D. 1000: An Encyclopedia of the Barbarian World. Ed. Peter Bogucki and Pam Crabtree. New York: Thomson Gale, 2004.

Encyclopedia of Barbarian Europe: Society in Transformation. By Michael Frassetto. Santa Barbara, CA: ABC-CLIO, 2003.

Encyclopedia of the Enlightenment [eighteenth-century French intellectual history]. Ed. Alan C. Kors. 4 vols. Oxford: Oxford University Press, 2003.

Encyclopedia of European Social History [1350–2000]. Ed. Peter N. Stearns. 6 vols. New York: Scribner, 2001. E-book version, Gale, 2005.

The Holocaust: An Encyclopedia and Document Collection. Eds. Paul R. Bartrop and Michael Dickerman. 4 vols. Santa Barbara, CA: ABC-CLIO, 2017.

Encyclopedia of the Renaissance. Ed. Paul F. Grendler. 6 vols. New York: Scribner, 1999.

Encyclopedia of the Renaissance and the Reformation. Rev. ed. Eds. Jennifer Speake and Thomas Goddard Bergin. New York: Facts on File, 2004.

Encyclopedia of Western Colonialism since 1450. Ed. Thomas Benjamin. Farmington Hills, MI: Macmillan Reference USA, 2007.

Europe 1450–1789: Encyclopedia of the Early Modern World. Ed. Jonathan Dewald. 6 vols. New York: Scribner, 2003.

Europe 1789–1914: Encyclopedia of the Age of Industry and Empire. 5 vols. New York: Scribner, 2006.

Europe since 1945: An Encyclopedia. Ed. Bernard A. Cook. 2 vols. New York: Garland, 2001.

The Oxford Encyclopedia of Martin Luther. Eds. Derek R. Nelson and Paul R. Hinlicky. 3 vols. New York: Oxford University Press, 2017.

Specialized encyclopedias for other specific eras or nations are listed separately, on pages 234–54.

Historical Encyclopedias — United States

The Encyclopedia of American Business History. Ed. Charles Geisst. 2 vols. New York: Facts on File, 2005.

Encyclopedia of American Foreign Policy. Ed. Glenn Hastedt. New York: Facts on File, 2004.

Encyclopedia of American History. Rev. ed. Ed. Gary B. Nash. 11 vols. New York: Facts on File, 2010.

The Encyclopedia of American Political History. Ed. Paul Finkelman and Peter Wallenstein. Washington, DC: CQ Press, 2001.

Encyclopedia of American Social History. Ed. Mary K. Cayton, Elliott J. Gorn, and Peter W. Williams. 3 vols. New York: Scribner, 1993.

Encyclopedia of the United States in the Nineteenth Century. Ed. Paul Finkelman. 3 vols. New York: Scribner, 2001.

Encyclopedia of the United States in the Twentieth Century. Ed. Stanley Kutler. 4 vols. New York: Scribner, 1996.

Encyclopedia of Urban America. Ed. Neil L. Shumsky. 2 vols. Santa Barbara, CA: ABC-CLIO, 1998.

Melton's Encyclopedia of American Religions. 8th ed. Ed. J. Gordon Melton. Detroit: Gale, 2009.

The Oxford Encyclopedia of American Military and Diplomatic History. Eds. Timothy J. Lynch. New York: Oxford University Press, 2013.

Women in American History: A Social, Political, and Cultural Document Collection. Eds. Peg A. Lamphier and Rosanne Welch. 3 vols. Santa Barbara, CA: ABC-CLIO: 2017.

Specialized U.S. encyclopedias for specific topics are listed separately, on pages 257–76.

Historical Atlases—World

David Rumsey Map Collection. **davidrumsey.com**. Emphasis is on North and South America in the eighteenth and nineteenth centuries. Hosted by Cartography Associates. Advanced graphics for side-by-side and overlay viewing.

Historical Atlas of the Islamic World. By David Nicolle. London: Mercury Books, 2004.

Historical Map Works Library Edition. ProQuest. Collection of over 1 million digital maps.

Oxford Atlas of the World. 24th ed. New York: Oxford University Press, 2017.

The Penguin Historical Atlas of Ancient Civilizations. Ed. John Haywood. London: Penguin Books, 2005.

The Perry-Castañeda Library Map Collection. University of Texas. **lib.utexas.edu /maps/**. An extensive collection of historical maps covering many areas of the world. Contains a large list of links to other historical map sites.

The Routledge Atlas of Jewish History. 8th ed. Ed. Martin Gilbert. London: Routledge, 2010.

Historical Atlases—United States

Map Collections of the Library of Congress, 1500–2003. Library of Congress, American Memory. **memory.loc.gov/ammem/gmdhtml/gmdhome.html**. A very large collection from many eras and areas. Strong search capabilities.

Mapping America's Past. By Mark C. Carnes and John A. Garraty with Patrick Williams. New York: Henry Holt, 1996. Emphasis on social and cultural maps.

Omni Gazetteer of the United States of America. Ed. Frank R. Abate. 11 vols. Detroit: Omnigraphics, 1991. A gazetteer is a list of place-names, including insignificant ones. This volume organizes places by region and state.

Osher Map Library. Smith Center for Cartographic Education, University of Southern Maine. **usm.maine.edu/maps/web_exhibit.html**. Over 600 maps and related documents, essays, and annotated bibliographies.

BIOGRAPHY COLLECTIONS AND DATABASES

The resources in this section will provide background information about a particular individual whose name you have come across in your research. An article in a biography collection will give you a brief (or in some cases a fairly comprehensive) description of an individual's life and will usually end with a list of sources to consult for further information. Each biography collection has its own criteria for determining which individuals to include. Take care to select the collection most likely to include the individuals on whom you are seeking information. Biography databases can contain an enormous amount of information. In many instances, they include the content of older print databases. You should be aware that a biography may have been written decades or even centuries ago. Take note of the sources that have been drawn upon to create these databases. More highly specialized biography collections for some countries are listed in the "Specialized Resources in World History" section of this appendix, which starts on page 234.

International Biography Collections

Biography and Genealogy Master Index. Ed. Miranda C. Herbert and Barbara McNeil. 8 vols. Detroit: Gale, 1980–. Now included in Gale: Biography Resource Center online.

Biography in Context. Gale/Cengage. Large online database of biographies as well as other resources that help put lives "in context."

Biography Reference Center. EBSCO Publishing. A comprehensive online database with many search features.

Biography Resource Center. Gale. A large, online collection of biographical databases. Strong search capabilities.

Current Biography. New York: H. W. Wilson, 1940–. A cumulative index was published in 2000. Content available through EBSCO Publishing online.

International Who's Who. London: Europa, 1935–. Now part of the Thomson Gale online database *Biography Resource Center.*

Marquis Biographies Online. Online database includes all "Who's Who" publications, including the "Who Was Who" collection. Emphasis is on more recent biographies.

Oxford Dictionary of National Biography: Earliest Times to 2000. 61 vols. Oxford: Oxford University Press, 2004.

Who Was Who. Vol. 1, 1897–1915; vol. 2, 1916–1928; vol. 3, 1929–1940; vol. 4, 1941–1950; vol. 5, 1951–1960; vol. 6, 1961–1970; vol. 7, 1971–1980; vol. 8, 1981–1990; vol. 9, 1991–1995; vol. 10, 1996–2000. A cumulative index for 1897–1990 was published in 1991. These collections of biographies are now part of the Thomson Gale online database *Biography Resource Center.*

United States Biography Collections

African-American National Biography. Ed. Henry Louis Gates and Evelyn Brooks Higginbothom. 8 vols. Oxford: Oxford University Press, 2008.

American Men and Women of Science. New York: Bowker, 1906–. Now part of the Thomson Gale online database *Biography Resource Center.*

American National Biography. Ed. John A. Garraty and Mark C. Carnes. 24 vols. New York: Oxford University Press and American Council of Learned Societies, 1999. Supplement, 2002. The most recent and most extensive print collection of U.S. biographies. Also available online.

American Reform and Reformers: A Biographical Dictionary. Ed. Randall M. Miller and Paul A. Cimbala. Westport, CT: Greenwood Press, 1996.

Biographical Dictionary of American Business Leaders. Ed. John N. Ingham. 4 vols. Westport, CT: Greenwood Press, 1983.

Biographical Dictionary of American Journalism. Ed. Joseph P. McKerns. Westport, CT: Greenwood Press, 1989.

Biographical Dictionary of American Labor. Rev. ed. Ed. Gary M. Fink. Westport, CT: Greenwood Press, 1984.

Biographical Dictionary of American Sports. Rev. ed. Ed. David L. Porter. Westport, CT: Greenwood Press, 2000.

Biographical Directory of the United States Congress, 1774–. U.S. Congress. **bioguide .congress.gov/biosearch/biosearch.asp**. Print and digital editions. Member biographies and information concerning the papers of U.S. senators and representatives.

Biographical Directory of the United States Executive Branch, 1774–1989. Ed. Robert Sobel. 3rd ed. Westport, CT: Greenwood Press, 1990.

Dictionary of American Biography. New York: Scribner, 1928–1996, including supplements. When using older editions or volumes of a print biography collection, note the date of publication because it will indicate which individuals might be included. A one-volume work containing shortened versions of these biographies is published under the title *Concise Dictionary of American Biography*, 5th ed., 1997. An index to the multivolume collection was published in 1996.

Heritage Quest Online. ProQuest. **heritagequestonline.com/hqoweb/library /do/index**. Very large database of sources for U.S. family history.

Notable American Women, 1607–1950: A Biographical Dictionary. Ed. Edward T. James. 3 vols. Cambridge, MA: Harvard University Press, 1971. Supplemented by *Notable American Women: The Modern Period*, ed. Barbara Sicherman and Carol Hurd Green, 1980, and *Notable American Women, A Biographical Dictionary, Volume 5: Completing the Twentieth Century*, ed. Susan Ware, 2005.

Who Was Who in America: Historical Volume, 1607–1896. Chicago: Marquis, 1967. If you are uncertain about your subject's date of death, check *Who Was Who in America: Index* (2002). These volumes are now part of the Thomson Gale online database *Biography Resource Center*, available by subscription.

Who Was Who in America, with World Notables, 1897–2002. 14 vols. Chicago: Marquis, 2002. The years covered in each volume indicate the dates of death of those included in it.

NEWSPAPER INDEXES AND DATABASES

If you need to find newspaper articles from the time period you are writing about, a newspaper **index** will tell you where copies of a particular newspaper can be found. Newspaper **databases** contain the full text of newspaper articles—but only for certain newspapers and only for a particular span of years. Most full-text newspaper databases are searchable, but they are usually available only by subscription. If your library does not have access to the online database that you want, check the **library catalog** to see if it has newspapers in other formats.

Newspaper Indexes and Databases—General

British Newspapers, 1800–1900. British Library online. **newspapers11.bl.uk/blcs**. Newspaper archives from many English cities. Some are full text and free.

Burney Collection: Newspapers. Gale. Online database. Newspapers of England, Scotland, and Ireland.

Canadian Online Historical Newspapers. Chadwyck-Healey. Fully searchable online collections of the *Toronto Star* and the *Globe and Mail.* Coverage begins in the mid-to-late nineteenth century.

Latin American Newspaper Series. Readex. Online database. Series 1: 1805–1922. Series 2: 1872–1922. Includes newspapers in English, Spanish, and Portuguese.

Newspaper Resources. EBSCO Publishing. A very large online database with special search features.

Palmer's Index to the Times [of London], *1790–1905.* Succeeded by *Official Index to the Times, 1906–1980.* Chadwyck-Healey. Chadwyck-Healey also has an *Index Online* from 1790 to 1905 and the full text from 1800 to 1870. Both are searchable online.

ProQuest Historical Newspapers and Periodicals. ProQuest. A very large collection. Emphasis is on UK and U.S. publications.

Trove: Digitized Newspapers. National Library of Australia. **trove.nla.gov.au /newspaper**. Keyword searchable database of over 76 million newspaper articles.

Newspaper Indexes and Databases — United States

Accessible Archives: American Newspapers. Accessible Archives. Online database covers the nineteenth and twentieth centuries.

American Historical Newspapers, 1690–1922. Readex. Online database. Nine separate series, each covering a different period of time. A very large number of papers, including ones from smaller cities. Continually being expanded.

Chronicling America: Historic American Newspapers. Library of Congress and National Endowment for the Humanities. **chroniclingamerica.loc.gov**. The main collection is "The National Digital Newspaper Program," currently covering the years 1836 to 1922. This database includes full text and is searchable by newspaper name and by topic. It contains a large selection of digitized newspapers from state archives, libraries, and institutions, many published in small towns and cities. Also available is the "U.S. Newspaper Directory, 1690–present." These newspapers are held by local repositories. This database is searchable by state, county, and newspaper title. It tells you when a particular newspaper was published, where archives of it are held, and in what form.

Ethnic-American Newspapers, 1799–1971. Readex. Online database featuring foreign-language and English newspapers.

Hispanic-American Newspapers, 1799–1971. Readex. Online database featuring mostly Spanish-language newspapers.

Historical Newspaper Project. Wisconsin Historical Society. **wisconsinhistory.org /libraryarchives/aanp/**. A fine collection of nineteenth-century northern newspapers, emphasizing African American newspapers and periodicals.

New York Times Index. New York: New York Times, 1851–. Many libraries have internet access to full-text articles. See, among others, *ProQuest Historical Newspapers.*

ProQuest Historical Newspapers. ProQuest. A very large collection of major urban newspapers. Also contains a modest number of "Black" and Jewish newspapers.

PERIODICAL INDEXES AND DATABASES

Articles in **periodicals** can be grouped into two categories: *magazine articles* written at the time of the events being discussed (usually **primary documents**) and *articles in scholarly journals* analyzing a variety of historical themes (**secondary sources**). Resources for finding articles of each type are in the next two lists.

Magazine indexes and databases help you to find contemporary articles in popular magazines concerning events, persons, or issues that are part of your topic. Some print indexes to magazine articles are in the reference section of your library. Most searchable magazine databases are online, and those available to you will be included in the library's online catalog under a heading such as "electronic," "digital," or "online" resources. Be sure that the database you are searching includes the kind of magazines most likely to have articles related to your topic.

Journal indexes and databases contain citations, abstracts, or full-text articles from scholarly journals. These articles are among the most important sources of secondary evidence for history research; however, many will be available to you only if your school or public library has paid for a subscription. Often, when a library has several subscriptions, each covering different journals, these groups of journals are "linked" so that you can search several of them at once. If your library does not subscribe to the most promising journal database listed below, try a different database.

NOTE: Journal databases also store book reviews that appear in scholarly journals. If you wish to know more about a particular book before deciding to use it in your research, use these databases to seek out book reviews written by scholars.

Magazine Indexes and Databases

LexisNexis Academic. This online database covers journals, magazines, news providers, and legal materials. It is particularly useful for researching current events.

Nineteenth Century Masterfile. ProQuest. A large online database featuring a wide range of media on a variety of subjects, including history. Also contains a large newspaper database.

Nineteenth-Century Periodicals: 1815–1900. Library of Congress, American Memory. **memory.loc.gov/ammem/ndlpcoop/moahtml/snchome.html**. A searchable collection of periodicals. Years of coverage of each periodical are indicated. Many articles are full text.

Poole's Index to Periodical Literature, 1802–1881. Boston: Houghton Mifflin, 1891. Now available online. See above, *Nineteenth Century Masterfile.*

Readers' Guide Full Text, Mega Edition. EBSCO Publishing. Searchable full text of magazines but only for articles published since 1994.

Readers' Guide to Periodical Literature. New York: H. W. Wilson, 1900–. Annual updates still available in print. Beginning with articles published in 1983, this *Guide* began to appear in online form by subscription only via EBSCO Publishing. The annual volumes for the period before 1983 are now in digital form in *Readers' Guide Retrospective: 1890–1982.*

Readers' Guide Retrospective: 1890–1982. H. W. Wilson. This online database allows you to search for articles among several hundred popular magazines going back to 1890. Note that many of the periodicals included were written for a popular rather than a scholarly audience. These magazines are valuable as records of popular opinions and interests.

Ulrich's International Periodicals Directory. 41st ed. New York: Bowker, 2003. Also available online.

Journal Indexes and Databases

Academic Search Premier. EBSCO Publishing. A large multidisciplinary online database.

America: History and Life [United States and Canada]. EBSCO Publishing. A large online database with abstracts of articles in 2,000 scholarly journals published since 1964. All topics in U.S. and Canadian history are covered. The print edition has been published since 1965 by ABC-CLIO. The latest print edition is 1995. The online edition has some full-text articles.

American Periodical Series Online. Chadwyck-Healey. Available online via ProQuest. Full-text archive of several thousand periodicals: scholarly, literary, scientific, and popular. Beginning in 1741. Mostly nineteenth century.

British Periodicals. ProQuest. A large collection of full-text journal articles and related materials.

Historical Abstracts: World History since 1450. EBSCO Publishing. This online database offers abstracts of articles from a great number of scholarly journals in all areas except the United States and Canada. Those two areas are covered by *America: History and Life.* Both of these are now online by subscription as part of *EBSCOhost.* The online edition has some full-text articles.

Historical Periodicals Directory. Ed. Eric H. Boehm, Barbara H. Pope, and Marie Ensign. Vol. 1, *United States and Canada.* Vol. 2, *Europe (West).* Vol. 3, *Europe (East).* Vol. 4, *Latin America.* Vol. 5, *Australia and New Zealand.* Santa Barbara, CA: ABC-CLIO, 1981–1986.

History Cooperative. Full text of recent articles in twelve major history journals. Now linked with *JSTOR* database.

Humanities Index. New York: H. W. Wilson, 1974–. Covers a wide range of journals in the humanities. Annual volumes. See also *Humanities Index Retrospective, 1907–1974.* Now available in online form via EBSCO Publishing.

JSTOR. Fully searchable online database includes the full text of articles in several hundred academic journals, including many prominent historical journals. The most current articles are not available in *JSTOR.* For more current articles in scholarly journals, see *Project Muse* and *History Cooperative* (above).

Periodicals Archive Online. ProQuest. Full-text articles from a large number of international journals in history and social science. Database articles run from 1802 to 2000.

Project Muse. Searchable online database of full text of recent articles in several hundred journals across many humanities and social science disciplines, including history.

PUBLIC DOCUMENTS

These general resources lead you to documents created by official bodies such as national governments. Only English-language documents are included here. More specialized public document collections are listed by region or nation, on pages 234–54 and 257–76.

Public Documents — International

International Organizations. Northwestern University Pritzger Legal Research Center. **law.northwestern.edu/library/research/international/organizations/**. Contains links to a large number of international organizations.

League of Nations. Library of Northwestern University. **library.northwestern .edu/govinfo/collections/league/search.html**. Several hundred League documents online.

Permanent Court of International Justice. League of Nations. **icj-cij.org/en/pcij**. Decisions and documents of the court from 1922 to 1946. Predecessor to the Court of International Justice, a body of the United Nations.

United Nations. UN Documentation Centre. **un.org/documents/**. The UN site is a large and complex one. If you are not familiar with searching for UN documents, begin with a portal at the Library of Northwestern University, **law.northwestern.edu/library/research/international/organizations/un/**, for links to the major bodies of the United Nations (Security Council, General Assembly, Economic and Social Council, etc.). Official documents of these bodies begin in 1946.

United Nations Documents: Comprehensive Collection. Readex. An online database of all documents from 1945 to the present for each of the major UN bodies: General Assembly, Security Council, Economic and Social Council, Secretariat, Trusteeship Council, International Court of Justice.

Public Documents — Britain, Australia, and Canada

Ancestry Library Edition. ProQuest. Searchable genealogical information from the United States and the United Kingdom taken from census, church, court, immigration, and other records.

British History Online. Institute of Historical Research. **british-history.ac**. Documents relating to British history concerning local, national, and international affairs. Searchable by subject or place.

Colonial Case Law of Australia. Macquarie Univ. **law.mq.edu.au/research /colonial_case_law**.

Government of Canada. See *Library and Archives Canada* for a large number of searchable topics on Canadian history.

House of Commons: Parliamentary Papers. Chadwyck-Healey. House of Commons "sessional" papers, 1715–. Bills, reports, accounts, and so on. Available online through ProQuest.

Penal Laws Statutes in Ireland. **library.law.umn.edu/irishlaw/**. Extracts from statutes, primarily 1691–1760.

State Papers Online: Government of Britain, 1509–1714. Gale/Cengage. State papers domestic and foreign for the Tudor and Stuart eras.

United Kingdom National Archives. **nationalarchives.gov.uk/records/our-online-records .htm**. Major categories of documents are "Family History" (including military records and wills), "Society and Law," "Home and Foreign Affairs," and "Military and Defense." There is a download fee for most documents. Some portions of the National Archives materials are now available on commercial databases.

Public Documents — United States

American State Papers, 1789–1838. Readex. A searchable online database of printed material from the legislative and executive branches of government.

ARC. Archival Research Catalog. **archives.gov/research/arc/**. This site allows users to search for U.S. government documents housed in regional archives. Only a small fraction of these documents are online.

Congressional Hearings Digital Collection. ProQuest. Text of all committee hearings, some formerly unpublished, in a searchable database.

Congressional Record Permanent Digital Collection. ProQuest. Searchable database of the *Congressional Record*, which records the proceedings, debates, and informal discussions on the floor of the chambers.

Foreign Relations of the United States. U.S. Department of State. Washington, DC: Government Printing Office, 1861–. These volumes are issued regularly and contain selected documents of diplomatic correspondence. Some documents for the period 1945–2000 are online at **state.gov/www/about_state /history/frus.html**.

National Archives and Records Administration. **archives.gov/research/**. A portal to an enormous collection of U.S. government documents. It contains an extensive searchable catalog. Only a small fraction of this huge collection of materials is available online.

Oyez: U.S. Supreme Court Media. Illinois Institute of Technology–Kent College of Law. **oyez.org**. Access to all audio recorded in the court since 1955.

Presidential Libraries and Museums. **archives.gov/presidential-libraries/**. Every president since Herbert Hoover has his own library of presidential papers. This site contains links to each of the libraries. Many primary documents are available at the libraries. As yet, only a small number of these documents have been placed online.

United States Congressional Documents and Debates, 1774–1875. Library of Congress, American Memory. **memory.loc.gov/ammem/amlaw/lawhome.html**. The largest collection of online documents of the legislative branch of the U.S. government. Among many others, it contains pre-Constitution documents, House and Senate documents and debates, and the official publications of Congress.

United States Congressional Serial Set, 1817–1994. Readex. Very large online collection of congressional documents. Strong search capabilities. Contains reports, documents, and the journals of the U.S. Senate and House.

United States House and Senate Journals, 1789–1817. Readex. Online records of the sessions of the U.S. Congress.

United States Public Documents Masterfile. Paratext. A large online database of U.S. government documents covering 1774 to the present.

United States Serial Set Digital Collection. LexisNexis. An online archive of congressional publications covering the period 1789–1969. Searchable.

United States Supreme Court Center. Justia.com. **supreme.justia.com/cases /federal/us**. An online database that contains unofficial text of Supreme Court opinions.

HISTORICAL STATISTICS

These resources lead you to a wide range of numerical data useful to research in such areas as political, economic, and social history.

Historical Statistics — General

Historical Tables, 58 B.C.–A.D. 1990. 12th ed. By Sigfrid H. Steinberg. New York: Tuttle, 1991.

International Historical Statistics. Ed. Brian R. Mitchell. 3 vols. New York: Palgrave Macmillan, 2008. See individual volume entries under the heading "Historical Statistics—National and Regional" for specific coverage areas.

League of Nations Statistical Yearbook. Northwestern University. **library.northwestern .edu/govinfo/collections/league/stat.html**. Full text of the yearbook from 1926 to 1944.

United Nations Demographic Yearbook. **unstats.un.org/unsd/demographic/products / dyb/dyb2.htm**. Statistical publications beginning in 1948.

United Nations Statistical Division. **unstats.un.org/unsd/methods/inter-natlinks /sd_natstat.asp**. Links to national statistical websites.

Historical Statistics — National and Regional

Africa South of the Sahara: African Statistics on the Internet. Stanford University. **www-sul.stanford.edu/depts/ssrg/africa/statistics.html**. This portal at Stanford University contains links to several different resources on statistical research in Africa.

Annual Abstract of Statistics. London: Office of National Statistics. Available in print and online. Earlier statistics are accessed through the link "Time Series" and are free to search and download.

The Arab World, Turkey and the Balkans, 1878–1914: A Handbook of Historical Statistics. Ed. Justin McCarthy. Boston: G. K. Hall, 1982.

Australian Historical Population Statistics. Australian Bureau of Statistics. **abs.gov .au/ausstats/abs@.nsf/mf/3105.0.65.001**. Last updated in 2008, this site provides historical population statistics dating back to 1788.

British Historical Statistics. Ed. B. R. Mitchell. Cambridge: Cambridge University Press, 1988.

British Labour Statistics: Historical Abstract, 1886–1968. London: Great Britain Department of Employment and Productivity, 1971.

The British Voter: An Atlas and Survey since 1885. By Michael Kinnear. London: Batsford, 1981.

Census Finder. U.S. Census Bureau. Links to census records for the United Kingdom, Canada, Sweden, and Norway available at **censusfinder.com/**. For U.S. data, see "Historical Statistics—United States."

The Gallup International Public Opinion Polls: Great Britain, 1937–1975; France, 1939, 1944–1975. By George H. Gallup. New York: Random House, 1976–1977.

HeritageQuest Online. ProQuest. A large database of nineteenth- and twentieth-century census statistics, most from the United States but also from the United Kingdom and Canada.

Historical Statistics of Canada. Statistics Canada. Ed. F. H. Leacy. **statcan.gc.ca**. Searchable online version of printed volume. Over 1,000 tables drawn from historical data for the period 1867 to 1970s.

International Historical Statistics: Africa, Asia, and Oceania: 1750–2005. 5th ed. Vol. 2. Ed. Brian R. Mitchell. New York: Palgrave Macmillan, 2008.

International Historical Statistics: The Americas: 1750–2005. 6th ed. Vol. 3. Ed. Brian R. Mitchell. New York: Palgrave Macmillan, 2008.

International Historical Statistics: Europe, 1750–2005. 6th ed. Vol. 1. Ed. Brian R. Mitchell. New York: Palgrave Macmillan, 2008.

Introduction to the Censuses of Canada, 1665 to 1871. Statistics Canada. [Printed: Ottawa, 1876.] Online version is at **statcan.gc.ca/bsolc/olc-cel/olc-cel?lang =eng&catno=98-187-X**.

The Montevideo-Oxford Latin American Economic History Database. **lac.ox.ac.uk /moxlad-database**. Statistical information on the economies and societies of Latin America, 1870–2010.

Statistical Abstract of Latin America. Ed. James W. Wilkie. Los Angeles: UCLA Center of Latin American Studies, 1955–.

Statistical Accounts of Scotland, 1791–1845. University of Edinburgh Library. Available by subscription online at **edina.ac.uk/stat-acc-scot/**.

Statistics in Africa. World Bank. This online resource allows you to search World Bank statistics related to Africa.

Twentieth-Century British Political Facts, 1900–2000. By David Butler and Gareth Butler. New York: Palgrave Macmillan, 2000.

United Kingdom Census Online: 1841–1911. **nationalarchives.gov.uk/census/**. Holds indexes to the census records of the United Kingdom. In some cases it describes document collections, but it does not give access to them. For this, readers are directed to commercial databases. See Appendix B.

Historical Statistics — United States

Census of Population and Housing, 1820–2010. U.S. Census Bureau. Portions of this data are available for download.

Datapedia of the United States: American History in Numbers. 4th ed. Ed. George Thomas Kurian and Barbara A. Chernow. Lanham, MD: Bernan Press, 2007. A one-volume compilation of U.S. statistics covering the nineteenth and twentieth centuries.

Federal Population Censuses 1790–1890: A Catalogue of Microfilm Copies of the Schedules. Washington, DC: National Archives and Records Administration. Index available online. A great deal of data from pre-1950 census results have been digitized. Much personal information is now available through commercial websites. The major sites are listed in Appendix B. For census "statistics" online, see sites such as *Heritage Quest Online* below.

The Gallup Poll. By George H. Gallup. New York: Random House and Scholarly Resources, 1935–.

The Gallup Poll Cumulative Index: Public Opinion, 1935–1997. Wilmington, DE: Scholarly Resources, 1999. Also available online, by subscription, at **brain.gallup.com**.

Gallup Polls. Gallup Organization. **brain.gallup.com**. Gallup polls beginning in the 1930s. Searchable database.

Heritage Quest Online. ProQuest. A large database of nineteenth- and twentieth-century census statistics, most from the United States but also some from the United Kingdom and Canada.

The Foreign-Born Population of the U.S. U.S. Census Bureau. **census.gov/topics /population/foreign-born.html**. This site provides census publications regarding the foreign-born population of the United States.

Historical Statistics of the United States, Colonial Times to 1970. Washington, DC: Bureau of the Census, 1976, and Government Printing Office, 1989. Also available online at **census.gov/library/publications/1975/compendia/hist _stats_colonial-1970.html**.

International Historical Statistics: The Americas: 1750–2005. 6th ed. Vol. 3. Ed. Brian R. Mitchell. New York: Palgrave Macmillan, 2008.

Measuring America: The Decennial Censuses from 1790 to 2000. U.S. Census Bureau. Does not contain data from censuses but rather a history of the forms used, questions asked, and the context in which information was collected. Available online at **census.gov/library/publications/2002/dec/pol_02-ma.html**.

National Historical Geographical Information System. University of Minnesota. **nhgis.org**. The site allows the user to aggregate and analyze U.S. census data for the period 1790–2010. Data is available for the national, state, county, census tract, and boundary files. Sophisticated interpretation is possible, but the site is complex and special software may be needed.

Roper Center for Public Opinion Research. University of Connecticut. **ropercenter .cornell.edu/**. This site offers access to data gathered from Roper opinion polls, archived collections, and the Roper magazine.

Statistical Abstract of the United States. U.S. Census Bureau. **census.gov/library /publications/time-series/statistical_abstracts.html**. Yearly collection of statistics. Files for most years are downloadable but are very large. Files are available for most years from 1878 to the present. Collection of data for this collection ceased in 2011.

GENERAL RESOURCES
IN WORLD HISTORY

Before examining the general resources in world history listed in this section, you should consult the historical dictionaries, encyclopedias, and atlases listed at the beginning of this appendix. They will enable you to choose and narrow a topic.

The general resources in this section consist of bibliographies and websites that cover large areas and many periods of world history. The specialized resources described later will be useful once you have chosen a topic and have a clear understanding of the kind of research you will need to do to develop and support your thesis. Even if you have already narrowed your topic, you should not ignore the following general resources, because many of them include sections on or links to specialized topics.

Reference Works and Bibliographies

A Dictionary of Twentieth-Century History, 1914–1990. Ed. Peter Teed. Oxford: Oxford University Press, 1992.

The Oxford Dictionary of Byzantium. Ed. Alexander P. Kazhdan. 3 vols. New York: Oxford University Press, 1991.

Slavery and Slaving in World History: A Bibliography, 1900–1991. Ed. Joseph C. Miller. New York: M. E. Sharpe, 1998.

Websites

Academic Info: Online Historical Documents. **academicinfo.net/histaalibrary.html**. This site categorizes and annotates links to history websites.

Advanced Papyrological Information System. APIS. **quod.lib.umich.edu/a/apis** (also **columbia.edu/cu/lweb/projects/digital/apis/index.html**). A consortium of academic institutions share this site, which displays originals and translations of some of the earliest written documents.

Al Mizan: Sciences and Arts in the Islamic World. Museum of the History of Science. **oxcis.ac.uk/almizan/index.html**. An online exhibition that explores the link between science and art in Muslim cultures.

Archive for the History of Economic Thought. McMaster University. **socserv.mcmaster .ca/econ/ugcm/3ll3/**. The full text of several hundred works on economic theory, third century BCE to mid-twentieth century.

ArchNet. MIT School of Architecture and Planning, University of Texas School of Architecture, and Aga Khan Development Network. **archnet.org/library**. Covers urban planning and design throughout the Muslim world; emphasis is on Islamic architecture. Large photograph collection organized by country, century, usage, style, and type. A site with great depth.

ARCL Women and Gender Studies Section. Association of College and Research Libraries and the American Library Association. **libr.org/wgss/**. A large collection of links to works covering many aspects of women's history in the United States and around the world.

Berkeley Digital Library SunSITE. **lib.berkeley.edu/**. Texts and images, including classical and medieval works, the Emma Goldman papers, and a strong collection relating to California.

Contagion: Historical Views of Diseases and Epidemics. Harvard Digital Collections. **ocp.hul.harvard.edu/contagion/**. An online collection featuring historical materials related to epidemiology and disease.

Dead Sea Scrolls. **ibiblio.org/expo/deadsea.scrolls.exhibit/intro.html**. Essays and brief translations.

Dissertation Abstracts International. ProQuest Dissertations and Theses Database. A database of non-U.S. dissertations. Abstracts available.

Expanded Academic ASAP. Gale/InfoTrac. A very large online database of newspapers, biographies, reviews, references, and primary and secondary sources covering both world and U.S. history.

Film Index International. Chadwyck-Healey. A searchable online database of information on 115,000 films from 170 countries. By subscription only.

The Geometry of War, 1500–1750. Museum of the History of Science. **mhs.ox.ac .uk/geometry/title.htm**. Documents and images concerning the application of mathematics to warfare.

George Ortiz Collection. **georgeortiz.com**. A large collection of art from a variety of ancient cultures.

Getty Digitized Library Collections. The J. Paul Getty Trust. **getty.edu/research /tools/digital_collections/index.html**. Digitized collections of decorative arts, manuscripts, paintings, drawings, photographs, and sculpture. Covers many eras and regions. One of the largest collections of this type in the world.

Historical Text Archive. **historicaltextarchive.com**. A searchable database of articles, books, and links.

History and the Social Sciences. Michigan State University. **digital.lib.msu.edu /collections**. A collection of public domain historical sources.

The History Guide. **historyguide.org/resources.html**. A gateway to a large number of online history sources.

History Studies Centre. Chadwyck-Healey. A large online collection of print and image resources. Nine separate collections.

Humanities E-Book. American Council of Learned Societies. **humanitiesebook .org**. Collection of digitized history books.

Index of Medieval Medical Images. UCLA Digital Library. **digital.library.ucla.edu**. Drawn from manuscripts created between 1250 and 1500. Five hundred medical-related images. Date, provenance, topic, physical characteristics, and annotation of the image.

InfoMine. University of California, Riverside. **library.ucr.edu/onesearch /infomine**. A large database of links to history and other websites. A nonsubscription database.

International Institute of Social History. **socialhistory.org**. Emphasis on social and economic history essays and documents.

International Mission Photography Archive. University of Southern California. **digitallibrary.usc.edu**. A searchable collection of 12,000 photographs covering images of mission work in many countries.

Internet History Sourcebooks. Paul Halsall, Fordham University. **fordham.edu /halsall/index.html**. Features full text of scholarly works organized by period, area, and, in a few cases, subject. Works appear without annotation. Some offsite links are no longer live.

Internet Public Library. **ipl.org/div/subject/**. This site offers free access to a very large number of magazines, newspapers, and books in the humanities.

Intute. **intute.ac.uk/**. Database containing a large number of links to a wide range of history websites. Emphasizes but is not confined to British resources. A nonsubscription database. (While Intute is still available and valuable, it ceased adding links in July 2011.)

ipl2: Information You Can Trust. **ipl2server-1.ipl.org/**. This site merged the collections from the Internet Public Library and the Librarian's Internet Index. Hosted and maintained by a number of universities. Annotates websites of interest to historians.

Lines of Faith: Instruments and Religious Practice in Islam. Museum of the History of Science. **mhs.ox.ac.uk/about/sphaera/sphaera-issue-no-7/lines-of-faith -instruments-and-religious-practice-in-islam/**. A 1998 exhibition on the influence of scientific instruments on Islamic religion.

Marxist Internet Archive. **marxists.org/subject**. Large collection of Marxist writings from all parts of the world.

Paratext Reference Universe. A large collection of databases, including one of reference works.

Project Gutenberg. **gutenberg.org/catalog/**. A very large, searchable database of books. Access to most of the books is unrestricted. Search by author, title, or subject.

ProQuest Research Library. A group of several databases, including "History Studies Center" and "Reference Works."

Questia. Questia Media America Inc. **questia.com/library/history**. A large database of books and articles on many areas and aspects of history. Fully searchable.

SAGE. Selected Archives at Georgia Tech and Emory Digital Archive Project. **sage.library.emory.edu/**. This site displays online multimedia exhibits.

Slave Movements during the Eighteenth and Nineteenth Centuries. Data and Programs Library Services, University of Wisconsin. **disc.wisc.edu/archive/slave /index.html**. Offers raw data and documentation of the Atlantic slave trade in the eighteenth and nineteenth centuries.

Slave Studies Net: European Studies Project. World Wide Web Virtual Library. Access to resources on the study of slavery. Global in scope.

Swarthmore Peace Collection. Swarthmore College. **swarthmore.edu/library /peace**. A large library of links on the topic of peace.

University of Pennsylvania Digital Library. **digital.library.upenn.edu/**. This site's Online Books page features over 25,000 books. It highlights banned books, female writers, and foreign-language texts.

Voice of the Shuttle History Page. University of California, Santa Barbara. **vos.ucsb .edu/browse.asp?id=2713**. Organizes a great number of links in an easily searchable format.

Women and Social Movements International. Ed. Kathryn Kish Sklar and Thomas Dublin. Alexander Street Press. Online database compiling primary sources related to women and social movements.

World History Compass. **worldhistorycompass.com/**. Organizes annotated links geographically and by subject and includes countries often underrepresented on such sites.

World History Matters. **worldhistorymatters.org**. A large index that gives thoughtful evaluations of websites in many areas and eras of history except for the United States. U.S. websites are evaluated at *History Matters:* **historymatters.gmu.edu/**.

WWW Virtual Library. **vlib.org/humanities**. A very large collection of links to history websites organized by topic, area, and era. Some materials not in English. Links not always reliable but still a valuable resource.

SPECIALIZED RESOURCES
IN WORLD HISTORY

Once you have chosen your topic with the aid of the historical dictionaries, encyclopedias, and atlases listed at the beginning of this appendix, you are ready to seek out primary and secondary sources that you will use to develop and support your thesis.

The world history resources in this section are organized by time period ("Ancient") and by region ("Africa"). The sources for each specialized period or region are separated into two groups. The first group contains reference works and bibliographies available in print form. The second group contains a list of websites organized alphabetically by the name of the site.

Ancient History

Ancient Europe 8000 B.C.–A.D. 1000: Encyclopedia of the Barbarian World. Ed. Peter I. Bogucki and Pam J. Crabtree. 2 vols. New York: Thomson Gale, 2004.

Biographical Encyclopedia of Ancient Natural Sciences. Ed. Paul Keyser and Georgia Irby-Massie. London: Routledge, 2009.

The Cambridge Ancient History. Cambridge: Cambridge University Press. 1st ed. 12 vols., 1924–1939. 2nd ed., 14 vols., 1970–2005. A multivolume work with extensive bibliographies.

The Encyclopedia of Ancient Civilizations of the Near East and Mediterranean. Ed. John Haywood. New York: M. E. Sharpe, 1997.

The Encyclopedia of Ancient Egypt. Ed. Helen Strudwick. London: Amber Books Ltd., 2017.

Encyclopedia of the Crusades. Ed. Alfred J. Andrea. Westport, CT: Greenwood Press, 2003.

Encyclopedia of Early Christianity. 2nd ed. Ed. Everett Ferguson et al. New York: Garland, 1998.

Encyclopedia of the Roman Empire. Rev. ed. Ed. Matthew Bunson. New York: Facts on File, 2002.

The Oxford Classical Dictionary. 4th ed. Ed. Simon Hornblower, Antony Spawforth, and Esther Edinow. Oxford: Oxford University Press, 2012.

The Oxford Encyclopedia of Ancient Egypt. Ed. Donald B. Redford. 3 vols. Oxford: Oxford University Press, 2001.

The Ancient Greek World. University of Pennsylvania Museum of Archaeology and Anthropology. **penn.museum/sites/greek_world/index.html**. Text and images that explore the history and culture of ancient Greece.

Ancient Mesopotamia: This History, Our History. University of Chicago, Oriental Institute Museum. **mesopotamia.lib.uchicago.edu/**. A small number of artifacts, photographs, and archaeological sites. Emphasis is on daily life. Also deals with elements of this civilization that were the basis for important aspects of modern civilizations.

Ancient Treasures and the Dead Sea Scrolls. Canadian Museum of Civilization Online Exhibits. **civilization.ca/cmc/exhibitions/civil/israel/isrele.shtml**. Examines the Dead Sea Scrolls and insights they offer on the peoples of that time, especially the Jewish people.

Centre for the Study of Ancient Documents. Oxford University. **csad.ox.ac.uk/**. Presents information on and links to the materials and scripts of ancient writing.

Diotima: Materials for the Study of Woman and Gender in the Ancient World. Ross Scaife, editor in chief. **stoa.org/diotima**. Large number of current translations of Greek, Latin, Egyptian, and Coptic texts, as well as bibliographies and links to other sources.

Duke Papyrus Archive. Duke University. **scriptorium.lib.duke.edu/papyrus/**. Texts and images of 1,300 papyri. These are summarized but not translated.

Egyptology Resources. Nigel Strudwick. **fitzmuseum.cam.ac.uk/er/**. Texts, images, and links to organizations, publications, archaeological digs, and museums about Egypt.

Electronic Antiquity: Communicating the Classics. Virginia Polytechnic Institute and State University. **scholar.lib.vt.edu/ejournals/ElAnt/**. Articles and book reviews relating to ancient Greece and Rome.

Electronic Text Corpus of Sumerian Literature. The Oriental Institute, Oxford University. **www-etcsl.orient.ox.ac.uk/**. Important texts, in transliterations and translations, from ancient Mesopotamia. Texts cover culture, history, poetry, and prayers.

Eternal Egypt. Supreme Council of Antiquities, Egyptian Center for Documentation of Cultural and Natural Heritage (CultNat), and IBM. **cultnat.org/ProgramDetails/13/Eternal_Egypt**. Images of 1,500 objects from the Pharaonic era. Also covers Roman, Byzantine, and Islamic periods. A very well-organized site with sophisticated multimedia and interactive presentations and a collection of scholarly articles on early Egypt.

Exploring Ancient World Cultures. University of Evansville. **edsitement.neh.gov/websites/exploring-ancient-world-cultures**. Includes essays and primary sources on the Near East, India, Egypt, China, Greece, Rome, Early Islam, and Medieval Europe.

Jerusalem Virtual Library. Hebrew University of Jerusalem. Al Quds University. **jewishvirtuallibrary.org/jerusalem**. A well-organized collection on the history of Jerusalem. Contains maps, plans, photographs, and inscriptions, among others.

LacusCurtius: Into the Roman World. William P. Thayer. **penelope.uchicago.edu/Thayer/E/Roman/home.html**. Online exhibitions of Roman archaeological sites. Primary and secondary sources and photographs of buildings and monuments. Latin and Greek primary texts with translations. Searchable by keyword.

Mohenjo Daro. Jonathan Mark Kenoyer, University of Wisconsin–Madison. **mohenjodaro.net**. A small collection of images and secondary sources from excavations at Mohenjo Daro in the Indus Valley (2600 to 1900 BCE). Emphasis is on daily life. Each image is accompanied by a detailed explanation. Unfortunately, this website includes advertisements.

Perseus Digital Library. Gregory Cane, editor in chief. **perseus.tufts.edu/**. Excellent collection of literature and archaeology from ancient Greek and Roman culture. Includes several hundred primary texts, plus images from museum collections and archaeological sites. English translations seem to be out of date.

Semitic Museum. Harvard University. **semiticmuseum.fas.harvard.edu**. Site includes film, images, and essays related to the material collected at the Semitic Museum at Harvard.

Vindolanda Tablets Online. Center for the Study of Ancient Documents, Oxford University. **vindolanda.csad.ox.ac.uk/**. The texts of hundreds of wooden tablets in Latin found at a Roman fortress at Vindolanda behind Hadrian's Wall in Britain. Written by German soldiers serving in the Roman Army in England (ca. second century CE). Each document is presented in both Latin transcription and English translation.

Women and Gender in Ancient Egypt. University of Michigan. **umich.edu/~kelseydb /Exhibits/WomenandGender/title.html**. The online version of a 1997 exhibit at the Kelsey Museum at the University of Michigan. Sources range from ca. 3100 BCE to 700 CE.

Europe — General

Celtic Culture: A Historical Encyclopedia. Ed. John T. Koch. 5 vols. Santa Barbara, CA: ABC-CLIO, 2006.

Dictionary of Scandinavian History. Ed. Byron J. Nordstrom. Westport, CT: Greenwood Press, 1986.

Encyclopedia of the Age of Imperialism, 1800–1914. Ed. Carl Hodge. 2 vols. Westport, CT: Greenwood Press, 2008.

Encyclopedia of European Social History [1350–2000]. Ed. Peter N. Stearns. 6 vols. New York: Scribner, 2001. E-book version, Gale, 2005.

Encyclopedia of the Industrial Revolution. Ed. Thomas Heinrich. 3 vols. New York: M. E. Sharpe, 2002.

Historical Dictionary of Germany. Ed. Wayne C. Thompson, Susan L. Thompson, and Juliet S. Thompson. Metuchen, NJ: Scarecrow Press, 1994.

Scandinavian History: 1520–1970. Comp. Stewart P. Oakley. London: Historical Association of London, 1984.

Women in European History. Gisela Bock, translated by Allison Brown. Malden, MA: Blackwell Publishers, 2002.

AdHoc [History of Christianity]. Yale University, Yale Divinity School. **web.library .yale.edu/digital-collections/adhoc-image-and-text-database-history -christianity**. Images and documents from all eras of the history of Christianity.

EuroDocs: Primary Historical Documents from European History. Brigham Young University. **eudocs.lib.byu.edu/index.php/Main_Page**. Covers all European countries. Legal documents, local history, eras from classical to present.

Translations from both primary and secondary sources are usually not the latest. A very large site. Some links may not be scholarly ones.

Gallica. National Library of France. **gallica.bnf.fr/?lang=en**. A very large national collection of thousands of digitized titles covering all eras and regions. You can search in English, but many of the documents are in French.

History Guide. **historyguide.de/**. Links, bibliographies, journals, and materials relating primarily to American and European history.

H-Slavery. H-Net: Humanities and Social Sciences Online. **networks.h-net.org /node/11465/pages/57412/what-other-h-net-networks-are-publishing -about-history-slaverywga.hu/index.html.**

United States Holocaust Memorial Museum. **ushmm.org/**. Multimedia exhibits and historical information relating to the Holocaust, World War II, and genocide.

Web Gallery of Art. **wga.hu/**. Images and information about the history of European art from 1100 to 1850. The database is searchable. Extensive annotation of artists and eras.

Europe — Medieval

Atlas of Medieval Europe. Ed. Angus Konstam and Roger Kean. New York: Facts on File, 2000.

Atlas of Medieval Europe. 2nd ed. Ed. David Ditchburn, Simon MacLean, and Angus MacKay. New York: Routledge, 2007.

Dictionary of the Middle Ages. Ed. Joseph R. Strayer. 13 vols. New York: Scribner, 1998. Supplement, 2003.

Encyclopedia of the Crusades. By Alfred J. Andrea. Westport, CT: Greenwood Press, 2003.

Medieval France: An Encyclopedia. Ed. William W. Kibler et al. New York: Garland, 1995.

Medieval Germany: An Encyclopedia. Ed. John M. Jeep. New York: Garland, 2001.

Medieval Italy: An Encyclopedia. Ed. Chris Kleinhenz. London: Routledge, 2004.

Medieval Jewish Civilization: An Encyclopedia. Ed. Norman Roth. New York: Routledge, 2002.

De Re Militari: Online Resources for Medieval Warfare. Society for Medieval Military History. **deremilitari.org/**. Excellent source for the study of medieval warfare: military, social, economic, political, religious, and geographic. Covers the late Roman period (fifth century CE) to the seventeenth century CE. Several hundred primary and secondary sources arranged by region and subject.

Early Manuscripts at Oxford University. Oxford University. **image.ox.ac.uk/**. Downloadable images "for personal study only." Over eighty manuscripts, although a number of them are incomplete.

Epistolae: Medieval Women's Latin Letters. Joan Ferrante, Columbia University, and Columbia Center for New Media, Teaching, and Learning. **epistolae .ccnmtl.columbia.edu/**. The lives of important women are examined through their letters. Covers fourth to thirteenth centuries CE. Historical notes and biographical sketches accompany each letter.

Florilegium Urbanum. Stephen Alsford. **trytel.com/~tristan/towns/florilegium /flor00.html**. This site is dedicated to the study of medieval English towns. Two hundred short primary sources and excerpts from longer texts. Translations are accompanied by historical context.

Index of Medieval Medical Images. UCLA Digital Library. **digital2.library.ucla .edu/**. Drawn from manuscripts created between 1250 and 1500. Five hundred medical-related images. Date, provenance, topic, physical characteristics, and annotation of the image.

ITER: Gateway to the Middle Ages and Renaissance. University of Toronto. **itergateway.org/**. A large, searchable database of journal articles on topics relating to Europe from 400 to 1700.

The Labyrinth: Resources for Medieval Studies. Georgetown University. **georgetown .edu/labyrinth/**. This site allows you to search bibliographies, discussion groups, images, and primary and secondary works by category.

LIBRO: The Library of Iberian Resources Online (Medieval Spain). **libro.uca.edu/**. A modest archive of full-text scholarly works in (or translated into) English. Covers the Iberian Peninsula from the fifth to the seventeenth centuries.

Medici Archive Project. Medici Archive Project. **medici.org**. Medici family archive beginning in the sixteenth century. A very large database of 3 million letters is searchable by word, topic, place, date, and person. Only summaries of the documents are available in English.

NetSERF: The Internet Connection for Medieval Resources. **netserf.org/**. An extensive and well-organized collection of annotated links to research sites.

Online Medieval and Classical Library (OMACL). **omacl.org**. European texts covering post-Homeric, preclassical Greek and Icelandic sagas, and others up to the sixteenth century CE.

Europe — Early Modern

Encyclopedia of Witchcraft: The Western Tradition. Ed. Richard M. Golden. 4 vols. Santa Barbara, CA: ABC-CLIO, 2006.

The Oxford Encyclopedia of the Reformation. Ed. Hans J. Hillerbrand. 4 vols. New York: Oxford University Press, 1996.

Renaissance and Reformation: Reference Library Cumulative Index. Detroit: U.X.L., 2002.

CERES. Cambridge English Renaissance Electronic Service. **open.conted.ox.ac .uk/resources/link/cambridge-english-renaissance-electronic-service-ceres.** A large database of links to Renaissance documents online.

ITER: Gateway to the Middle Ages and Renaissance. University of Toronto. **itergate way.org/**. A large, searchable database of journal articles on topics relating to Europe from 400 to 1700.

Renascence Editions [Renaissance]. **luminarium.org/renascence-editions/**. Provides online access to texts printed in English between the late fifteenth century and the end of the eighteenth century.

The Revolt of the Netherlands. Leiden University. **dutchrevolt.leiden.edu/english /Pages/default.aspx**. A large collection of documents on the history of the Dutch struggle for independence (1568–1648). This site is an English-language one.

Witchcraft Collection. Cornell University. **historical.library.cornell.edu/witchcraft /browse.html**. A collection of digitized books on witchcraft, principally in Europe.

Europe — Modern

Encyclopedia of European Social History (1350–2000). Ed. Peter N. Stearns. 6 vols. New York: Scribner, 2001. E-book version, Gale, 2005.

Encyclopedia of the Industrial Revolution. Ed. Thomas Heinrich. 3 vols. New York: M. E. Sharpe, 2002.

Europe, 1789–1914: Encyclopedia of the Age of Imperialism and Empire. Ed. John Merriman and Jay Winter. 5 vols. New York: Scribner, 2006.

The European Powers in the First World War: An Encyclopedia. Ed. Spencer C. Tucker. New York: Garland, 1999.

Europe since 1945: An Encyclopedia. Ed. Bernard A. Cook. 2 vols. New York: Garland, 2001.

French Culture, 1900–1975. Ed. Catharine Savage Brosman and Tom Conley. Detroit: Gale Research, 1995.

Historical Dictionary of the French Fourth and Fifth Republics, 1946–1991. Ed. Wayne Northcutt. Westport, CT: Greenwood Press, 1992.

A Historical Dictionary of Germany's Weimar Republic, 1918–1933. Ed. C. Paul Vincent. Westport, CT: Greenwood Press, 1997.

Historical Dictionary of Modern Italy. 2nd ed. Mark Gilbert and Robert K. Nilsson. Lanham, MD: Scarecrow Press, 2007.

Historical Dictionary of Modern Spain, 1700–1988. Ed. Robert W. Kern. Westport, CT: Greenwood Press, 1990.

Historical Dictionary of the Spanish Civil War, 1936–1939. Ed. James W. Cortada. Westport, CT: Greenwood Press, 1982.

Historical Dictionary of the Third French Republic, 1870–1940. Ed. Patrick H. Hutton, Amanda S. Bourque, and Amy J. Staples. 2 vols. Westport, CT: Greenwood Press, 1986.

The Longman Handbook of Modern European History, 1763–1997. 3rd ed. Ed. Chris Cook and John Stevenson. New York: Longman, 1998.

Modern Germany: An Encyclopedia of History, People and Culture, 1871–1900. Ed. Dieter K. Buse and Juergen C. Doerr. 2 vols. New York: Garland, 1998.

Modern Italian History: An Annotated Bibliography. Comp. Frank J. Coppa and William Roberts. Westport, CT: Greenwood Press, 1990. A companion to *Dictionary of Modern Italian History.*

Nazism, Resistance, and the Holocaust in World War II: A Bibliography. Ed. Vera Laska. Metuchen, NJ: Scarecrow Press, 1985.

Women in German History: From Bourgeois Emancipation to Sexual Liberation. Ute Frevert. New York: Bloomsbury Publishing, 1990.

Women in Western European History: A Select Chronological, Geographical, and Topical Bibliography; The Nineteenth and Twentieth Centuries. Ed. Linda Frey, Marsha Frey, and Joanne Schneider. Westport, CT: Greenwood Press, 1984.

Anarchism Pamphlets. Labadie Collection of the University of Michigan. **hti.umich.edu/l /labadie/**. A searchable database of several hundred anarchist books and pamphlets.

Bibliotec National de France. **bnf.fr/en/collections_and_services.html**. Digital collections of the National Library of France.

Cold War International History Project. Woodrow Wilson International Center for Scholars. **wilsoncenter.org/program/cold-war-international-history-project**. Publications and documents relating to the study of international relations during the Cold War. Many documents from former Soviet archives.

Einstein Archives Online. Hebrew University of Jerusalem. **alberteinstein.info/**. A large collection of Einstein's nonscientific writings, many in German, some in English.

Encyclopedia of 1848 Revolutions. **ohio.edu/chastain/contents.htm**. Online encyclopedia with the author of each article noted.

German History in Documents and Images. German Historical Institute. **germanhis torydocs.ghi-dc.org/Index.cfm?language=english**. A moderately sized, self-contained site. It presents many aspects of German history, from 1500 to the present, with a series of well-organized exhibits, each containing an introduction, documents, images, and maps. Exhibits integrate each of these elements. All sources are documented.

Inquisitio: Manuscript and Print Sources for the Study of Inquisition History. University of Notre Dame. **inquisition.library.nd.edu/collections/RBSC-INQ:COLLECTION**. Documents in several languages, especially Latin and Spanish.

Italian Life under Fascism. University of Wisconsin–Madison. **library.wisc.edu /exhibits/online-exhibits/special-collections/italian-life-under-fascism -selections-from-the-fry-collection/**. This online exhibit features materials from the Fry Collection, organized thematically.

Liberty, Equality, Fraternity: Exploring the French Revolution. George Mason University, Center for History and New Media. **chnm.gmu.edu/revolution// searchfr.php**. Overview of the French Revolution in more than 600 images, texts, maps, and songs. Generally excellent context provided along with some in-depth scholarly essays.

Nazi and East German Propaganda. **calvin.edu/academic/cas/gpa**. English translations of a large group of Nazi-era and East German (GRD) propaganda material.

The Nuremberg War Crimes Trials. Avalon Project at Yale Law School. **avalon.law .yale.edu/subject_menus/imt.asp**. A large number of online documents from the official records of the trials.

The Siege and Commune of Paris, 1870–71. Northwestern University. **library .northwestern.edu/spec/siege/index.html**. A database of a wide range of documents and images from besieged Paris.

Southworth Spanish Civil War Collection. University of California, San Diego. **library.ucsd.edu/research-and-collections/collections/special-collections -and-archives/collections/southworth.html**. Propaganda posters, children's drawings, newspapers, poems, and other primary resources.

Spartacus Educational. **spartacus-educational.com/**. Short hyperlinked essays focusing mostly on modern European political history. Degree of documentation for essays varies. Separate collections for many aspects of modern European history and also for some non-European topics.

WWI: The World War I Document Archive. Brigham Young University. **lib.byu.edu /~rdh/wwi/**. Government documents, maps, photographs, and biographies.

Britain — General

British Trials, 1660–1900. Chadwyck-Healey. Index of thousands of trials. Descriptions range from brief outlines to verbatim transcripts. Microfilm.

Dictionary of National Biography [United Kingdom]. Ed. Leslie Stephen and Sidney Lee. Oxford: Oxford University Press, 1908–. A summary of this large multivolume collection can be found in *A Concise Dictionary of National Biography, from Earliest Times to 1985.* The book is now online.

English Poor Laws, 1639–1890. UMI. A collection of contemporary books, pamphlets, and public papers from England, Scotland, and Ireland focusing on the poor and the unemployed as public issues. Microfiche. By subscription only.

Historical Atlas of Britain. Ed. Malcolm Falkus and John Gillingham. New York: Crescent Books, 1987.

The Routledge Atlas of British History: From 45 BC to the Present. 4th ed. By Martin Gilbert. London: Routledge, 2007.

Archive Finder. ProQuest. Online finding aids for UK Archives. **proquest.com /products-services/archives_usa.html.**

Bibliography of British and Irish History. Royal Historical Society. **history.ac.uk /projects/bbih**. Online database containing over 500,000 records on British and Irish history.

British Cartoon Archive. British Cartoon Archive at the University of Kent. **cartoons.ac.uk/**. An archive of 120,000 newspaper cartoons covering 200 years. It has a searchable artist index with a collection of each one's work. Little historical context.

British Foreign and Colonial Offices: Confidential Print Series: Africa, Latin America, Middle East. Adam Matthew Digital. Internal documents dealing with these areas from the 1830s to the 1960s.

British History—BBC. BBC. **bbc.co.uk/history/british**. Short scholarly essays with images for a series of exhibits such as Anglo-Saxons, Normans, Middle Ages, Civil War, Tudors, Empire, the Victorian era, World War I, World War II, and modern Britain.

British History Online. Institute of Historical Research. **british-history.ac.uk/**. Primary and secondary documents from the medieval to the modern periods and for a wide array of subjects. Searchable by subject or by place.

British Library. **bl.uk/onlinegallery/index.html**. Thirty thousand resources, especially on the history of Britain. Also contains a pathbreaking exhibit, "Turning the Pages," where the viewer can "turn" the leaves of the original volume of, for example, the notebooks of Leonardo Da Vinci, the Magna Carta, and other such treasures of the library.

British Periodicals. ProQuest. Full text of several hundred popular periodicals, seventeenth through nineteenth centuries.

Hansard: Official Reports of Parliamentary Debates, 1803–2005. **hansard .millbanksystems.com/**. Reports of the business of the House of Lords and the House of Commons. Searchable by date.

History of Parliament. British Online History. **histparl.ac.uk/**. This collection contains studies of parliamentary elections, the lives of members, and

Parliament as an institution. It includes records of the House of Commons (1386–1832) and House of Lords (1660–1832).

In the First Person: An Index to Letters, Diaries, Oral Histories, and Personal Narratives. Alexander Street Press. **inthefirstperson.com/firp/index.shtml**. A strong search capability for a very large online database. Citations and full text. Covers the United States also.

Oral History Online. Alexander Street Press. Online index to oral histories. Links to recordings when available. Includes thousands of pages of printed interviews.

Oxford Dictionary of National Biography. Oxford University Press. **oxforddnb .com/**. Fully searchable, regularly updated UK online biography collection.

Parliamentary Publications. Parliamentary Archives. **parliament.uk/business /publications/**. Contains the archives of the UK Parliament. Includes links to digital sources.

UK National Archives. **discovery.nationalarchives.gov.uk/**. Major categories of documents are "Family History" (military records, wills), "Society and Law," "Home and Foreign Affairs," and "Military and Defense." There is a download fee for most documents.

Britain before 1800

The Blackwell Encyclopedia of Anglo-Saxon England. Ed. Michael Lapidge, John Blair, Simon Keynes, and Donald Scragg. New York: Blackwell, 2000.

The Kings of Medieval England, c. 560–1485: A Survey and Research Guide. Ed. Larry W. Usilton. Lanham, MD: Scarecrow Press, 1996.

Medieval England: An Encyclopedia. Ed. Paul E. Szarmch et al. New York: Garland, 1998.

Tudor England: An Encyclopedia. Ed. Arthur F. Kinney and David W. Swain. New York: Garland, 2000.

Women in Early Modern England. Sara Mendelson and Patricia Crawford. New York: Oxford University Press, 2000.

Bodleian Library, Broadside Ballads. Bodleian Library, University of Oxford. **ballads.bodleian.ox.ac.uk/**. Printed texts of 30,000 song-sheets. Searchable by topic. Includes thirteen sound files as examples of popular tunes.

Britannia History Index: The Age of Empire. **britannia.com/history/h80.html**. Documents, chronologies, articles, biographies, and links relating to Great Britain during the Age of Empire (1689–1901).

Britannia History Index: Reformation and Restoration [England, 1486–1689]. **britannia .com/history/h70.html**. Documents, chronologies, articles, biographies, and links relating to England during the Reformation, Civil War, and Restoration.

British History Online. University of London and the History of Parliament Trust. **british-history.ac.uk/subject.aspx**. Thousands of primary and secondary documents from the medieval, early modern, and modern periods of British history. These cover such subjects as government, church, economy, local history, Parliament, London, and maps, among others.

The British Library. **bl.uk/**. This site offers online access to historical newspapers and a variety of special exhibits.

CERES. Cambridge English Renaissance Electronic Service. **open.conted.ox.ac .uk/resources/link/cambridge-english-renaissance-electronic-service-ceres**. A large database of links to Renaissance documents online.

Civil War and Revolution. BBC. **bbc.co.uk/history/british/civil_war_revolution**. A series of segmented essays by scholars with images and bibliographies.

Cobbetts Parliamentary History, 1700–1806. Oxford Digital Library. **www2.odl .ox.ac.uk/gsdl/cgi-bin/library?site=localhost&a=p&p=about&c=modhis06 &ct=0&l=en&w=iso-8859-1**. Part of a large collection of works on the history of Parliament.

Colonial State Papers, 1574–1757. ProQuest. Papers presented to the Privy Council and the Board of Trade.

Early English Books Online, 1475–1700. ProQuest. Provides access to more than 125,000 digital books.

Early Manuscripts at Oxford University. Oxford University. **image.ox.ac.uk/**. Eighty digitized manuscripts that can be viewed for personal use only.

Eighteenth Century Collections Online [1701–1800]. Gale. A large full-text database of eighteenth-century materials printed in Britain.

Eighteenth Century Entertainment Ephemera. Oxford Digital Library–Scholarly Editions. **www2.odl.ox.ac.uk/gsdl/cgi-bin/library?site=localhost&a=p&p=about &c=bodjjo05&ct=0&l=en&w=iso-8859-1**. A large collection of newspaper articles, advertisements, and handbills, organized into topics such as theater, circuses, exhibits, "freaks," and wax museums. Some are open to view, others not.

Eighteenth-Century Resources—History. Rutgers, Newark. **andromeda.rutgers .edu/~jlynch/18th/history.html**. A large number of annotated links; particularly strong in American and British history, but covers related areas as well.

The Middle Ages. BBC. **bbc.co.uk/history/british/middle_ages**. A series of segmented essays by scholars, with images and bibliographies.

The Normans. BBC. **bbc.co.uk/history/british/normans/**. A series of segmented essays (and linked images) by scholars.

The Parliament Rolls of Medieval England. Scholarly Digital Editions. **british-history .ac.uk/no-series/parliament-rolls-medieval**. Contains the full text and translation of the meetings of Parliament, 1272–1504.

Proceedings of the Old Bailey, London's Central Criminal Court, 1674 to 1913. **oldbaileyonline.org/**. A searchable collection of nearly 200,000 criminal trials at London's central criminal court.

Tudor History. **tudorhistory.org/texts**. A small archive of texts and documents from the Tudor period as well as commentaries on it.

The Tudors. BBC. **bbc.co.uk/history/british/tudors**. A series of segmented essays by scholars, with images and bibliographies.

Virginia Company Archives, 1590–1790. Adam Matthew Digital. Keyword searchable documents from the Virginia Company Archives.

Britain since 1800

British Economic and Social History: A Bibliographical Guide. 3rd ed. Ed. R. C. Richardson and W. H. Chaloner. Manchester, UK: Manchester University Press, 1996.

The Cambridge Historical Encyclopedia of Great Britain and Ireland. Ed. Christopher Haigh. Cambridge: Cambridge University Press, 1990.

Modern England, 1901–1984: A Bibliographical Handbook. 2nd ed. Comp. Alfred F. Havighurst. Cambridge: Cambridge University Press, 2004.

The Oxford History of England: Consolidated Index. Comp. Richard Raper. Oxford: Clarendon/Oxford University Press, 1991.

Victorian Britain: An Encyclopedia. Ed. Sally Mitchell. New York: Garland, 1988.

Britannia History Index: The Age of Empire. **britannia.com/history/h80.html**. Documents, chronologies, articles, biographies, and links relating to Great Britain during the Age of Empire (1689–1901).

British and Irish Women's Letters and Diaries. Alexander Street Press. **alexanderstreet.com/products/british-and-irish-womens-letters-and-diaries**. A large online collection of personal writings from the sixteenth to the twentieth centuries.

British Empire and International Relations. Victorian Web. **victorianweb.org /history/index.html**. A well-organized set of documents and commentary covering nineteenth-century British imperialism with an emphasis on India.

C19: The Nineteenth Century Index. ProQuest. Indexes to a very large variety of sources for research into the nineteenth century. Links to full-text collections.

Foreign Office Files for India, Pakistan, and Afghanistan, 1947–1980. Adam Matthew Digital. A series of document collections from the UK Foreign and Colonial Office.

The Internet Library of Early Journals. Bodleian Library, Oxford University. **bodley .ox.ac.uk/ilej/**. Full text of six eighteenth- and nineteenth-century British journals. Browsable by journal, date, and page.

Nineteenth Century Parliamentary Papers. Chadwyck-Healey/ProQuest. Keyword searchable online database covering the years 1801–1900.

Spartacus Educational. **spartacus-educational.com/**. Short hyperlinked essays focusing mostly on modern European political history. The degree of documentation for the essays varies. This section deals with the modern United Kingdom.

Twentieth Century Parliamentary Papers: House of Commons, 1901–2005. ProQuest. Full text of all printed documents of the House of Commons.

Victoria Research Web. Patrick Leary. **victorianresearch.org**. A wide-ranging research-oriented site.

Victorian Census Project. University of Staffordshire. **arch.oucs.ox.ac.uk/detail /93202/index.html**. Databases from the 1831 and 1861 censuses.

Victorian Popular Culture. Adam Matthew Digital. Visual and print items from circuses, music halls, early film, etc.

The Victorian Web. **victorianweb.org/history**. Site content and links relating to Victorian-era culture, history, art, economics, science, politics, and imperialism. Resources include contemporary periodicals, cartoons, and bibliographies.

The Workhouse. Oxford University. **workhouses.org.uk/**. An excellent archive of linked resources examining the legal and actual treatment of the poor in England, Ireland, Scotland, and Wales in the eighteenth, nineteenth, and twentieth centuries.

Ireland and Scotland

A Bibliography of Works Relating to Scotland, 1916–1950. Ed. P. D. Hancock. Edinburgh: Edinburgh University Press, 1959–1960.

Celtic Culture: A Historical Encyclopedia. Ed. John T. Koch. Santa Barbara, CA: ABC-CLIO, 2006.

A Chronology of Irish History since 1500. Ed. J. E. Doherty and D. J. Hickey. Savage, MD: Rowman & Littlefield, 1990.

Encyclopedia of Irish History and Culture. Ed. James S. Donnelly Jr. et al. New York: Macmillan Reference USA, 2004.

Bibliography of British and Irish History. Royal Historical Society. **history.ac.uk /projects/bbih**. Online database containing over 500,000 records on British and Irish history.

British and Irish Women's Letters and Diaries. Alexander Street Press. A large online collection of personal writings from the sixteenth to the twentieth centuries.

CELT: Corpus of Electronic Texts. University College Cork. **celt.ucc.ie//**. Links to journals, bibliographies, and archives for research in Irish studies.

EPPI: Enhanced British Parliamentary Papers on Ireland, 1801–1922. University of Southampton Library. **dippam.ac.uk/eppi/**. A selection of parliamentary acts and publications relating to Ireland. Searchable through the catalog of the Southampton Library, which recommends you type "EPPI" along with your keywords. **www-lib.soton.ac.uk/**.

The Highland Clearances. **theclearances.org/clearances/main.php**. A large number of well-organized, annotated documents concerning the nineteenth-century displacement of Scottish farmers and the emigration of many. Last updated in 2005.

Irish History Online. Royal Irish Academy. **iho.ie/**. A project to place online the very large bibliography published in print since the 1930s.

Irish Resources in the Humanities. **irith.org/index.jsp**. A collection of links to archives and other academic resources in Irish history.

National Archives of Ireland. **nationalarchives.ie/search-the-archives/**. A description of each collection of documents is available. Some documents are online, but not a great number.

National Library of Scotland—Map Library. **maps.nls.uk/**. Selected from a very important collection of maps covering Scotland and other areas. Historical context offered. Display of maps excellent.

Scottish History: Ancient to Modern. BBC. **bbc.co.uk/history/scottishhistory /index.shtml**. Essays and materials related to the ten-part TV series *In Search of Scotland.*

Stormont Papers: 50 Years of Northern Ireland Parliamentary Debates Online. **stormontpapers.ahds.ac.uk/index.html**. Searchable by keyword or subject. In some cases full text is available. Materials concern parliamentary debates from June 7, 1921, until March 28, 1972.

The Word on the Street: Broadsides at the National Library of Scotland. **digital.nls.uk /broadsides/**. A searchable database of broadsides from 1650 to 1910. Many are transcribed and downloadable.

Eastern Europe

Encyclopedia of Eastern Europe. Ed. Richard Frucht. New York: Garland, 2000.

Historical Atlas of East Central Europe. Rev. ed. Ed. Paul R. Magocsi. Seattle: University of Washington Press, 2002.

Independent Ukraine: A Bibliographical Guide to English-Language Publications, 1989–1999. Ed. Bohdan S. Wynar. Englewood, CO: Ukrainian Academic Press, 2000.

Yugoslavia: A Comprehensive English-Language Bibliography. Ed. Francine Friedman. Wilmington, DE: Scholarly Resources, 1993.

The American Bibliography of Slavic and East European Studies (ABSEES) Online. EBSCO Publishing, American Association for the Advancement of Slavic and East European Studies. A bibliography of books, journal articles, online resources, and so on. Includes many disciplines. The online version is available by subscription only.

Bulgaria's History. OMDA Library. **omda.bg/engl/common/history.htm**. A series of short hypertext essays on a variety of historical topics.

Czech and Slovak History: An American Bibliography. Ed. George J. Kovtun. **loc.gov /rr/european/cash/cash1.html**. An extensive bibliography of books and articles in English. Contains works written before 1994.

Radio Prague's History Online Virtual Exhibit. Radio Prague. **beta.clio-online.de /webresource/id/webresource-3069**. A short essay on Czech history with images and links to further explanation of key topics.

Russia and the Soviet Union

The Blackwell Encyclopedia of the Russian Revolution. Ed. Harold Shukman. Cambridge, MA: Blackwell Reference, 1994.

Encyclopedia of Russian History. Ed. James R. Millar. 4 vols. New York: Macmillan Reference USA, 2004.

The Russian Revolution, 1905–1921: A Bibliographic Guide to the Works in English. Ed. Murray Frame. Westport, CT: Greenwood Press, 1995.

Soviet Foreign Policy, 1918–1945: A Guide to Research and Research Materials. Ed. Robert H. Johnston. Wilmington, DE: Scholarly Resources, 1991.

The Soviet Union: A Biographical Dictionary. Ed. Archie Brown. New York: Macmillan, 1991.

The American Bibliography of Slavic and East European Studies (ABSEES) Online. EBSCO Publishing, American Association for the Advancement of Slavic and East European Studies. A bibliography of books, journal articles, online resources, and so on. Includes many disciplines. The online version is available by subscription only.

Beyond the Pale: The History of Jews in Russia. **friends-partners.org/partners /beyond-the-pale/**. A series of brief essays with visuals.

Revelations from the Russian Archives. **loc.gov/exhibits/archives/**. Documents from the Soviet era focusing on repression and espionage.

Russia Engages the World: 1453–1825. New York Public Library. **russia.nypl.org/**. A collection of documents on Russia and the West (and also Asia) in the fifteenth to nineteenth centuries.

Seventeen Moments in Soviet History. James von Geldern and Lewis Siegelbaum. **soviethistory.msu.edu/**. Extensive introductory essays, hundreds of audio and video clips, and thousands of archival documents. Written material is translated into English. Free registration is required to access some resources.

Africa

Africana: The Encyclopedia of the African and the African American Experience. 2nd ed. Ed. Kwame Anthony Appiah and Henry Louis Gates Jr. 5 vols. New York: Oxford University Press, 2005.

Dictionary of African Biography. Ed. Emmanuel Kwaku Akyeampong and Henry Louis Gates Jr. New York: Oxford University Press, 2012.

Encyclopedia of African Nations and Civilizations. Ed. Keith Lye. New York: Facts on File, 2002.

Encyclopedia of Africa South of the Sahara. Ed. John Middleton. 4 vols. New York: Scribner, 1997.

Encyclopedia of Twentieth-Century African History. Ed. Paul Tiyambe Zeleza and Dickson Eyoh. New York: Routledge, 2002.

Historical Dictionary of Pre-Colonial Africa. Ed. Robert O. Collins. Lanham, MD: Scarecrow Press, 2001.

New Encyclopedia of Africa. 2nd ed. Ed. John Middleton and Joseph C. Miller. New York: Scribner, 2008.

Africa South of the Sahara: Selected Internet Resources. Stanford University. **library .stanford.edu/africa-south-sahara**. Links relevant to African cultures and history by country and topic.

Africa Studies Collection. University of Wisconsin. **uwdc.library.wisc.edu/collections /africanstudies**. Primary and secondary sources on African studies from the University of Wisconsin Digital Collections.

AFRICABIB. **africabib.org**. Features five bibliographic databases: African Periodical Literature; African Women; Women Travelers, Explorers, and Missionaries to Africa; Islam in Contemporary Sub-Saharan Africa; and Kenyan Coast.

African National Congress: Historical Documents. **anc.org.za/**. A collection of documents by and about the ANC and about organizations that supported the ANC struggle.

African Posters. Melville J. Herskovitz Library of African Studies, Northwestern University. **library.northwestern.edu/libraries-collections/herskovits-library /index.html**. Three hundred and fifty posters focusing primarily on South Africa and the struggle against apartheid. The collection covers domestic and international aspects of the movement.

African Studies. Columbia University Libraries. **library.columbia.edu/indiv /global/africa.html**. A collection of links to sources of research on Africa.

African Studies Quarterly. University of Florida. **africa.ufl.edu/asq/**. Online access to the journal's articles and book reviews.

African Voices. Smithsonian, National Museum of Natural History. **mnh.si.edu /africanvoices/**. Historical and contemporary images and text for African history and culture. Modest number of maps, photographs, drawings, and paintings. Subsections organized chronologically and thematically. Emphasis on material culture.

Afriterra, The Cartographic Free Library. Afriterra Foundation Library. **afriterra .org/**. More than 1,000 maps of Africa by European mapmakers from the late fifteenth century to the twentieth century. Images can be examined in a variety of ways.

Atlantic Slave Trade and Slave Life in the Americas: A Visual Record. Jerome S. Handler and Michael L. Tuite Jr., for the Virginia Foundation for the Humanities and the Digital Media Lab at the University of Virginia Library. **search.lib.virginia.edu/catalog/u3912409**. One thousand images emphasizing a pan-Atlantic perspective. Topics include culture, politics, economics, geography, and military. Easily searchable by keyword or by subject. Images accompanied by annotations, but some are very brief.

Digital Innovation South Africa. **disa.ukzn.ac.za/**. Essays and resources focusing on South Africa, particularly during the years 1950–1994.

National Archives of South Africa. **www.national.archsrch.gov.za/sm300cv/smws /sm300dl**. Excellent search facility for fourteen databases of the nation's archives. At this time online access only to document summaries.

National Museum of African Art. Smithsonian Institution. **africa.si.edu/collections /index.htm**. An online permanent exhibit featuring a large number of annotated images.

Studies in the History of the African Diaspora. York University Library. **yorku.ca /nhp/shadd/shadd.htm**. Essays and documents on the African Diaspora. Many are in English.

Trans-Atlantic Slave Trade Database. Emory University. **slavevoyages.org/**. Searchable databases of voyages, quantitative data, and images.

Middle East and North Africa

Encyclopedia of the Arab-Israeli Conflict: A Political, Social, and Military History. Ed. Spencer C. Tucker. 4 vols. Santa Barbara, CA: ABC-CLIO, 2008.

Encyclopedia of the Modern Middle East and North Africa. 2nd ed. Ed. Philip Mattar et al. 4 vols. Detroit: Macmillan Reference USA, 2004.

Encyclopedia of the Ottoman Empire. Ed. Gábor Ágoston and Bruce Masters. New York: Facts on File, 2008.

Grove Encyclopedia of Islamic Art and Architecture. Ed. Jonathan M. Bloom and Sheila S. Blair. 3 vols. Oxford: Oxford University Press, 2009.

The Oxford Encyclopedia of the Modern Islamic World. Ed. John L. Esposito. 4 vols. New York: Oxford University Press, 1995. Covers the eighteenth century to the present.

Index Islamicus: Index to the Literature on Islam. Cambridge University Library. A large database of literature on Islam, the Middle East, and the Muslim world.

Middle Eastern and Islamic Studies. Columbia University Libraries. **library.columbia .edu/locations/global/mideast.html**. A large collection of links to resources on the Middle East.

Question of Palestine: History. United Nations. **unispal.un.org/**. This UN multimedia document discusses the history of Palestine since 1917.

The Topkapi Palace Museum. Bilkent University. **ee.bilkent.edu.tr/~history /topkapi.html**. More than one hundred objects of Islamic art from the collections of the Ottoman dynasty.

Asia — General

Bibliography of Asian Studies. Ann Arbor: Association for Asian Studies, 1956–1991. Succeeded by *BAS Online* (see below).

Encyclopedia of Asian History. Ed. Ainslie T. Embree. 4 vols. New York: Scribner, 1988.

Southeast Asia: A Historical Encyclopedia, from Angkor Wat to East Timor. Ed. Ooi Keat Gin. 3 vols. Santa Barbara, CA: ABC-CLIO, 2004.

Vietnam Studies: An Annotated Bibliography. Ed. Carl Singleton. Lanham, MD: Scarecrow Press, 1997.

Asian Division, Area Studies. Library of Congress. **lcweb.loc.gov/rr/asian**. Information on the Library of Congress's Asian studies collections, as well as a Korean bibliography and a Japanese Documentation Center with a searchable database.

Asian Studies Search Engines. T. Matthew Ciolek. **ciolek.com/SearchEngines .html**. Onsite access to a series of offsite search engines, including H-Nets. Also a database of images. Last updated in 2009.

Bibliography of Asian Studies (BAS) Online. Association for Asian Studies. A fully searchable database of journal articles and other scholarly resources on Asia.

Formosa. Reed College. **academic.reed.edu/formosa/formosa_index_page /Formosa_index.html**. An archive of U.S. writings on "Formosa" in the nineteenth century. Also features maps, art, and photographs.

Huntington Archive of Buddhist and Related Art. Ohio State University. **hunting tonarchive.osu.edu/database.php**. A searchable database of photographed images of art from Asia and South Asia.

Philippine Bibliography. Library of Congress. **lcweb2.loc.gov/asian/philhtml /philhome.html**. An online bibliography of the Library of Congress's Philippine history collection.

Southeast Asian Archive. University of California, Irvine. **seaa.lib.uci.edu**. Virtual exhibits and annotated links to Southeast Asian resources.

SouthEast Asian Images and Texts. University of Wisconsin Digital Collections. **uwdc .library.wisc.edu/collections/seait/**. Focuses on the Philippines and Laos. Collection of primary and secondary resources, including 3,600 photographs from the early 1900s to the 1940s. Contains a series of short scholarly articles.

Viettouch. **viettouch.com**. Essays covering Vietnamese history, with internal links to art, chronology, and so on. Especially strong in ancient Vietnam.

South Asia — India, Pakistan, and Sri Lanka

The Cambridge Encyclopedia of India, Pakistan, Sri Lanka, Nepal, Bhutan and the Maldives. Ed. Francis Robinson. Cambridge: Cambridge University Press, 1989.

Encyclopedia of India. Ed. Stanley A. Wolpert. 4 vols. New York: Scribner, 2005.

A Historical Atlas of South Asia. 2nd ed. Ed. Joseph E. Schwartzberg. New York: Oxford University Press, 1992.

Digital South Asia Library. University of Chicago. **dsal.uchicago.edu**. Categorizes resources useful in South Asian research, including documents, books, newspapers, references, journals, bibliographies, and maps.

GandhiMedia. Gandhi Serve Foundation. **gandhimedia.org/**. A searchable archive of Gandhi's correspondence, published writings, and other materials.

Harappa: Glimpses of South Asia before 1947. **harappa.com/index.html**. Text and images from early Indus Valley civilizations. Also, images, sound, and film from the decades prior to independence and partition.

Mohenjo Daro. Jonathan Mark Kenoyer, University of Wisconsin–Madison. **mohenjodaro.net**. A small collection of images and secondary sources from excavations at Mohenjo Daro in the Indus Valley (2600 to 1900 BCE). Emphasis is on daily life. Each image is accompanied by a detailed explanation. Unfortunately, website includes advertisements.

Primary Documents for the Study of Indian History, c. 1890–2000. **sscnet.ucla.edu/southasia/MAIN/research.html**. A bibliography, part of a larger site on the history of India.

South Asia Resource Access on the Internet [SARAI]. Columbia University. **columbia.edu/cu/lweb/indiv/southasia/cuvl/**. Links to journals, organizations, and topical guides on South Asian history.

China

China: A Historical and Cultural Dictionary. Ed. Michael Dillon. Richmond, Surrey, UK: Curzon, 1998.

Modern China: An Encyclopedia of History, Culture, and Nationalism. Ed. Wang Kewen. New York: Garland, 1998.

Academic Info: Chinese History. **academicinfo.net/chinahist.html**. Selected, annotated links to chronologies, databases, bibliographies, journals, and dictionaries. Site has some advertisements.

Chinese Posters: Propaganda, Politics, and Art. **chineseposters.net/index.php**. Hundreds of Chinese posters covering 1925–2006. Organized by theme.

The Gate of Heavenly Peace. Long Bow Group. **pbs.org/wgbh/pages/frontline/gate/**. Digital material organized around a PBS documentary on the Tiananmen Massacre of June 4, 1989. Includes background material and a variety of perspectives on the event. Articles, essays, audio, video, and artwork.

John Fairbank Memorial Chinese History Virtual Library. Chinese News Digest. **cnd.org/fairbank/**. Information about the Qing period, the Republican era, and the People's Republic of China.

Japan and Korea

The Cambridge History of Japan. Ed. John Whitney Hall. 6 vols. Cambridge: Cambridge University Press, 1988–1999.

Concise Dictionary of Modern Japanese History. Ed. Janet E. Hunter. Berkeley: University of California Press, 1984.

Japan and Korea: A Critical Bibliography. Ed. Bernard S. Silberman. Whitefish, MT: Literary Licensing, LLC, 2013.

Japanese History and Culture from Ancient to Modern Times: Seven Basic Bibliographies. Ed. John W. Dower and Timothy S. George. New York: M. Wiener, 1997.

Modern Japan: An Encyclopedia of History, Culture and Nationalism. Ed. James L. Huffman. New York: Garland, 1998.

Studies on Korea: A Scholar's Guide. Ed. Han-Kyo Kim. Honolulu: University of Hawaii Press, 1980.

Asian Division, Area Studies. Library of Congress. **loc.gov/rr/asian/**. Information on the Library of Congress's Asian studies collections.

Asuka Historical Museum. **asukanet.gr.jp/asukahome/**. Exhibits on the Japanese Nara culture, seventh century.

Japanese Studies Resources. Duke University Libraries. **library.duke.edu/research/international/japan**. An extensive compilation of bibliographies, journals, dictionaries, reference works, and other materials useful to the study of Japan.

J Guide: Stanford Guide to Japan Information Resources. **jguide.stanford.edu/**. Covers all aspects of Japanese culture and history, with extensive links.

Joseph Berry Keenan Digital Collection. Harvard Law School Library. **law.harvard.edu/library/digital/keenan-digital-collection.html**. Manuscript materials and photographs concerning the Japanese War Crimes Trials.

Korean Bibliography. Library of Congress. **lcweb2.loc.gov/misc/korhtml/korbibhome.html**. A searchable database of books on Korea in English.

Korean History: A Bibliography. University of Hawaii. **hawaii.edu/korea/biblio/BiblioOpen.html**. An online bibliography organized by period.

Kyoto National Museum. **kyohaku.go.jp/eng/syuzou/index.html**. An extensive online collection of pre-1800 Japanese art.

Australia and New Zealand

Australian Dictionary of Biography. Ed. Douglas Pike et al. 16 vols. Carlton, Victoria: Melbourne University Press, 1966–. Also available online at **adb.anu.edu.au/**.

Australian Federation Full Text Database. University of Sydney. **adc.library.usyd.edu.au/index.jsp?database=ozfed&page=home**. Transcribed debates and related writings on the Federation movement.

Australian Studies Resources. University of Sydney. **setis.library.usyd.edu.au/oztexts/**. A large digital collection of Australian literary and historical texts and journals.

Colonial Case Law—Australia. Macquarie University Law School. **law.mq.edu.au/research/colonial_case_law/**. A selection of court records, including colonial case law in New South Wales and Tasmania, privy council decisions, and colonial cases.

National Library of Australia. **nla.gov.au/app/eresources/browse**. A list of serious websites on Australian history.

National Library of New Zealand: Papers Past. **paperspast.natlib.govt.nz/**. A digital collection of nineteenth-century New Zealand newspapers and periodicals.

Trove: Journals, Articles and Datasets. National Library of Australia. **trove.nla.gov .au/article**. Keyword searchable journal articles, reports, book chapters, reviews, working papers, data sets, newspapers, and magazines.

Latin America and the Caribbean

Encyclopedia of Brazilian History and Culture. Ed. E. Riedinger. London: Routledge, 2009.

Encyclopedia of Latin American History and Culture. 2nd ed. Ed. Jay Kinsbruner and Erik Langer. 5 vols. New York: Scribner, 2008.

Handbook of Latin American Studies. Cambridge, MA: Harvard University Press, 1936–1947; and Gainesville: University of Florida Press, 1948–. Annual volume. Also a searchable database on the website of the Library of Congress at **rs6.loc.gov/hlas**.

Hispanic Culture of South America. Ed. Peter Standish. Detroit: Gale Research, 1995.

Historical Dictionary of Mexico. 2nd ed. By Marvin Alisky. Lanham, MD: Scarecrow Press, 2008.

Historical Dictionary of the Spanish Empire, 1402–1975. Ed. Sam L. Slick. Westport, CT: Greenwood Press, 1991.

The History Atlas of South America. Ed. Edwin Early. New York: Macmillan, 1998.

Mexico: An Encyclopedia of Contemporary Culture and History. Ed. Don M. Coerver, Suzanne B. Pasztor, and Robert Buffington. Santa Barbara, CA: ABC-CLIO, 2004.

The Oxford Encyclopedia of Mesoamerican Cultures: The Civilizations of Mexico and Central America. Ed. David Carrasco. 3 vols. Oxford: Oxford University Press, 2001.

Castro Speech Database. University of Texas. **lanic.utexas.edu/la/cb/cuba/castro .html**. English translations of Fidel Castro's speeches.

Central American Archives. ProQuest. Primary documents from the national archives of several Central American nations. Mostly in Spanish, for the period 1519–1898.

Cuban Heritage Digital History Collection. University of Miami Libraries. **merrick .library.miami.edu/digitalprojects/chc.php**. Includes manuscripts, photographs, and other resources culled from the University of Miami Libraries Cuban Heritage Collection.

Latin American Network Information Center. University of Texas. **lanic.utexas.edu /la/region/history/**. This site organizes online history resources on Latin America. Some sites are in Spanish.

Latin American Newspapers. Readex. 1805–1922. Online database includes newspapers in English, Spanish, and Portuguese.

Latin American Pamphlet Digital Collection. Harvard University. **vc.lib.harvard.edu /vc/deliver/home?_collection=LAP**. A large collection of full-text pamphlets.

Mexico: From Empire to Revolution. Getty Research Institute. **getty.edu/research /tools/guides_bibliographies/mexico/**. A photographic archive of Mexico covering the years 1857–1923.

The Perry-Castañeda Library Map Collection. University of Texas. **lib.utexas.edu /maps/index.html**. An extensive collection of historical maps covering many areas of the world.

PreColumbian Portfolio. Foundation for the Advancement of Mesoamerican Studies. **research.famsi.org/kerrportfolio.html**. A database of 2,000 artifacts from several pre-Columbian cultures in Central and South America. Mythology, daily life, religion.

Realms of the Sacred in Daily Life: Early Written Records of Mesoamerica. University of California, Riverside. **lib.uci.edu/about/publications/exhibits/meso/sacred .html**. An annotated collection of "Codices"—documents in the native "languages" of the Aztec, Maya, and Mixtec people of Mexico and Central America.

Sources and General Resources on Latin America. **oberlin.edu/faculty/svolk /latinam.htm**. A large collection of links to Latin American history sites.

The Strachwitz Frontera Collection of Mexican and Mexican American Recordings. UCLA, Arhoolie Foundation, Los Tigres del Norte Foundation. **frontera.library.ucla .edu/**. Thirty thousand phonograph recordings in Spanish representing Mexican American vernacular music. A browsable list of subjects. Except for users on the UCLA campus, only fifty-second sound clips are available.

Templo Mayor Museum. **templomayor.inah.gob.mx/english**. This site guides you through the halls of the museum, dedicated to ancient Mexican history and artifacts. Last updated in 2000.

Vistas: Visual Culture in Spanish America, 1520–1820. Dana Leibsohn, Smith College, and Barbara Mundy, Fordham University. **smith.edu/vistas**. Focuses on art and architecture of the Spanish colonial period in the Americas. One hundred and fifty images of objects, buildings, sculptures, drawings, and maps. Each image includes an explanation of its use, origin, and significance.

Canada

Bibliography of Ontario History, 1867–1976: Cultural, Economic, Political and Social. By Olga B. Bishop. 2 vols. Toronto: University of Toronto Press, 1980. Supplement, 1976–1986. Toronto: Dunburn Press, 1989.

The Canadian Encyclopedia, 2000. Ed. James H. March. Toronto: McClelland and Stewart, 2000. See below for online version.

Canadian Reference Sources: An Annotated Bibliography. Ed. Mary E. Bond and Martine M. Caron. Vancouver: University of British Columbia Press, 1996.

Canadian Who's Who. 37 vols. Toronto: University of Toronto Press, 2011. Also available online by subscription.

Dictionary of Canadian Biography. Toronto: University of Toronto Press, 1966–. A print index covers *Volumes I to XII, 1000 to 1900.* See also below, *Dictionary of Canadian Biography Online.*

Historical Atlas of Canada. Ed. R. Cole Harris et al. 3 vols. Toronto: University of Toronto Press, 1987–1993.

American Journeys: Eyewitness Accounts of Early American Exploration and Settlement. Wisconsin Historical Society. **americanjourneys.org/**. One hundred and eighty texts written by explorers, traders, missionaries, settlers, and Native Americans.

Documents range from works by early Viking explorers to the journals of nineteenth-century North Americans. All documents in English translation. Site includes a large number of drawings, maps, photographs, and paintings.

Canada's Digital Collections. Government of Canada. **epe.lac-bac.gc.ca/100 /205/301/ic/cdc/E/Alphabet.asp**. An alphabetical index to a large number of online sites concerning many aspects of Canadian history.

The Canadian Encyclopedia. **thecanadianencyclopedia.com/**. This site allows you to search 50,000 articles, many relating to Canadian history. Created for beginning researchers.

The Canadian West. Library and Archives Canada. **collectionscanada.gc.ca/05 /0529/052901_e.html**. A broad-ranging essay with links and images concerning the experience of Natives and Europeans on the Canadian "frontier." No longer updated.

Dictionary of Canadian Biography Online. **biographi.ca/index-e.html**. A searchable database of Canadians who lived or were well known before 1930. This date will move forward as the database is updated.

Early Canadiana Online. **canadiana.org/eco/english/collect.html**. A centralized, rapidly growing collection of documents relating to Canadian history through the early twentieth century. Some collections available to subscribers only.

First Peoples of Canada. Canadian Museum of Civilization, Online Exhibits. **civilization.ca/exhibitions/online-exhibitions/first-peoples**. Many subsections to the topic, each with its own introduction. Maps, bibliographies, and illustrations. Other online exhibits include "Gateway to Aboriginal History."

The Last Best West, Advertising for Immigrants to Western Canada, 1870–1930. Canadian Museum of Civilization. **civilization.ca/cmc/exhibitions/hist/advertis /adindexe.shtml**. Text and images concerning the effort to attract European immigrants to western Canada.

Library and Archives Canada. Government of Canada. **collectionscanada.gc.ca /index-e.html**. Wide-ranging collections of primary source materials and research guides. Includes monographs and periodicals.

Peopling North America: Population Movements and Migration. University of Calgary. **ucalgary.ca/applied_history/tutor/migrations/**. A historical overview of migratory movements. Includes the Native American peoples of the United States as well.

GENERAL RESOURCES IN UNITED STATES HISTORY

Before examining the general resources in U.S. history listed in this section, you should consult the historical dictionaries, encyclopedias, and atlases listed at the beginning of this appendix. They will enable you to choose and narrow a topic.

The general resources in this section consist of bibliographies and websites that cover large areas and many periods of U.S. history. The specialized resources described later will be useful once you have chosen a topic and have a clear understanding of the kind of research you will need to do to develop and support your thesis. Even if you have already narrowed your topic, you should not ignore the following general resources, because many of them include sections on or links to more specialized topics.

Reference Works and Bibliographies

The American Historical Association's Guide to Historical Literature. 3rd ed. Ed. Mary Beth Norton. 2 vols. New York: Oxford University Press, 1995. This guide contains a large section on U.S. history.

A Companion to American Thought. Ed. Richard Wightman Fox and James T. Kloppenberg. Malden, MA: Blackwell Publishers, 1998.

Directory of Oral History Collections. Ed. Allen Smith. Phoenix: Oryx, 1988.

Encyclopedia of the American Constitution. 2nd ed. Ed. Leonard Levy. 6 vols. New York: Macmillan, 2000.

Encyclopedia of American Cultural and Intellectual History. Ed. Mary Kupiec Cayton and Peter W. Williams. 3 vols. New York: Scribner, 2001.

Encyclopedia of American History. Rev ed. Ed. Gary B. Nash. 11 vols. New York: Facts on File, 2010.

The Reader's Companion to American History. Ed. Eric Foner and John A. Garraty. Boston: Houghton Mifflin, 1991.

Websites

Amdocs. World Wide Web Virtual Library. **vlib.us/amdocs**. A large collection of primary documents relating to North America and covering the large span from 800 CE to 2005.

American Antiquarian Society: Historical Periodicals Collection, 1691–1877. EBSCO Publishing. Five series of 10–20 years each.

American Journeys: Eyewitness Accounts of Early American Exploration and Settlement. Wisconsin Historical Society. **americanjourneys.org**/. One hundred and eighty texts written by explorers, traders, missionaries, settlers, and Native Americans. Documents range from works by early Viking explorers to the journals of nineteenth-century North Americans. All documents in English translation. Site includes a large number of drawings, maps, photographs, and paintings.

American Memory. Library of Congress. **memory.loc.gov**/. This site features more than 7 million documents relating to American history. This URL will take you to the main page of the site. It is a good place to start your research into a wide variety of topics in U.S. history.

American Periodicals Series Online. ProQuest. Magazines and journals for the seventeenth, eighteenth, and nineteenth centuries.

American State Papers, 1789–1838. Library of Congress. **memory.loc.gov /ammem/amlaw/lwsp.html**. Legislative and executive documents of Congress. Search by keyword or browse by subject.

American Studies at the University of Virginia. **xroads.virginia.edu**. A variety of multimedia and hypertext sources, exhibits, timelines, and other resources of use for studying American history, with a special section on the 1930s.

An American Time Capsule: Three Centuries of Broadsides and Other Printed Ephemera. Library of Congress, American Memory. **memory.loc.gov/ammem/rbpehtml**.

A searchable collection of 17,000 posters, advertisements, leaflets, propaganda pieces, and business cards dating from the seventeenth century to the present.

Archive Finder. Chadwyck-Healey/ProQuest. A searchable online directory of over 5,000 archives of primary source material in the United States. Updates and supersedes *Directory of Archives and Manuscript Repositories in the United States* (Phoenix: Oryx, 1988) and includes the National Union Catalogue of Manuscript Collections (NUCMC) and ArchivesUSA.

Avalon Project: Documents in Law, History and Diplomacy. Yale Law School. **avalon .law.yale.edu/**. Documents in law, history, and diplomacy from many periods in American history, organized by century.

Berkeley Digital Library SunSITE. **sunsite.berkeley.edu/**. Texts and images, including classical and medieval works, the Emma Goldman papers, and a strong collection relating to California.

Chronicling America: Historic American Newspapers. Library of Congress and National Endowment for the Humanities. **chroniclingamerica.loc.gov.** The main collection, "The National Digital Newspaper Program," currently covers the years 1836–1922. This database includes full text and is searchable by newspaper name and by topic. It contains a large selection of digitized newspapers from state archives, libraries, and institutions, many published in small towns and cities. Also available is the "U.S. Newspaper Directory, 1690–Present." These newspapers are held by local repositories. This database is searchable by state, county, and newspaper title. It tells you when a particular newspaper was published, where archives of it are held, and in what form.

Core Historical Literature of Agriculture. Cornell University. **chla.library.cornell .edu/**. A collection of primary and secondary documents on agriculture in the nineteenth and twentieth centuries, including over 800 monographs.

Duke University David M. Rubenstein Rare Book and Manuscript Library. **library .duke.edu/rubenstein/**. Highly specialized and in-depth collections of digital materials on a variety of subjects but especially in the areas of advertising, the history of women, African American history, and Native American history.

The Great Chicago Fire and the Web of Memory. **greatchicagofire.org/**. Essays, images, and primary documents about the fire of 1871 and its legacies.

History Matters. George Mason University. **historymatters.gmu.edu.** Includes over 1,000 primary documents in text, image, and audio and an annotated list of over 850 sites for serious research in U.S. history on the web.

H-Reviews. **h-net.org/reviews**. A searchable online collection of full-text book reviews in all fields of history.

In the First Person: English Language Letters, Diaries, Autobiographies, Memoirs and Oral Histories. Alexander Street Press. A strong search capability for a very large online database.

Karpeles Manuscript Museum Libraries. **rain.org/~karpeles/list.html**. Collection of U.S. manuscripts and historical documents.

Making of America. University of Michigan. **quod.lib.umich.edu/m/moa/**. Scanned images of books and magazine articles (over 10,000 books and 50,000 journal articles) from nineteenth-century America. The focus is on social history in the period 1850–1876. Searchable, full-text access. See also the next item.

Making of America. Cornell University Library. **ebooks.library.cornell.edu/m /moa/**. Complements coverage by the University of Michigan site (preceding item) with its own collection of nineteenth-century books and articles. Full-text access.

National Historical Geographic Information System (NHGIS). **nhgis.org**. Provides a range of GIS-compatible data for the United States since 1790.

National Museum of American History. Smithsonian Institution. **americanhistory .si.edu/collections/**. Searchable library and archival exhibitions drawn from the museum's larger collection.

The National Union Catalog of Manuscript Collections. Washington, DC: Library of Congress, 1959–1993. **loc.gov/coll/nucmc/**. A searchable catalog, with complex search rules, of manuscript materials held by universities, libraries, archives, historical associations, and so on. Now included in Archives USA and in Archive Finder, both from Chadwyck-Healey.

The Nineteenth Century in Print. Library of Congress, American Memory. **memory .loc.gov/ammem/ndlpcoop/moahtml/ncphome.html**. A large, searchable collection of nineteenth-century books and periodicals.

ProQuest Dissertations and Theses Database. Citations to all U.S. dissertations (since 1861). Abstracted after 1980. Full text to most dissertations added since 1997.

ProQuest History Studies Center. A large database of reference works, media, journals, and so on. All by subscription. Find out which of the individual information collections can be accessed from your library.

Questia Net Library. Questia. **questia.com/library/history/united-states-history**. A large database of digitized research sources on all eras and aspects of U.S. history.

Reviews in American History. Johns Hopkins University Press. Full-text reviews of recent books. Back issues through *JSTOR*. Also available in print.

Sabin Americana, 1500–1926. Gale. A large collection of print material about the American continent. Most material published before 1900.

U.S. Congressional Serial Set, 1817–1994. Readex. Very large online collection of congressional documents. Strong search capabilities.

VAST: Academic Video Online. Alexander Street Press. A major video collection. Includes many humanities disciplines. Most in English and created by U.S. or UK producers.

WWW-VL History: United States. **vlib.iue.it/history/USA**. This site categorizes links and materials by media, topic, and era. A very large site: some links are not available and others not reliable.

SPECIALIZED RESOURCES
IN UNITED STATES HISTORY

Once you have chosen your topic with the aid of the historical dictionaries, encyclopedias, and atlases listed at the beginning of this appendix, you are ready to seek out primary and secondary sources that you will use to develop and support your thesis. The U.S. history resources in this section are organized by subject, and the resources listed for each subject are divided into two groups. The first group contains reference works and bibliographies available in print form. The second group contains a list of websites organized alphabetically by the name of the site.

Regional, State, and Local

A Bibliography of American County Histories. Comp. P. William Filby. Baltimore: Genealogical Publishing, 1985.

Directory of Historical Organizations in the United States and Canada, 2002. 15th ed. Comp. Mary Bray Wheeler. Nashville: American Association for State and Local History, 2002.

Encyclopedia of the American West. 4 vols. New York: Simon and Schuster/Macmillan, 1996.

Encyclopedia of Local History. Ed. Carol Kammen and Norma Prendergast. Walnut Creek, CA: Alta Mira Press, 2000.

Encyclopedia of Southern Culture. Ed. Charles Reagan Wilson and William Ferris. Chapel Hill: University of North Carolina Press, 1989.

Genealogical and Local History Books in Print. 5th ed. 4 vols. Washington, DC: Genealogical Books in Print, 1996–1997.

The New Encyclopedia of the American West. Ed. Howard R. Lamar. New Haven: Yale University Press, 1998.

American County Histories to 1900. Accessible Archives. Online database organized by state. Texts of county histories primarily published between 1870 and 1900.

Center for the Study of Southern Culture. University of Mississippi. **olemiss.edu /depts/south/#**. A series of documentary collections on southern popular culture. Contains a large media archive at **olemissmedia.com/**.

Directory of State Archives. **statearchivists.org/connect/resources-state/**. A linked list of state archives throughout the United States.

Documenting the American South. University of North Carolina. **docsouth.unc .edu/**. A wide array of primary sources relating to the American South before 1940, especially North Carolina.

The First American West: The Ohio River Valley, 1750–1820. Library of Congress, American Memory. **memory.loc.gov/ammem/award99/icuhtml/fawhome .html**. A searchable collection of documents, images, and other resources in a multimedia format.

The Handbook of Texas Online. Texas State Historical Society with the University of North Texas. **tshaonline.org/handbook/about-handbook**. Thousands of full-text articles and essays on Texas history, especially the Spanish and Mexican periods. Searchable by county, town, subject, and era.

History of the American West, 1860–1920. Library of Congress, American Memory; Denver Public Library. **memory.loc.gov/ammem/award97/codhtml/haw phome.html**. Over 30,000 photos, most taken between 1860 and 1920, of Colorado towns, mining industry, and Indian communities. Keyword searchable.

Online Archive of California. California Digital Libraries. **oac.cdlib.org/**. Digital resources relating to the history of California. Several collections are more broad in scope.

State Digital Resources: Memory Projects, Online Encyclopedias, Historical & Cultural Materials Collections. **loc.gov/rr/program/bib/statememory/**. A linked list of materials on state archive websites.

Westward by Sea: A Maritime Perspective on American Expansion, 1820–1890. Library of Congress, American Memory. **memory.loc.gov/ammem/award99/mymhihtml /mymhihome.html**. A searchable collection of documents, images, and other resources in a multimedia format.

Colonial, Revolutionary, and Early National, 1607–1800

The American Revolution, 1775–1783: An Encyclopedia. Ed. Richard L. Blanco. 2 vols. New York: Garland, 1993.

The Blackwell Encyclopedia of the American Revolution. Ed. Jack P. Greene and J. R. Pole. Cambridge, MA: Blackwell, 1994.

Colonial Wars of North America, 1512–1763: An Encyclopedia. Ed. Alan Gallay. New York: Routledge, 2015.

Encyclopedia of the North American Colonies. Ed. Jacob E. Cooke. 3 vols. New York: Scribner, 1993.

James Madison and the American Nation, 1751–1836: An Encyclopedia. Ed. Robert A. Rutland. New York: Scribner, 1994.

American Journeys: Eyewitness Accounts of Early American Exploration and Settlement. Wisconsin Historical Society. **americanjourneys.org/index.asp**. One hundred and eighty texts written by explorers, traders, missionaries, settlers, and Native Americans. Documents range from works by early Viking explorers to the journals of nineteenth-century North Americans. All documents in English translation. Site includes a large number of drawings, maps, photographs, and paintings.

The Birth of the Nation: The First Federal Congress, 1789–1791. George Washington University. **www2.gwu.edu/~ffcp/exhibit/**. Selected documents on the first federal Congress of the United States.

Calendar of State Papers, Colonial (America and the West Indies, 1574–1738). **british-history.ac.uk/**. Wide-ranging, keyword searchable site contains British government records on relations with its colonies in America.

Continental Congress and Constitutional Convention: 1774–1789. Library of Congress, American Memory. **memory.loc.gov/ammem/collections/continental/**. A searchable collection of documents.

Documents of the American Revolution, 1774–1776. Northern Illinois University. **dig.lib.niu.edu**. Several thousand U.S. and UK documents.

Doing History: Martha Ballard's Diary Online. Film Study Center, Harvard University. **DoHistory.org**. The diary of an eighteenth-century midwife.

Early American Imprints. Readex. Series 1, 1639–1800. Online database containing books, pamphlets, and broadsides. Series 2 covers 1801–1819.

Early American Newspapers, Series 1, 1690–1876. NewsBank/Readex. A searchable online archive of over 600 newspapers, most from the eighteenth century.

Early Americas Digital Archive. University of Maryland. **mith.umd.edu/eada/**. A very good source for early material on North America between 1492 and 1826. Mostly full text.

Early Encounters in North America: Peoples, Cultures, and the Environment. Alexander Street Press. A large online collection of primary materials by and about the Native and European American peoples from 1534 to 1850.

Eighteenth-Century Resources—History. Rutgers, Newark. **andromeda.rutgers .edu/~jlynch/18th/**. Annotated links; particularly strong in American and British history.

George Washington Papers at the Library of Congress, 1741–1799. Library of Congress, American Memory. **rs6.loc.gov/ammem/gwhtml/gwhome.html**. This URL brings you to a number of Washington-related documents.

James Madison: 1723–1836. Library of Congress, American Memory. **memory .loc.gov/ammem/collections/madison_papers/index.html**. A searchable collection of papers.

The Papers of John Jay. Columbia University Libraries. **columbia.edu/cu/lweb /digital/jay**. One of the largest collections of documents relating to the U.S. chief justice.

Papers of the U.S. War Department, 1784–1800. **wardepartmentpapers.org.** A very large collection of documents.

Pennsylvania Gazette. Accessible Archives. **accessible-archives.com/collections /the-pennsylvania-gazette/**. This database includes the full range of the publication—1728 to the early 1800s. A wide range of search options is available.

Plimoth Plantation [colonial America, 1620–1692]. **plimoth.org**. Multimedia educational materials about colonial America and the Plymouth Colony.

Plymouth Colony Archive Project. Ed. Patricia Scott Deetz, Christopher Fennell, and J. Eric Deetz, University of Virginia. **histarch.uiuc.edu/plymouth/index .html**. Documents and analytical essays; social history of Plymouth Colony from 1620 to 1691.

Religion and the Founding of the American Republic. Library of Congress. **loc.gov /exhibits/religion/**. Documents and visual images; significance of religion for early American history; manuscripts, letters, books, prints, paintings, artifacts, and music.

Salem Witch Trials: Documentary Archive and Transcription Project. University of Virginia. **etext.virginia.edu/salem/witchcraft/home.html**. Trial transcripts, contemporary narratives, pamphlets, and sermons. Also a historical overview and links to relevant organizations and archives.

The Thomas Jefferson Digital Archive. University of Virginia. **etext.virginia.edu/jef ferson**. A very large collection of writings about Jefferson, covering 1826 to 1997. Also included are extracts from Jefferson's writings, a large number of his letters (organized by topic), and some papers for Alexander Hamilton.

Thomas Jefferson Papers. Library of Congress, American Memory. **memory.loc .gov/ammem/collections/jefferson_papers/**. About 27,000 documents, including Jefferson's letters, notes, and official writings. Reading the handwriting can be slow going.

Virginia Company Archives, 1590–1790. Adam Matthew Digital. Keyword searchable documents from the Virginia Company Archives.

Native American

American Indian Religious Tradition: An Encyclopedia. Ed. Suzanne J. Crawford and Dennis F. Kelly. 3 vols. Santa Barbara, CA: ABC-CLIO, 2005.

Atlas of American Indian Affairs. Ed. Francis Paul Prucha. Lincoln: University of Nebraska Press, 1990.

Encyclopedia of American Indian History. Ed. Bruce E. Johansen and Barry M. Pritzker. 4 vols. Santa Barbara, CA: ABC-CLIO, 2007.

Encyclopedia of the Great Plains Indians. Ed. David J. Wishart. Lincoln: University of Nebraska Press, 2007.

Handbook of North American Indians. Ed. William C. Sturtevant. 17 vols. Washington, DC: Smithsonian Institution, 1978–2001.

Native American Periodicals and Newspapers, 1828–1982: Bibliography, Publishing Record, and Holdings. Comp. Maureen E. Hady. Ed. James P. Danky. Westport, CT: Greenwood Press, 1984.

A Native Americas Encyclopedia: History, Culture and Peoples. Ed. Barry M. Pritzker. New York: Oxford University Press, 2000.

UXL Encyclopedia of Native American Tribes. 3rd ed. Ed. Sharon Malinowski et al. 5 vols. Detroit: Gale, 2012. Also available as an e-book.

Early Encounters in North America: Peoples, Cultures, and the Environment. Alexander Street Press. A large online collection of primary materials by and about the Native and European American peoples from 1534 to 1850.

NativeWeb. **nativeweb.org**. This site, which is updated and expanded regularly, features information about Native American studies.

The Newberry Library: Ayer Art Digital Collection [of American Indian History]. **newberry.org/american-indian-and-indigenous-studies**. A collection of over 500 images representing the history of North American Indians.

North American Indian Thought and Culture. Alexander Street Press. An online collection featuring over 100,000 pages worth of firsthand accounts.

Slavery and the Civil War
(See also "African American," pp. 263–64.)

Dictionary of Afro-American Slavery. Updated ed. Ed. Randall M. Miller and John David Smith. Westport, CT: Greenwood Press, 1997.

Encyclopedia of the Confederacy. Ed. Richard N. Current. 4 vols. New York: Simon and Schuster, 1998.

The Abraham Lincoln Papers. Library of Congress, American Memory. **memory .loc.gov/ammem/alhtml/malhome.html**. A searchable collection of 20,000 documents, mostly from the 1850s until his death in 1865.

The African-American Mosaic: Abolition. Library of Congress. **loc.gov/exhibits /african/afam005.html**. A multimedia exhibit guiding users through African

American history, particularly the abolition movement. Part of the larger *African-American Mosaic* at the Library of Congress.

The American Civil War: Letters and Diaries. Alexander Street Press. A 100,000-page online collection, indexed and searchable.

American Civil War Reference Library. Gale Reference Library. Detroit: U.X.L., 2003. A searchable e-book.

American Civil War Research Database. Alexander Street Press. This online database has extensive search capabilities for finding individuals connected with the Civil War.

The Anti-Slavery Literature Project. Arizona State University and Iowa State University. **antislavery.eserver.org/**. A broad variety of texts and images can be found on this site. Very good documentation. Well-maintained site. Free registration required.

Born in Slavery: Slave Narratives from the Federal Writers' Project, 1936–1938. Library of Congress, American Memory. **lcweb2.loc.gov/ammem/snhtml/snhome .html**. Over 2,000 firsthand accounts of slavery; introductory essay discusses the significance of slave narratives.

The Coming of the Civil War. World Wide Web Virtual Library. **vlib.us/eras/war .htm**. Links to eighty documents and forty longer works. Last updated in January 2010.

The Dred Scott Case Collection. Washington University Libraries. **digital.wustl .edu/d/dre/index.html**. This site features the papers of the Dred Scott case, as well as a chronology and information about the papers.

Freedmen's Bureau Online. **freedmensbureau.com**. Freedmen's Bureau records, including materials on the supervision of relief and education activities for refugees and freedmen; issuing rations, clothing, medicine; issues concerning confiscated land; labor contracts; and a variety of other records and reports.

Geography of Slavery in Virginia. Virginia Center for Digital History and University of Virginia. **www2.vcdh.virginia.edu/gos**. Over 4,000 runaway slave newspaper advertisements published in newspapers in Virginia and Maryland between 1736 and 1803.

Gilder Lehrman Center for the Study of Slavery, Resistance and Emancipation. Gilder Lehrman Institute. **glc.yale.edu/**. A collection of over 200 documents, including speeches, letters, cartoons, interviews, and articles.

Journal of the Congress of the Confederate States of America. Library of Congress, American Memory. **memory.loc.gov/ammem/amlaw/lwcc.html**. Contains extensive materials on the Confederate Congress, 1861–1865.

North American Slave Narratives, Beginnings to 1920. William Andrews, University of North Carolina, Chapel Hill. **docsouth.unc.edu/neh/**. Over 200 full-text documents; all known published slave narratives; many published biographies of slaves.

Reconstruction Era Reference Library. Gale Reference Library. 3 vols. Detroit: U.X.L., 2005. Covers the social and political history of Reconstruction. Features include biographies and primary sources.

Samuel J. May Anti-Slavery Collection. Cornell University Library. **digital.library .cornell.edu/m/mayantislavery**. A rich collection of antislavery and Civil War materials. Over 10,000 pamphlets, leaflets, broadsides, local antislavery society newsletters, sermons, and essays. Slave trade and emancipation; 300,000 full-text pages. Searchable. Many links to other collections.

Slaves and the Courts, 1740–1860. Library of Congress, American Memory. **memory.loc.gov/ammem/sthtml/sthome.html**. Pamphlets, books, and primary documents illustrate the treatment of slaves and slavery by the U.S. courts prior to emancipation.

The Trans-Atlantic Slave Trade Database. Ed. David Eltis. **slavevoyages.org/**. Searchable, interactive databases of almost 35,000 slaving voyages. Includes itineraries, ship lists, quantitative data, and images.

Uncle Tom's Cabin and American Culture. University of Virginia. **utc.iath.virginia .edu/**. An excellent multimedia archive created around Harriet Beecher Stowe's famous novel. Draws on a wide range of documents to trace the origins of the book, its reception, and the evolution of the debate about slavery and race in America.

The Valley of the Shadow: Two Communities in the American Civil War. Ed. Edward Ayers et al., University of Virginia. **valley.vcdh.virginia.edu/**. Documents from a northern county and a southern county throughout the Civil War, offering primary sources and secondary narrative and analysis.

African American

Africana: The Encyclopedia of the African and the African American Experience. 2nd ed. Ed. Kwame Anthony Appiah and Henry Louis Gates Jr. 5 vols. New York: Oxford University Press, 2005.

Black Women in America: An Historical Encyclopedia. 2nd ed. New York: Oxford University Press, 2005.

Encyclopedia of African-American Culture and History. Ed. Jack Salzman, David L. Smith, and Cornel West. 5 vols. New York: Macmillan, 1996. Supplement, 2000.

Encyclopedia of African-American Culture and History: The Black Experience in the Americas. 2nd ed. Ed. Colin A. Palmer. 6 vols. Detroit: Macmillan, 2006.

Encyclopedia of African-American History, 1619–1895: From the Colonial Period to the Age of Frederick Douglass. Ed. Paul Finkelman. 3 vols. New York: Oxford University Press, 2006.

Encyclopedia of African American History, 1896 to the Present: From the Age of Segregation to the Twenty-First Century. Ed. Paul Finkelman. 5 vols. New York: Oxford University Press, 2009.

Encyclopedia of African-American Religions. Ed. Larry G. Murphy et al. New York: Garland, 1993.

Encyclopedia of the Harlem Renaissance. Ed. Cary D. Wintz and Paul Finkelman. 2 vols. New York: Routledge, 2004. E-book, Taylor & Francis, 2004.

The African-American Mosaic. Library of Congress. **loc.gov/exhibits/african /afam001.html**. This online multimedia exhibit guides the reader through annotated images of many aspects of African American history.

African American Newspapers: Nineteenth Century. Accessible Archives. Full text of articles from major nineteenth-century African American newspapers. Searchable online.

African-American Perspectives: Pamphlets from the Daniel A. P. Murray Collection, 1818–1907. Library of Congress, American Memory. **memory.loc.gov /ammem/aap/aaphome.html**. Focuses on the late nineteenth and early twentieth centuries in America, with the bulk of the material published between 1875 and 1900.

African-American Religion: A Documentary History Project. Amherst College. **amherst.edu/~aardoc/menu.html**. Materials span 1441 to the present. Includes limited information and sample documents.

African-American Women. Duke University, David M. Rubenstein Rare Book and Manuscript Library. **library.duke.edu/rubenstein/collections/digitized /african-american-women**. Published and unpublished writings, most from the nineteenth century.

African American Women Writers of the 19th Century. New York Public Library. **digital.nypl.org/schomburg/writers_aa19/**. Fifty-two digitized books, novels, pamphlets, and poetry from the period before 1920.

Africans in America: America's Journey through Slavery. PBS Online. **pbs.org/wgbh /aia**. Complements a four-part television series covering the seventeenth to the nineteenth centuries. Contains several hundred documents, images, and maps, as well as comments by a large number of historians.

Afro-Louisiana History and Genealogy, 1718–1820. Gwendolyn Midlo Hall. **ibiblio .org/laslave/**. A searchable database of the genealogy and life of slaves in the Gulf of Mexico region.

Black Studies Center. Chadwyck-Healey. A large online collection of full-text journals, bibliographies, and historical newspapers useful for black studies research.

Black Thought and Culture. Alexander Street Press. A large online database of publications and documents written by leaders of the black community. Covers the eighteenth to the twentieth centuries.

Digital Schomburg. Schomburg Center for Research in Black Culture, New York Public Library. **nypl.org/locations/tid/64/node/65914**. Oral histories, online exhibits, images, books, and multimedia presentations drawn from the Schomburg Center's vast collections on black history.

In Motion: The African-American Migration Experience. Schomburg Center for Research in Black Culture, New York Public Library. **inmotionaame.org /home.cfm**. An excellent collection of texts, maps, and images examining the many migrations of Africans and African Americans from the era of the slave trade to the late twentieth century.

The University of Southern Mississippi Digital Collections. University of Southern Mississippi. **digilib.usm.edu/cdm/**. A searchable collection of images and documents, with an emphasis on the civil rights movement of the 1960s.

Up South: African American Migration in the Era of the Civil War. American Social History Project (ASHP). **ashp.cuny.edu/ashp-documentaries/up-south/**. A documentary on the Great Migration, one of a series of short documentaries done by the American Social History Project.

W. E. B. Du Bois Institute for Afro-American Research. Harvard University. **dubois .fas.harvard.edu/dubois**. Links to recent projects and research, including databases, bibliographies, and other materials.

Women's

The Female Experience in Eighteenth- and Nineteenth-Century America: A Guide to the History of American Women. Ed. Jill K. Conway, Linda Kealey, and Janet E. Schulte. New York: Garland, 1982.

Handbook of American Women's History. 2nd ed. Ed. Angela M. Howard and Frances M. Kavenik. Thousand Oaks, CA: Sage, 2000.

Women's Studies Encyclopedia: History, Philosophy, and Religion. Vol. 3. Ed. Helen Tierney. Westport, CT: Greenwood Press, 1991.

Civil War Women. David M. Rubenstein Rare Book and Manuscript Library, Duke University. **library.duke.edu/rubenstein/collections/digitized/civil-war-women/**. Diaries, letters, and other writing by women during the Civil War.

Discovering American Women's History Online. Middle Tennessee State University. **digital.mtsu.edu/cdm/landingpage/collection/women**. A database for locating and viewing primary sources on the history of American women. Includes links to audio, video, images, oral histories, and documents.

Documents from the Women's Liberation Movement. David M. Rubenstein Rare Book and Manuscript Library, Duke University. **library.duke.edu/rubenstein /scriptorium/wlm/**. A database of primary texts from the 1960s and 1970s. Keyword searching is not fully functional.

The Emma Goldman Papers. University of California, Berkeley. **ucblibrary3 .berkeley.edu/Goldman/**. Online exhibitions, multimedia presentations, bibliographies, and primary sources on Emma Goldman.

The Ida B. Wells Papers, 1884–1976. University of Chicago Library. **lib.uchicago .edu/e/scrc/findingaids/view.php?eadid=ICU.SPCL.IBWELLS**. Guide to the University of Chicago's Ida B. Wells collection. Includes digitized documents.

North American Women's Letters and Diaries. Alexander Street Press. A large online collection of primary sources by women from a variety of backgrounds and circumstances. Excellent searching facilities. Full text of documents from colonial times to 1950.

Trails of Hope: Overland Diaries, 1846–1869. Brigham Young University. **overlandtrails.lib.byu.edu/**. Diaries, maps, images, and trail guides of the westward migration on the Mormon, California, Oregon, and Montana trails.

Votes for Women: Selections from the National American Woman Suffrage Association Collection, 1848–1921. Library of Congress, American Memory. **memory.loc .gov/ammem/naw/nawshome.html**. A searchable collection of books and pamphlets.

Women's History. Library of Congress, American Memory. **memory.loc.gov /ammem/browse/ListSome.php?category=Women's%20History**. Allows searching of seven Library of Congress collections related to American women. Many sources are full text; some are not. An important collection is *Votes for Women* (see preceding item).

Women Working, 1800–1930. Harvard University Library. **ocp.hul.harvard.edu /ww/**. A large archive of manuscripts, pamphlets, and photographs on the role of women in the U.S. economy. Several of the subcollections examine social, cultural, racial, and gender issues.

Immigrant and Ethnic

American Immigrant Cultures. Ed. David Levinson and Melvin Ember. 2 vols. New York: Macmillan, 1997.

Asian American Studies: An Annotated Bibliography and Research Guide. Ed. Hyung-chan Kim. Westport, CT: Greenwood Press, 1989.

Dictionary of Asian American History. Ed. Hyung-chan Kim. Westport, CT: Greenwood Press, 1986.

Dictionary of Mexican American History. Ed. Matt S. Meier and Feliciano Rivera. Westport, CT: Greenwood Press, 1981.

Encyclopedia of American Immigration. 2nd Ed. James Ciment. 4 vols. New York: Routledge, 2014.

Encyclopedia Latina: History, Culture and Society in the United States. Ed. Ilan Stavans and Harold Augenbraum. 4 vols. Danbury, CT: Grollier Academic Reference, 2005.

European Immigration and Ethnicity in the United States and Canada: A Historical Bibliography. Ed. David L. Brye. Santa Barbara, CA: ABC-CLIO, 1983.

Harvard Encyclopedia of American Ethnic Groups. Ed. Stephan Thernstrom et al. Cambridge, MA: Harvard University Press, 1980.

Hispano Music and Culture from the Northern Rio Grande: The Jan B. Rael Collection. Library of Congress, American Memory. **memory.loc.gov/ammem/rghtml/rghome.html**. Religious and secular music of southern Colorado and northern New Mexico. One hundred and forty-six sound recordings with brief annotations for each. Songs can be searched by title and performer. Site includes research notes and publications by renowned folklorist Jan B. Rael.

The Italian-American Experience: An Encyclopedia. Ed. Salvatore J. LaGumina et al. New York: Garland, 1999.

American Family Immigration History Center. The Statue of Liberty–Ellis Island Foundation. **ellisisland.org/**. Much useful advice about conducting family history. Search of passenger lists beginning in 1892. Full access requires membership.

Calisphere: A World of Primary Sources and More. University of California. **calisphere.universityofcalifornia.edu/**. Though intended for use by teachers, this site features essays, documents, and images relating to California history since 1780.

Castle Garden. The Battery Conservancy. **castlegarden.org/index.php**. A nonprofit organization that offers free access to a database of information on 11 million immigrants from 1820 through 1892, who arrived in America's first immigration center, Castle Garden.

The Chinese in California: 1850–1925. Library of Congress, American Memory. **memory.loc.gov/ammem/award99/cubhtml/cichome.html**. A searchable collection of documents, images, and other resources in a multimedia format.

Columbia River Basin Ethnic History Archive. Washington State University. **library.vancouver.wsu.edu/archive/crbeha**. A searchable multimedia database of materials relating to each of the many ethnic groups that live in the portions of Oregon, Washington, and British Columbia (in Canada) surrounding the Columbia River.

Hispanic-American Newspapers, 1808–1980. Readex. Online database. Most newspapers are in Spanish.

Immigration: The Changing Face of America. Library of Congress, American Memory. **loc.gov/teachers/classroommaterials/presentationsandactivities /presentations/immigration/alt/introduction.html**. A multimedia exhibit of immigration to America from many different parts of the world.

Immigration History Research Center. University of Minnesota. **ihrc.umn.edu/**. A searchable archive of personal papers and images of immigrants, with a brief abstract for each collection. Digital content can be found in the University of Minnesota UMedia Archive at **umedia.lib.umn.edu/node/5494**.

Immigration to the United States, 1789–1930. Harvard University. **ocp.hul.harvard .edu/immigration/**. An online collection of photographs, diaries, biographies, and other writings from immigrants.

Japanese American Relocation Digital Archive. University of California. **calisphere .universityofcalifornia.edu/jarda/**. A large collection of primary sources and images concerning the World War II internment of Japanese Americans.

Japanese American Relocation Digital Archive. University of Southern California Digital Library. **digitallibrary.usc.edu/cdm/landingpage/collection/p15799coll75**. Over 200 newspaper photos and captions from the period 1941–1946.

Japanese Immigrants to the United States, 1887–1924. Brigham Young University. **abish.byui.edu/specialCollections/fhc/Japan/index.asp**. A collection of biographical data on Japanese in the West. Searchable by name only.

Korean American Archive Photograph Inventory. East Asian Library and Korean Heritage Library at the University of Southern California. **libraries.usc.edu /locations/east-asian-library/korean-heritage-library**. Primary materials, mostly photographs, related to Koreans living in the United States from 1903 to 1965.

The Latino-Hispanic American Experience. EBSCO Publishing. Books, articles, pamphlets, and newspapers pertaining to U.S. Latinos and Hispanics during the late nineteenth and twentieth centuries. Eighty percent of content is in Spanish.

North American Immigrant Letters, Diaries, and Oral Histories. Alexander Street Press. A large online collection of primary sources by immigrants. Materials begin around 1840 and focus on the period from 1890 to 1920.

Puerto Rico at the Dawn of the Modern Age: Nineteenth- and Early-Twentieth-Century Perspectives. Library of Congress, American Memory. **memory.loc.gov /ammem/collections/puertorico/**. Primary sources and essays on the early history of the commonwealth of Puerto Rico. This site also contains a searchable collection of books and pamphlets for the American Memory topic "Puerto Rico Books and Pamphlets, 1831–1929."

The Strachwitz Frontera Collection of Mexican and Mexican American Recordings. UCLA, Arhoolie Foundation, Los Tigres del Norte Foundation. **frontera.library.ucla .edu/**. Thirty thousand phonograph recordings in Spanish representing Mexican American vernacular music. A browsable list of subjects. Except for users on the UCLA campus, only fifty-second sound clips are available.

Social and Cultural

The Cambridge History of American Theater. Ed. Don B. Wilmeth and Christopher Bigsby. 3 vols. Cambridge: Cambridge University Press, 1998–2000.

Encyclopedia of American Education. 3rd ed. Ed. Harlow G. Unger. 3 vols. New York: Facts on File, 2007.

Encyclopedia of American Social History. Ed. Mary K. Cayton, Elliott J. Gorn, and Peter W. Williams. 3 vols. New York: Scribner, 1993.

Encyclopedia of Early Cinema. Ed. Richard Abel. New York: Routledge, 2005; Reprint, 2010.

Encyclopedia of Lesbian and Gay Histories and Cultures. Ed. Bonnie Zimmerman. New York: Garland, 1999.

Encyclopedia of Social Welfare History in North America. Ed. John M. Herrick and Paul H. Stuart. Thousand Oaks, CA: Sage, 2005.

Historical Dictionary of American Education. Ed. Richard J. Altenbaugh. Westport, CT: Greenwood Press, 1999.

History of the Mass Media in the United States: An Encyclopedia. Ed. Margaret A. Blanchard. Chicago: Fitzroy Dearborn, 1998.

The New Grove Dictionary of Jazz. 2nd ed. Ed. Barry Kernfeld. 3 vols. New York: Oxford University Press, 2003.

The Oxford Encyclopedia of American Social History. Ed. Lynn Dumenil. 2 vols. New York: Oxford University Press, 2012.

Social Reform and Reaction in America: An Annotated Bibliography. Santa Barbara, CA: ABC-CLIO, 1984.

Ad*Access: John W. Hartman Center for Sales, Advertising, and Marketing History. Duke University Library Digital Collections. **library.duke.edu/digitalcollections /adaccess/**. Newspaper advertisements between 1911 and 1955; over 7,000 examples in such fields as beauty, hygiene, radio, television, transportation, and World War II.

American Film Institute Catalog. Chadwyck-Healey. An online catalog of (almost) every American film from 1893 to 1975, with full or short records for films from 1976 to 2011. Includes plot summaries, director and actor entries, and other information on 45,000 films.

Americans' First Look into the Camera: Daguerreotype Portraits and Views, 1839–1864. Library of Congress, American Memory. **memory.loc.gov/ammem/daghtml /daghome.html**. Over 700 early photographs, primarily daguerreotypes. A short introduction to the daguerreotype medium.

The American Social History Project and Center for Media and New Learning. The Graduate Center at the City University of New York. **ashp.cuny.edu/**. Features documentaries, primary sources, and other innovative research materials.

An American Time Capsule: Three Centuries of Broadsides and Other Printed Ephemera. Library of Congress, American Memory. **memory.loc.gov/ammem/rbpehtml**. A searchable collection of 17,000 posters, advertisements, leaflets, propaganda pieces, and business cards dating from the seventeenth century to the present.

American Variety Stage: Vaudeville and Popular Entertainment, 1870–1920. Library of Congress, American Memory. **memory.loc.gov/ammem/vshtml/vshome .html**. Scripts, theater programs, playbills, motion pictures, sound recordings, and photos.

Clash of Cultures in the 1910s and 1920s. Ohio State University. **ehistory.osu.edu /exhibitions/clash/default**. Explains the cultural turmoil of the early twentieth century by focusing on the Scopes trial, Prohibition, immigration restriction, the Ku Klux Klan, and the "New Woman."

Dime Novels and Penny Dreadfuls. Stanford University. **www-sul.stanford.edu /depts/dp/pennies**. Over 2,000 images of covers, nine full-text selections, weekly story papers, and essays. Searchable by subject.

Emergence of Advertising in America, 1850–1920. Duke University Libraries Digital Collections. **library.duke.edu/digitalcollections/eaa/**. Over 3,300 advertising items and publications from the period 1850 to 1920. Advertising ephemera, trade cards, calendars, almanacs, postcards, broadsides, and advertising cookbooks. Searchable by keyword or ad content.

Film Literature Index Online. Film and Television Documentation Center and Indiana University. **webapp1.dlib.indiana.edu/fli/index.jsp**. An online database of over 700,000 citations to articles, film reviews, and book reviews published between 1976 and 2001.

Helios: The Smithsonian American Art Museum Photography Collection. Smithsonian American Art Museum. **2.americanart.si.edu/exhibitions/online/helios/index .html**. Three hundred photos; 175 daguerreotypes. Scholars discuss images, landscape photos, and the history of daguerreotypes, among other topics.

Historic American Sheet Music. Duke University Libraries Digital Collections. **library.duke.edu/digitalcollections/hasm/**. Digital images of 3,000 examples of sheet music from the period 1850 to 1920. Background essays.

Medicine and Madison Avenue. Duke University Libraries Digital Collections. **library.duke.edu/digitalcollections/mma/**. Traces the evolution and complexity of twentieth-century health-related marketing. Over 600 health-related ads from 1850 to 1920. Also, transcripts of 1,930 radio commercials, plus medical journal articles.

New Deal Stage: Selections from the Federal Theater Project, 1935–1939. Library of Congress, American Memory. **memory.loc.gov/ammem/fedtp/fthome .html**. Over 13,000 images; 71 play scripts; 168 documents from Federal Theater Project records.

Performing Arts in America, 1875–1923. New York Public Library for the Performing Arts. **digital.nypl.org/lpa/nypl/sitemap/sitemap.cfm**. Over 16,000 items relating to the performing arts in the late nineteenth and early twentieth centuries: documents, photographs, clippings, films, theater programs, and sheet music.

Red Hot Jazz Archive: A History of Jazz before 1930. Scott Alexander. **redhotjazz .com**. Biographical information, photos, and audio and video files for more than 200 jazz bands and musicians active from 1895 to 1929; biographical essays, discographies, and short jazz films.

September 11 Digital Archive. Center for History and New Media, George Mason University; American Social History Project, City University of New York. **911digitalarchive.org/**. Annotated resources connected with 9/11: firsthand accounts, emails, digital images, posters, press releases, brochures, and newsletters.

Social Welfare and Visual Politics: The Story of Survey Graphic. New Deal Network, Franklin and Eleanor Roosevelt Institute/Columbia University. **explorepahistory .com/citation.php?wciteId=1-E-653**. A series of articles from this journal. Includes a collection of online resources in U.S. social history.

Southern Mosaic: The John and Ruby Lomax 1939 Southern States Recording Trip. Library of Congress, American Memory. **memory.loc.gov/ammem/lohtml /lohome.html**. In 1939, John Lomax, curator of the Library of Congress

Archive of American Folk Songs, and his wife Ruby took a 6,500-mile journey and recorded 700 folk tunes, available in these audio files.

Southern Oral History Program. Center for the Study of the American South, University of North Carolina, Chapel Hill. **sohp.org**/. Audio and transcripts for a large number of oral history interviews. See also the section *Oral Histories of the American South* (**docsouth.unc.edu/sohp/**) presented by the Center for the Study of the American South and Documenting the American South.

Temperance and Prohibition. K. Austin Kerr, Ohio State University. **prohibition .osu.edu**/. A collection of images, speeches, newspaper and journal articles, advertisements, reports, and statistics.

TV News Archive. Vanderbilt University. **tvnews.vanderbilt.edu**/. Major network news programs since 1968.

Twentieth Century Advice Literature: North American Guides on Race, Sex, Gender, and the Family. Alexander Street Press. Online collection includes how-to books, professional manuals, employee manuals, workplace and government literature, works on sex education, and other advice literature published in the twentieth century.

Political

Dwight D. Eisenhower: A Bibliography of His Times and Presidency. Comp. R. Alton Lee. Wilmington, DE: Scholarly Resources, 1991.

Encyclopedia of the American Left. 2nd ed. Ed. Mari J. Buhle, Paul Buhle, and Dan Georgakas. Oxford: Oxford University Press, 1998.

Encyclopedia of American Political History: Studies of the Principal Movements and Ideas. Ed. Jack P. Greene. 3 vols. New York: Scribner, 1984.

Encyclopedia of the American Presidency. Rev. ed. Ed. Michael A. Genovese. New York: Facts on File, 2010.

Encyclopedia of the Cold War. Ed. Ruud van Dijk. 2 vols. New York: Routledge, 2008.

The Great Depression in America: A Cultural Encyclopedia. Ed. William H. Young and Nancy K. Young. 2 vols. Westport, CT: Greenwood Press, 2007.

The Great Depression and the New Deal: A Thematic Encyclopedia. Ed. Steven Danver et al. 2 vols. Santa Barbara, CA: ABC-CLIO, 2009.

Historical Dictionary of the Gilded Age. Ed. Leonard Schlup and James G. Ryan. Armonk, NY: M. E. Sharpe, 2003.

Historical Dictionary of the Progressive Era, 1890–1920. Ed. John D. Buenker and Edward R. Kantrowicz. Westport, CT: Greenwood Press, 1988.

Political Parties and Elections in the United States: An Encyclopedia. Ed. L. Sandy Maisel. 2 vols. New York: Garland, 1991.

Protest, Power and Change: An Encyclopedia of Non-Violent Action from ACT-UP to Women's Suffrage. Ed. Roger S. Powers and William B. Vogele. New York: Garland, 1997.

Abraham Lincoln Historical Digitization Project. Drew VandeCreek, Northern Illinois University. **lincoln.lib.niu.edu**. Illinois history focusing on Lincoln's years there (1831–1860).

The Abraham Lincoln Papers. Library of Congress, American Memory; Lincoln Studies Center, Knox College. **memory.loc.gov/ammem/alhtml/malhome .html**. A searchable collection of 20,000 documents, mostly from the 1850s until Lincoln's death in 1865.

America in the 1930s. American Studies Program, University of Virginia. **xroads .virginia.edu/~1930s/front.html**. Offers audio, visual, and textual sources to survey the culture and politics of the time.

The American President Project. University of California, Santa Barbara. **presidency .ucsb.edu/index_docs.php**. An archive of presidential documents: speeches, press conferences, party platforms, election data, and so on. A wide range of public documents for each presidency.

Brooklyn Daily Eagle (1841–1902). Brooklyn Public Library. **bklyn.newspapers .com/**. A well-organized long run of an important newspaper. Full text available.

By the People, For the People: Posters from the WPA, 1936–1943. Library of Congress, American Memory. **memory.loc.gov/ammem/wpaposters/wpahome.html**. A searchable collection of posters.

Center for Oral History and Cultural Heritage. University of Southern Mississippi. **usm.edu/oral-history/projects**. This site features an oral history bibliography, oral history transcripts, and a civil rights timeline. Organized by topic, by holding institution, and by name of person interviewed.

Franklin D. Roosevelt Presidential Library and Digital Archives. Franklin D. Roosevelt Library and Museum, Marist College. **fdrlibrary.marist.edu**. Ten thousand documents from FDR's presidency: correspondence, reports, memoranda, and so on.

Free Speech Movement Archives. University of California, Berkeley. **fsm-a.org/**. An archive of documents concerning student activism at the university in the early 1960s.

The Gilded Age. Alexander Street Press. A large online archive of primary and secondary works on the social, economic, and political history of this period.

The Gilded Page. Scott Nelson. **teachinghistory.org/history-content/website -reviews/22831**. Documents and links to materials relating to the American Gilded Age (1866–1901). Not all links are active.

Living Room Candidate: A History of Presidential Campaign Commercials, 1952–2012. Museum of the Moving Image. **livingroomcandidate.org/**. Over 300 political TV commercials.

Martin Luther King, Jr. Research and Education Institute. Stanford University. **mlk-kpp01.stanford.edu/**. This site features materials relating to the life and works of Dr. King and includes his writings, speeches, and sermons, and audio files, chronologies, and analysis.

A New Deal for the Arts. National Archives. **archives.gov/exhibits/new_deal_for _the_arts/**. A description of the various government programs for artists from 1933 until 1943. Describes and displays their art.

The New Deal Network. Franklin and Eleanor Roosevelt Institute/Columbia University. **neh.gov/humanities/2000/januaryfebruary/feature/the-new-deal -network**. An online library of 900 documents and 5,000 images, as well as bibliographies and other materials pertaining to the era.

Newspaper Collection. The State Historical Society of Missouri. **shs.umsystem .edu/newspaper/index.shtml**. A growing collection of Missouri newspapers, including those from small towns as well as cities.

Populism. Worth Robert Miller, Missouri State University. **courses.missouristate .edu/bobmiller/Populism/Texts/populism.htm**. Articles, documents, cartoons, and bibliographies on the Populist era.

Presidential Elections, 1860–1912. Harpweek LLC. **elections.harpweek.com/**. Annotated political cartoons, campaign overviews, and biographical sketches.

The President John F. Kennedy Assassination Records Collection. National Archives. **archives.gov/research/jfk/**. Documentation of the assassination and its investigation. Includes 194 digitized images.

Prosperity and Thrift: The Coolidge Era and the Consumer Economy, 1921–1929. Library of Congress, American Memory. **memory.loc.gov/ammem/cool html/coolhome.html**. A collection of documents illustrating the economic and political forces at work in the 1920s.

Radical Responses to the Great Depression. University of Michigan Special Collections Library. **lib.umich.edu/radical-responses-great-depression/**. Part of a large collection of documents concerning American radicalism. Search and browse materials on the Scottsboro Boys, the Spanish Civil War, labor organization, and other topics.

Radicalism Collection. Michigan State University Libraries. **lib.msu.edu/spc /collections/radicalism/**. Books, pamphlets, periodicals, posters, and ephemera on radicalism in the United States. Many documents available online.

Red Scare, 1918–1921. William and Anita Newman Library, Baruch College, CUNY. **newman.baruch.cuny.edu/digital/redscare/default.htm**. A searchable image database.

Senate Executive Journals, 1789–1980. Readex–Newsbank. Online records of the nonlegislative sessions of the U.S. Senate. Includes military events, judicial appointments, and foreign affairs.

Truman Presidential Museum and Library. Harry S. Truman Library. **trumanlibrary .org/library.htm**. An archive of hundreds of government documents from Truman's presidency.

Woodrow Wilson eLibrary. Woodrow Wilson Presidential Library. **woodrowwilson .org/library-archives/wilson-elibrary**. Five thousand online documents and 1,000 images drawn from the Woodrow Wilson Library. Transcribed documents can be downloaded or printed.

Foreign Relations, International, and War

American Foreign Relations since 1600: A Guide to the Literature. 2nd ed. Ed. Robert Beisner. Santa Barbara, CA: ABC-CLIO, 2003.

American Naval History: A Guide. 2nd ed. Ed. Paolo E. Coletta. Lanham, MD: Scarecrow Press, 2000.

The Encyclopedia of United States Foreign Relations. Ed. Bruce Jentleson and Thomas Patterson. 4 vols. New York: Oxford University Press, 1997.

Encyclopedia of United States–Latin American Relations. Ed. Thomas M. Leonard et al. Washington, DC: CQ Press, 2012.

Encyclopedia of the Vietnam War: A Political, Social, and Military History. Ed. Spencer C. Tucker. New York: Oxford University Press, 2001.

Guide to the Sources of United States Military History. By Robin Higham. Hamden, CT: Archon Books, 1975. Supplements, 1981, 1986, 1993, 1998.

Historical Dictionary of United States–Middle East Relations. By Peter L. Hahn. Lanham, MD: Scarecrow Press, 2007.

The New Cambridge History of American Foreign Relations. 5 vols. Ed. Warren I. Cohen. New York: Oxford University Press, 2014.

Reference Guide to United States Military History, 1607–1815. Ed. Charles Reginald Shrader. New York: Replica Books, 1999.

The United States in the First World War: An Encyclopedia. Ed. Anne Cipriano Venzon. New York: Garland, 1999.

Central Intelligence Agency Freedom of Information Act Electronic Reading Room. Central Intelligence Agency. **foia.cia.gov/**. The CIA has digitized thousands of formerly secret documents. These documents were declassified to comply with requests made under the Freedom of Information Act. Keyword searchable.

Cold War International History Project. Woodrow Wilson International Center for Scholars. **wilsoncenter.org/program/cold-war-international-history-project**. Lists publications and information relating to the study of international relations during the Cold War.

The Decision to Drop the Bomb. Truman Presidential Library. **trumanlibrary.org /whistlestop/study_collections/bomb/large/index.php**. A series of documents on this topic selected from the Truman Library collection. Documents cover March 1945 through 1964.

Experiencing War: Stories from the Veterans History Project Library. Library of Congress, American Folklife Center. **loc.gov/folklife/vets/stories/ex-war-home.html**. Oral histories from American veterans of twentieth-century wars; memoirs, letters, diaries, photo albums, scrapbooks, poetry, artwork, and official documents.

Foreign Relations of the United States. U.S. Department of State, Office of the Historian. **state.gov/r/pa/ho/frus/**. Contains foreign policy-primary documents covering 1945 to 1976. Earlier documents (dating to the 1860s) are in the print version.

Joseph Berry Keenan Digital Collection. Harvard Law School Library. **law.harvard .edu/library/digital/keenan-digital-collection.html**. Manuscript materials and photographs concerning the Japanese war crimes trials.

The Mexican-American War and the Media, 1845–1848. Virginia Polytechnic Institute and State University. **history.vt.edu/MxAmWar/INDEX.HTM**. A digital archive of newspaper articles related to the war.

National Security Archive. George Washington University. **nsarchive.gwu.edu/**. Declassified U.S. government documents relating to many countries and to many aspects of U.S. foreign policy since 1945. Contains several different collections of documents, some open and others by subscription through Chadwyck-Healey/ProQuest.

The Stars and Stripes: The American Soldiers' Newspaper of World War I, 1918–1919. Library of Congress, American Memory. **memory.loc.gov/ammem/sgphtml /sashtml/sashome.html**. Searchable collection of all issues.

Terrorism and U.S. Policy, 1968–2002. Digital National Security Archive, Chadwyck-Healey/ProQuest. An online collection of declassified U.S. government documents, with introductory essay and bibliography. Searchable.

The United States and Its Territories, 1870–1925: The Age of Imperialism. University of Michigan. **quod.lib.umich.edu/p/philamer/**. Four thousand publications and 2,000 photographs. Emphasis is on the Philippines, but Cuba, Puerto Rico, U.S.-Pacific relations, and U.S.-Caribbean relations are also included. Searchable by subject.

U.S. Nuclear Nonproliferation Policy, 1945–1991. Digital National Security Archive, Chadwyck-Healey/ProQuest. Online database featuring declassified U.S. government documents along with annotations and a bibliography.

Veterans History Project. Library of Congress. **lcweb2.loc.gov/diglib/vhp/html /search/search.html**. A growing collection of digitized interviews with veterans.

The Vietnam Center and Archive. Texas Tech University. **vietnam.ttu.edu/**. Over 200 recorded oral histories. More than 63,000 documents.

Vietnam War Bibliography. Clemson University. **edmoise.sites.clemson.edu /bibliography.html**. A list of books and articles relevant to the study of the Vietnam War.

Voices of World War II: Experiences from the Front and at Home. University of Missouri–Kansas City Libraries. **info.umkc.edu/news/tag/voices-of-world -war-ii-experiences-from-the-front-and-at-home/**. An archive of U.S. radio broadcasts.

WWI: The World War I Document Archive. Brigham Young University. **lib.byu.edu /~rdh/wwi/**. Government documents, maps, photographs, and biographies.

Science, Technology, Environment, and Medicine

Encyclopedia of Environmental Issues. Rev. ed. Ed. Craig W. Allin. Pasadena, CA: Salem Press, 2011.

The History of Science and Technology in the United States: A Critical and Selective Bibliography. Ed. Marc Rothenberg. New York: Garland, 1993.

The History of Science in the United States: An Encyclopedia. Ed. Marc Rothenberg. New York: Garland, 2001.

ECHO: Exploring and Collecting History Online—Science, Technology, and Industry. Center for History and New Media, George Mason University. **echo.gmu .edu/**. A directory of history of science websites; has over 5,000 entries. Search by keyword or browse by time period and content.

The Evolution of the Conservation Movement: 1850–1920. Library of Congress, American Memory. **lcweb2.loc.gov/ammem/amrvhtml/conshome.html**. A searchable collection of documents, images, and other resources in a multimedia format.

Medicine in the Americas, 1610–1865. U.S. National Library of Medicine. **collections.nlm.nih.gov/muradora**. Also includes Canadian and Latin American materials.

National Library of Medicine: History of Medicine Division. **nlm.nih.gov/hmd/**. Images, texts, and exhibits relating to all aspects of the history of medicine.

Nature Transformed: The Environment in American History. National Humanities Center. **nationalhumanitiescenter.org/tserve/nattrans/nattrans.htm**. Historical documents and related commentary in three exhibits: "Native Americans and the Land," "Wilderness and American Identity," and "The Use of the Land."

Seeing Is Believing: 700 Years of Scientific and Medical Illustration. New York Public Library. **seeing.nypl.org**. Traces the impact of illustrative technique on progress in medicine.

Labor, Business, Economic, and Urban

American Economic History: An Annotated Bibliography. Ed. John Braeman. Englewood Cliffs, NJ: Salem Press, 1994.

Class in America: An Encyclopedia. Ed. Robert E. Weir. 3 vols. Westport, CT: Greenwood Press, 2007.

Encyclopedia of American Urban History. Ed. David Goldfield. 2 vols. Thousand Oaks, CA: Sage, 2007.

Encyclopedia of U.S. Labor and Working-Class History. Ed. Eric Arnesen. 3 vols. London: Routledge, 2006.

A Financial History of the United States. Ed. Jerry W. Markham. 3 vols. New York: M. E. Sharpe, 2002.

Gale Encyclopedia of United States Economic History. 2nd ed. Ed. Thomas Carson. 2 vols. Detroit: Gale, 2005. Also available in e-book format as part of *Gale Virtual Reference Library.*

Labor in America: A Historical Bibliography. Santa Barbara, CA: ABC-CLIO, 1985.

Urban History: A Guide to Information Sources. Ed. John D. Buenker. Detroit: Gale, 1981.

Chicago Anarchists on Trial: Evidence from the Haymarket Affair: 1886–1887. Library of Congress, American Memory. **loc.gov/item/2001561575/**. A searchable collection of documents, images, and other resources in a multimedia format.

Emergence of Advertising in America, 1850–1920. Duke University Libraries Digital Collections. **library.duke.edu/digitalcollections/eaa/**. Over 3,300 advertising items and publications from the period 1850 to 1920. Advertising ephemera, trade cards, calendars, almanacs, postcards, broadsides, and advertising cookbooks. Searchable by keyword or ad content.

Like a Family: The Making of a Southern Cotton Mill World. University of North Carolina, Chapel Hill. **ibiblio.org/sohp/laf**. A selection of essays, images, and oral histories pertaining to life in southern textile mill towns from 1880s to 1930s. Topics include mill work, company towns, and labor protests.

Remembering the 1911 Triangle Factory Fire. Cornell University—ILR School. **ilr.cornell.edu/trianglefire/**. A collection of essays connect documents and images relating to immigrant sweatshop labor in the early twentieth century. Also includes bibliographies and materials on the fire's legacies.

Religious

Atlas of American Religion: The Denominational Era, 1776–1990. Ed. William M. Newman and Peter L. Halvorson. Walnut Creek, CA: Alta Mira Press, 2000.

Encyclopedia of American Religious History. Ed. Edward L. Queen et al. 3 vols. New York: Facts on File, 2009.

Encyclopedia of Fundamentalism. Ed. Brenda E. Brasher. New York: Routledge, 2001.

Encyclopedia of Protestantism. Ed. J. Gordon Melton. New York: Facts on File, 2005.

Encyclopedia of Religion in the South. 2nd ed. Ed. Samuel S. Hill and Charles H. Lippy. Macon, GA: Mercer University Press, 2005.

New Historical Atlas of Religion in America. Ed. Edwin Scott Gaustad and Philip L. Barlow. New York: Oxford University Press, 2001.

AdHoc: Image and Text Database on the History of Christianity. Yale University, Yale Divinity School. **web.library.yale.edu/digital-collections/adhoc-image-and -text-database-history-christianity**. A large collection of images and texts drawn from the history of Christianity.

ATLA-CDRI. American Theological Library Association and Cooperative Digital Resource Initiative. **atla.com/digitalresources/browsecoll.asp**. An extensive online archive of texts and images concerning many religious topics, including the history of Christian missionary work.

ATLA Religious Database with ATLASerials. EBSCO Publishing. A large index of journal articles, book reviews, and essays from the American Theological Library Association. Includes an online collection of religion and theology journals.

Divining America: Religion in American History. National Humanities Center. **nationalhumanitiescenter.org/tserve/divam.htm**. A site for teachers but also useful for student researchers. Essays and a series of links on religion and U.S. culture. Covers seventeenth to twentieth centuries. Includes essays by scholars.

International Mission Photography Archive. University of Southern California Libraries. **digitallibrary.usc.edu/cdm/landingpage/collection/p15799coll123**. A searchable database of 12,000 photographs, with emphasis on U.S. missionary activity.

APPENDIX
B

Historical Sources in
Your Own Backyard

The history that surrounds you is local history. Wherever you live, that place has its own historical record, and you can research it as you would any other historical research **topic**. Local history is something that you can, literally, reach out and touch. The documents and **artifacts** recording local history are easily available to you. Just about every town (or city, or county, or region) has its own historical **archive**. This repository usually has a name such as "Anytown Historical Society." Whatever the official name, it houses old books, documents, illustrations, artifacts, and photographs, among other historical items. You begin your research by walking in the door. Unless the items you want to see are very rare or delicate, you can hold many of them in your hands. These are the **primary sources** for the history of this particular place. The research skills set out in this book will enable you to make sense of those primary sources and to relate them to whatever you have learned about "Anytown" from traditional historical resources.

Wherever you live, or wherever your school is located, you are probably not more than a short drive from a local history archive. Find the address and make a visit. Ask the archivist to see, say, a hundred-year-old photograph of the town or the deed to the very building you have walked into. You can hold in your hand a token used to pay "car fare" on the trolleys that took people around the town and to nearby towns before most people owned automobiles. You can open a box filled with letters written by a mother to her son fighting in France in World War I. If you know something about "Anytown," and about the era in which the deed, the token, and the letter were parts of daily life, you can begin to draw in your mind a picture of the town of a hundred years ago. Those primary sources could become part of a research project just as valid and just as serious as a study of town transportation in 1900 or of the impact of World War I on people's lives. In fact, the token and the letter would be vital **evidence** in supporting a **thesis** on either of these topics.

NOTE: In addition to your own research, as a volunteer you might assist a local historical society to organize items in its archives. Experience in archival work would be an important asset if you were to become interested in a professional career in that field.

Some of the most rewarding historical research focuses on the people, events, and places that provide the **historical context** for your own life. The experiences of your parents and grandparents are pieces of history that have touched you more than any other aspect of the past—even if you are not aware of those experiences. The more you discover about the history of your family, the more you will learn about yourself. The primary documents of your family's history (even if yours is not a "traditional" family) exist. They may lie in an old trunk in "grandma's" attic or be stuffed into a shoe box at the back of a closet. Family papers may consist of letters; old photograph albums; birth, marriage, and death records; citizenship papers and military service records; genealogies; old newspaper articles; report cards; and everything else that someone in the family decided to keep or didn't have the heart to throw out. You might discover a dozen neat boxes with clear labels, or you might find only a worn envelope with faded directions to a cemetery. Most likely, you will find a range of clues to your family's past: a dress that your grandmother told your mother had belonged to her own mother; a postcard in Chinese mailed to someone in your family and dated "Hong Kong, October 24, 1938"; a photograph of a house in Cincinnati, Ohio, with a note on the back saying "Uncle Boris's house." Not much to go on. Still, you have more than you may think. Armed with nothing more than your family's name, a place where family members once lived (in this or another country), the postcard from Hong Kong, and the photo of the house in Cincinnati, you can search public records. Many pieces of your ancestors' lives may be in the archives of state and county courts and historical societies: wills, estate records, land records, church and business records, and "vital" records of birth, marriage, and death.

HOW TO RESEARCH YOUR FAMILY HISTORY

The effort to reconstruct your family's history is very personal, and each discovery an exciting event. Each discovery also is evidence of the connection between the members of your family and the world around them. Your ancestors' lives were touched—perhaps deeply—by the events of their day. The postcard from Hong Kong, when translated, says that your great-uncle was desperate to leave China for America because of the growing civil conflict in China. Uncovering the history of your family makes you aware of the ways, however indirect, in which your own life has been touched by large historical events. Knowledge of your family's history and its meaning can give you a sense of your social and cultural roots—something that will strengthen you throughout your lifetime.

The private evidence of your family's past (however slight) and the public records of its existence can be fleshed out by the most important kind of evidence: the memories of your living relatives. Once you are as familiar as you can be about the relationships, places, and events of your family's history, you are ready to interview as many of your older relatives as you can find.

If you have the opportunity to interview some of your family members or family friends, such interviews provide a way of uncovering the day-to-day nature of your family's life. With the recollections of these people, you can discover more information than only the barest outline of your family's history.

In preparing for this crucial aspect of family research, you must familiarize yourself with the basic history of your family so that you can place in proper historical context the information you obtain from the people you interview. You will need to prepare your questions beforehand, focusing on important aspects of family life and of the larger social and political life surrounding your family. Be sure that your questions establish the basics: the names, relationships, and principal home and workplace activities of each member of the family in each generation, going as far down the trunk and out on the limbs of the family tree as possible given the scope of your project and the memories of your relatives. Look for information that will enable you to make comparisons between generations of your family and between your family and other families. Investigate such topics as types of dwelling and neighborhoods, parent-child and husband-wife relationships, authority and status patterns, and income and social mobility. When you come across major family events—immigration, military service, job and residence changes, involvement in political movements—probe the reasons for these events because the reasons will illuminate the ties between your family and the nation's history.

When actually conducting the interview, use your research questions, taking care to make them as open-ended as possible—for example, "What was the neighborhood like when you lived there?" not "What was your address in 1956?" When you get an answer that seems to lead in the direction of important material, ignore your prepared questions temporarily and probe further. Don't interrupt an answer even when the point seems unimportant. Your informants are the experts on their own lives, and their memories, even if not always factually correct, are essential ingredients of family history.

Finally, because the intricate web of your relatives' feelings is as important as the milestones of their lives, it is best to record (audio or video) the interview rather than rely on written notes. Record it all, and then collect from your tapes the information that, on the one hand, best reflects your informants' testimony about their lives and, on the other, enables you to say something of importance about those lives and the times in which they were lived. If you have the needed skills and software, you could upload facts, sounds, and pictures to a website so that you could share them.

If important pieces of the story are still missing—your great-grandfather's birthplace, for instance, or the age at which your grandmother married—you can supplement your own family's records and memories with official sources. Listed below are the best sources both for county and local history and for family history research. As more and more public records are placed online, the web becomes increasingly important to family history research.

SOURCES FOR COUNTY
AND LOCAL HISTORY

Census Finder. **censusfinder.com/**. This site has a large collection of free census data, although its links often go to commercial sites. At this site, you can access historic state census data, county maps, other census sites, and more.

Directory of Historical Organizations in the United States and Canada. American Association for State and Local History. A large list of historical organizations in all states and provinces. Print edition, 2001. A larger list of state and regional historical offices, organizations, museums, and so on, appears on the organization's website: **aaslh.org/**.

Directory of State Archives and Records Programs. Council of State Archivists. **statearchivists.org/connect/resources-state/**. Links to each of the state archives.

Encyclopedia of [U.S.] Local History. Walnut Creek, CA: Alta Mira Press, 2000.

Genealogical and Local History Books in Print. Comp. and ed. Marian Hoffman. 4 vols. Baltimore, MD: Genealogical Publishing, 1996–1997.

Historical Museum Guide. CensusFinder. **censusfinder.com/guide_to_historical _museums.htm**. Links to history museums and historical sites in all states.

National Register of Historic Places. National Park Service. **nps.gov/nr/**. Links to national historic preservation sites throughout the United States.

State Censuses: An Annotated Bibliography of Censuses of Population Taken after 1790 by States and Territories of the United States. New York: Burt Franklin, 1969.

United States Census Bureau. **census.gov/population/www/censusdata/hiscendata .html**. A source for data from historical censuses by year and state. Contains Census Bureau reports on census data across time.

United States Local History. Library of Congress. 5 vols. Baltimore, MD: Magna Carta, 1974.

SOURCES FOR FAMILY HISTORY AND
GENEALOGICAL RESEARCH

American Family Immigration History Center. **ellisisland.org/**. Much useful advice about conducting family history research. You can search ships' passenger lists beginning in 1892. Full access requires membership.

Ancestry.com. **ancestry.com**. One of the largest sites for genealogical research. By subscription only.

Ancestry Library Edition. ProQuest. Genealogical information for the United States, United Kingdom, and Canada taken from census, church, court, immigration, and other records. Searchable. By subscription only.

Census Finder. **censusfinder.com/**. General census information is available here, as are many good links. But information on specific individuals is on the commercial genealogical sites, which require fee-based membership of some kind.

Encyclopedia of American Immigration. Ed. J. Ciment. 4 vols. New York: M. E. Sharpe, 2001.

European Immigration and Ethnicity in the United States and Canada: A Bibliography. Ed. David L. Brye. Santa Barbara, CA: ABC-CLIO, 1983.

Family History Center. Brigham Young University. **sites.lib.byu.edu/familyhistory/**. A large number of digital collections centering on local and family history.

Family Search. The Church of Jesus Christ of Latter-Day Saints. **familysearch .org/**. A very large surname database including the 1880 U.S. Census. Access to most elements of the site is free. An excellent resource.

Find a Grave. **findagrave.com**. Inscriptions and photographs from tombstones.

Heritage Quest Online. ProQuest. A very large database of sources on family history. By subscription only.

Immigrant Ships. Immigrant Ships Transcribers Guild. **immigrantships.net/**. A nonprofit group of transcribers has placed on this site passenger lists (most from Europe to the United States) from several thousand ships. Where the records are complete, searches are by name of person or name of ship. It takes some work, but is worth it.

Immigration History Research Center. University of Minnesota. **ihrc.umn.edu /research/familyhistory.php**. A valuable set of links to immigrant history. The center's own collection of family history resources is impressive.

NARA— Genealogists/Family Historians. U.S. National Archives. **www.archives .gov/research/arc/topics/genealogy**. There are several important NARA (National Archives and Records Administration) records of interest to family historians. The online catalogs are an important aid in family history research. However, most NARA records themselves are not online except for summaries. The records must be seen at regional depositories.

U.S. Department of the Interior, General Land Office, Bureau of Land Management. **glorecords.blm.gov**.

The USGenweb Census Project. **us-census.org/inventory/**. One of the few nonprofit census sites. Here volunteers transcribe information from federal census data and digitize it. This is an immense task, and only a small fraction of all census data is available here. The existing material can be searched by location, date, or name.

Glossary

abstract: A brief description of the content of a short piece of writing such as a scholarly article. An abstract usually appears at the beginning of the piece. Periodical databases often contain abstracts. See also **periodical database**; **scholarly article**.

active voice: A sentence in which the subject is the actor and the verb describes what the subject is doing. Contrast **passive voice**.

ahistorical view: A misinterpretation resulting from applying contemporary values, understandings, and so on, to the past. A failure to place the past in its proper historical context. Sometimes referred to as "presentism." Contrast **historical context**.

annotation: Written notes in the margin of a reading summarizing main points and raising questions to be pursued later.

appendix: Supplementary information placed at the end of a research paper or after the final chapter of a book. This material (for example, tables, visuals, lists of addresses or websites) is separated from the body of the text because of its length.

archive: A place in which public records and historical documents are preserved. Online: a site where historical documents are available in digital form.

argument: A thesis, especially the principal ideas and evidence that directly support a thesis. See also **evidence**; **thesis**.

artifact: A physical object made and used by people in the past, such as a tool, clothing, machinery, a building.

atlas: A bound collection of maps, often including illustrations, informative tables, and textual matter. See also **historical atlas**.

bias: A perspective or prejudice that a person has about a particular subject. Hidden, inherent biases of the author or creator of a primary source can be uncovered by close examination of the source. Secondary sources often reflect the bias of the historian studying the primary evidence. Bias is similar to a "point of view," but is more closely associated with "prejudice."

bibliography: An alphabetical list, often annotated with descriptive or critical comments, of works relating to a particular subject, period, or author; in student papers, a list of the works referred to or consulted. See also **working bibliography**.

biographical dictionary: A specialized reference work containing detailed information about important historical figures.

book review: An essay that comments on a particular work or series of works on a single subject.

call number: A combination of letters and numbers assigned to a book to indicate its place on a library shelf.

causation: The process by which one historical event influences another.

cheating: See **plagiarism**.

citation: A reference to a source of information used in preparing a written assignment; usually takes the form of a footnote or endnote. See also **documentation**.

coherent: The clear flow of arguments as the author moves from one point to the next.

conclusion: The final section of a written document in which the writer summarizes findings and interpretations. More generally, a finding or discovery that a researcher makes about a particular piece of historical evidence.

context: In a text, the material that surrounds a particular statement and affects that statement's meaning. Quoting a statement out of its context can misrepresent the original author's meaning. See also **historical context**.

continuity: In writing, the clarity and unity of meaning for an essay or other writing.

counterevidence: Evidence that contradicts a thesis.

cyclical view: View of history that holds that history repeats itself, that essential forces of nature and human nature are changeless, and that past patterns of events recur.

database: A large collection of digital data organized for rapid search and retrieval. See also **periodical database**.

date range: The period of time covered by a large collection of books, articles, newspapers, and other documents.

dissertation: An extended, usually written, treatment of a subject; specifically a paper submitted for a doctorate.

documentation: The use of historical or other evidence to support a statement or argument; usually takes the form of footnotes or endnotes or material such as pictures, graphs, tables, and copies of documents.

draft: See **rough draft**.

ellipsis mark: Three spaced dots (. . .) indicating the omission of words from a quotation.

encyclopedia: A work that contains information on all branches of knowledge or that comprehensively treats a particular branch of knowledge; usually comprises entries arranged alphabetically by subject. Online encyclopedias can be searched electronically. See also **historical encyclopedia**.

endnote: See **note**.

evidence: A historical source that supports an argument or thesis. Evidence takes the form of, among other things, written sources as well as nonwritten sources that may be visual, aural, or physical. See also **primary source; secondary source**. Contrast **counterevidence**.

footnote: See **note**.

headnote: A brief introduction that usually includes biographical information about a source's author or creator and provides historical context for the time when the source was written or made.

historical atlas: A collection of maps that illustrate important changes over time and that provide visual representations of such changes.

historical context: The complex environment in which a historical topic is embedded. The historical context includes social, political, cultural, economic, and other factors.

historical dictionary: A dictionary that contains brief explanations of historical terms.

historical encyclopedia: An encyclopedia that contains alphabetically organized short essays on historical topics.

historicism: The view that truly objective examination of the past is not possible, that historical data does not represent "laws" of history, and that interpretation by historians is necessary to give data meaning. Contrast **positivism**.

historiography: The study of changes in the methods, interpretations, and conclusions of historians over time.

index: An alphabetical list of persons and subjects and the page numbers where they are discussed in a book. More generally, any list arranged by subject or by letter (alphabetical) of a specific kind of information source such as magazine articles and books.

interlibrary loan: The lending of a book by one library to another.

introduction: The beginning section of a book or a multipage paper; the introduction sets out the writer's thesis.

journal: For students, a written record, created by a student, of some aspect of a course. Contrast **scholarly journal**.

journal database: A large collection of articles from scholarly journals in electronic, searchable form. A journal database may contain article titles only, titles and abstracts, or the full text of articles.

keyword: Specific word or words associated with a particular research topic. In a keyword search, the search engine looks for the researcher's chosen term in all the records of the database or catalog, or on all the sites in the directory. Contrast **subject search**.

library catalog: A catalog that organizes all the holdings of a library; most library catalogs can be searched by title, author, or keyword. See also **online catalog**.

library stacks: Shelves on which a library's books and journals are stored.

linking paragraph: A paragraph that indicates how and why an essay is moving from one important point to another.

linking sentence: A sentence that ties together the points made in two paragraphs. It almost always comes at the end of one paragraph or at the beginning of the very next one.

microfiche: A sheet of microfilm containing pages of printed matter in reduced form.

microfilm: A film bearing a photographic record on a reduced scale of printed or other graphic matter.

monograph: A book-length study of one specific topic.

note: A note of reference, explanation, or comment. A note placed at the end of an essay or paper is called an "endnote"; a note placed below the text on a printed page is called a "footnote." See also **documentation**.

note cards: Small paper cards (3-by-5 or 4-by-6) that are convenient for note taking and the indexing of notes when researching. Such "cards" can also take the form of computer "files."

online catalog: An electronic catalog that enables the user to search the holdings of a library or database.

oral history: The systematic collection of living people's testimony about their own experiences.

paraphrase: A restatement of a passage, idea, or work in different words. Like direct quotations, paraphrases of original work require proper documentation. See also **plagiarism**; **summary**. Contrast **quotation**.

passive voice: A sentence in which the subject is the receiver of the action and the verb describes what is happening to the subject rather than what the subject is doing. Contrast **active voice**.

peer editing: See **peer reviewing**.

peer reviewing: Examining the work (usually written) of a classmate or colleague. The purpose is to offer constructive comments so that the work can be improved. Articles in scholarly or academic journals are often peer-reviewed or vetted to ensure that the scholarship is of high quality. See also **refereed article**.

periodical: A publication that appears on a regular basis—daily, weekly, monthly, quarterly.

periodical database: A large collection of articles from journals, magazines, or newspapers in electronic, searchable form. Periodical databases may contain article titles only, titles and abstracts, or the full text of articles.

perspective: A general way of understanding something; an author's view of his or her subject.

plagiarism: Presenting someone else's ideas or words as if they were one's own; using material without crediting its source; presenting as new and original an idea or product derived from an existing source. Plagiarism is a serious act of academic dishonesty. See also **paraphrase**; **quotation**; **summary**.

point of view: Similar to "perspective" but usually refers to an author's attitude toward a particular subject rather than a broad subject.

positivism: The view that historical "truth" can be uncovered by objective examination. Contrast **historicism**.

postmodernism: View of history that questions whether we can truly uncover the past.

primary document: See **primary source**.

primary source: Firsthand evidence—published or unpublished, written or nonwritten—that comes directly from a historical actor such as a person or an organization. Written primary sources include letters and diaries, newspaper articles, official records and statistics, and transcripts of legal proceedings and interviews. Nonwritten primary sources include photographs, audiotapes, videos, and artifacts. See also **artifact**. Contrast **secondary source**.

progressive view: View of history that holds that human history illustrates neither endless cycles nor divine intervention but continual progress, and that the situation of humanity is constantly improving.

proofreading: A careful rereading of written work to correct errors of style or grammar.

providential view: View of history that holds that the course of history is determined by God and that the flow of historical events represents struggles between forces of good and evil.

quotation: A statement that repeats a source exactly, word for word. Such a statement must be enclosed in quotation marks and be properly documented. See also **plagiarism**. Contrast **paraphrase**; **summary**.

refereed article: An academic article that is published only after a group of scholars has agreed that it represents high-quality scholarship. See also **peer reviewing**.

reference source: A work, such as an atlas, a dictionary, or an encyclopedia, containing useful facts or information.

research paper: A formal writing assignment on a specific topic that requires the reading and synthesis of primary and secondary sources, as well as documentation by means of notes and a bibliography.

research question: A carefully framed question that guides research on a specific topic and later serves as the basis for a thesis.

research strategy: A plan for organizing research tasks: what kind of sources to look for, which to read, and in what order.

revise: To look over again in order to correct or improve; to make a new, amended, improved, or up-to-date version of an essay or paper.

revisionism: The replacement of one historical interpretation of a topic by another. Later historians often "revise" the findings of earlier ones.

rough draft: The first version of a written assignment; it is polished and revised in later drafts.

scholarly article: An article, the product of serious scholarly research, on an academic topic. Such articles usually appear in scholarly journals.

scholarly journal: A periodical containing peer-reviewed articles on scholarly topics. See also **peer reviewing**.

secondary source: The work of a researcher who did not have firsthand knowledge of a topic and whose findings came from his or her examination of primary sources. Contrast **primary source**.

source card: The first in a series of note cards or computer files that a writer creates to hold (and later organize) information from a particular source. The source card contains all the information the writer will need to cite that source in a note or list it in a bibliography.

stacks: See **library stacks**.

subject bibliographies: Lists of books, articles, and other material organized by subject.

subject headings: Words or phrases that are assigned to materials in a library catalog or database in order to classify them.

subject hierarchy: A series of subjects that moves from the broadest category to the narrowest. Most online library catalogs and databases base their subject hierarchy on the official set of headings compiled by the Library of Congress.

subject search: A search by subject of a library catalog, database, or web directory. A subject search finds all of the information in the catalog, database, or directory that is categorized under a given subject heading. Contrast **keyword**.

summary: A brief restatement *in the writer's own words* of facts or ideas taken from a source. See also **paraphrase**; **plagiarism**. Contrast **quotation**.

thesis: A clear statement, usually appearing at the beginning of an essay or research paper, that informs the reader of the central point or claim the writer intends to make. See also **argument**; **working thesis**.

topic: A broad subject area chosen or assigned for research.

working bibliography: A list of sources that may be needed to research a topic for a formal paper; it includes publication information and the location of the materials.

working thesis: A tentative thesis that helps the writer organize research tasks. As research proceeds, it may need to be revised. See also **thesis**.

yearbook: A book that is published yearly and contains a report or summary of statistics or facts.

Index